T0167285

BIRTH OF A LEGEND

The Bomber Mafia and the Y1B-17

The Story of the Pre-WWII Army Air Corps Visionaries'
Quest for Strategic Airpower

CAPT ARTHUR H. WAGNER, USCG (RET)
AND
LTCOL LEON E. (BILL) BRAXTON USAF (RET)

Order this book online at www.trafford.com
or email orders@trafford.com

Most Trafford titles are also available at major online book retailers.

Printed in the United States of America.

ISBN: 978-1-4669-0602-0 (sc)
ISBN: 978-1-4669-0604-4 (hc)
ISBN: 978-1-4669-0603-7 (e)

Library of Congress Control Number: 2011961733

Trafford rev. 01/21/2012

 www.trafford.com

North America & International
toll-free: 1 888 232 4444 (USA & Canada)
phone: 250 383 6864 ♦ fax: 812 355 4082

CONTENTS

ACKNOWLEDGEMENTS

A book such as this would take many years to gather the foundational data and information. We were fortunate to find willing hands to assist us in the research needed to bring the story of the Y1B-17 to life. Among them were:

1. Susan Connor, Director of Archives, *Daily Press* of Newport News, VA.
2. Susan Braxton, Research Librarian, Univ. of Illinois, Champaign, IL
3. Daniel F. Harrington, civilian historian, Air Combat Command, Langley Field, VA
4. John Little (Museum Director) and Amy Heidrick (photo archives), Museum of Flight, Seattle, WA.
5. Benjamin K. Christensen, Archives Technician, NWCS Still Pictures Reference, A11, FM 5360, National Archives and Records Administration, 8601 Adelphi Road, College Park,, MD 20740.

A heartfelt "Thank You" to all of them.

DEDICATION

The National Defense Act of 1920 authorized a maximum Regular Army officer strength of 17,726 and a maximum Regular Army enlisted strength of 280,000 men, but the actual enlisted and officer strengths would depend on the amount of money appropriated annually, and budgets fell well short. It also created the Air Service. In 1926, the Air Corps Act gave authorization to carry out a five-year expansion program with expansion to 1,800 airplanes, 1,650 officers, and 15,000 enlisted men.

Within this small band of officers and men were men who dared to push flight envelopes, fought the administrative bureaucracies and established the doctrinal pathways that paved the way for the unbelievable build-up for WWII. This book is dedicated to those early visionaries and the long lines of bomber crews and support personnel that followed them and to this day, form a stalwart leg of our strategic military posture.

CHAPTER
I

The Early Years

Company of Aeronauts (Compagnie D'Aérostiers)

The casual reader usually considers the dashing aviators in their fragile open cockpit aeroplanes of WWI as the nascent use of airpower by the military. It's not so. The ancient Chinese recognized the importance of carrying the war into the air and in the second and third centuries used manned kites for reconaisance and communication. They also mounted massive aerial fire arrow attacks; the first air-to-ground support of ground troops. About the same time, the Chinese used hot-air balloons to rise above the battlefield and provide that over-the-horizon intelligence so vital in ground conficts.

The world's first Air Force was actually the French Company of Aeronauts (compagnie d'aérostiers), founded in 1794, who used balloons, primarily for reconnaissance[1]. During the French Revolutionary War, there were suggestions for the use of balloons by the military. Despite unsatisfactory initial testing[2], the Committee of Public Safety was eventually successful in fostering the creation of hydrogen without sulfuric acid, and it was approved for the use in tethered balloons[3]. By November 1793, chemist Jean-Marie-Joseph Coutelle and his assistant, engineer Nicolas Lhomond, were sent to join the Army of the North, but were turned back to Paris by General Jean-Baptiste Jourdan with a request for more men, not balloons.

Back in Paris, the Committee of Public Safety ordered further tests on the balloon technology and the Aerostatic Development Centre was founded[4]. Their research in shapes, sizes and lifting gas led eventually to the issuing of an Act creating the Aerostatic Corps on 2 April 1794[5]. This Act creating the corps envisaged three roles: reconnaissance, signaling and the distribution of propaganda.

In May 1794, the new corps joined Jourdan's troops once again at Mauberge, bringing one balloon: L'Entreprenant. On June 2, 1794, the balloon was used for reconnaissance during an enemy bombardment[6]. On June 22nd, the Corps received orders to move the balloon to the plain of Fleurus, and twenty soldiers dragged the inflated balloon across thirty miles of ground and for the three following days, an officer ascended to make further observations.

**Moving L'Entreprenant
to the Battle at Fleurus**

On June 26th, the Battle of Fleurus was fought, and the balloon remained afloat for nine hours, during which notes on the movements of the Austrian Army were dropped and messages were sent using semaphore[7]. Perhaps it was the high logistics requirements which dictated limited mobility, or the lack of realization of the potential of an airborne military, or the subsequent interment of the corps upon defeat in September 1796 at the Battle of Würzburg, but in any case, the corps was disbanded and essentially disappeared by 1799[8].

Union Army Balloon Corps

The Civil War was a nation-changing event for the United States, as brother fought brother, and the split between the North and South became a chasm as casualties built to unbelievable numbers. There were precious few families that did not feel the impact of these tumultuous times. So too was it an inflection point in the machinery of war, with the introduction of the rifled bore cannon, breech loading rifles, machine guns, and the melding of the railroads into the important logistics requirements for large armies on the move. A few visionaries saw the advantage of getting a manned aerial vehicle into the action.

In June 1861, scientist and inventor Professor Thaddeus S. C. Lowe, mostly self-educated in the fields of chemistry, meteorology, and aeronautics, left his work in the private sector as a scientist/balloonist, and offered his services as an aeronaut to President Lincoln. He had already established himself as a pioneer in ballooning, building and piloting his first balloon in 1857. He had also attempted two trans-Atlantic flights using strong prevailing westerly winds.

The transmission of a telegraph message from the balloon *Enterprise* over Washington, DC convinced Lincoln that a manned airborne vehicle could aid the Union effort[9]. Lowe was introduced to the commanders of the Topographical Engineers as it was initially thought that balloons could be used for preparing better maps.

His balloon was put to use at the First Battle of Bull Run in July of 1961 with General Irvin McDowell and the Army of Northeastern Virginia. His performance was impressive, though he had the misfortune of having to land behind enemy lines. Fortunately he was found by members of the 31st New York Volunteers before the enemy could discover him, but after landing, he had twisted his ankle and was not able to walk out with them. They returned to Fort Corcoran to report his position. Eventually his wife Leontine, disguised as an old hag, came to his rescue with a buckboard and canvas covers and was able to extract him and his equipment safely[10].

In another demonstration, Lowe was called to Fort Corcoran by artillery General W. F. Smith and he ascended to a given altitude in order to spot rebel encampments at Falls Church, VA. With semaphore flag signals, he directed artillery fire onto the sleeping encampment and General Smith said "The signals from the balloon have enabled my gunners to hit with a fine degree of accuracy an unseen and dispersed target area". By October, Lowe had orders in hand to build four balloons with portable hydrogen gas generators for use in aerial reconnaissance. When President Lincoln learned of the successes, he ordered General Winfield Scott to see to Lowe's formation of a balloon corps, with Lowe as Chief Aeronaut. However, even with that high level direction, it was almost four months before Lowe received orders and provisions to construct four (eventually seven) balloons equipped with mobile hydrogen gas generators. He soon assembled a band of men whom he would instruct in the methodology of military ballooning. The Balloon Corps remained a civilian contract organization, never receiving military commissions, a dangerous position lest anyone of the men be captured as spies and summarily executed[11].

Lowe Aboard *Intrepid* at Fair Oaks

Lowe next was assigned to the Army of the Potomac, now under General George McClellan, with his new military balloon the *Eagle*, though his generators were not ready. He performed ascensions over Yorktown, after which the Confederates retreated toward Richmond. Understanding the need for mobility to follow the retreat, Lowe was given use of a converted coal barge, the *George Washington Parke (GWP) Custis*, onto which he loaded two new balloons and two new hydrogen gas generators, and he made the first observations over water thereby making the *GWP Custis* the first ever aircraft carrier. In Lowe's Official Report to the Secretary of War, he stated, "I have the pleasure of reporting the complete success of the first balloon expedition by water ever attempted."[12]

Lowe went on to serve in the Peninsula Campaign of 1862, making observations over Mechanicsville, VA, and the ensuing Battle of Seven Pines or Fair Oaks. The image above shows Lowe's ascent in the *Intrepid* over the Battle of Seven Pines, where his observations of the oncoming Confederate Army and the timely manner in which he reported troop movements saved the isolated army of General Samuel P. Heintzelman. The muddy bogs around Fair Oaks and the Chickahominy River gave rise to many exotic diseases such as typhoid and malaria. Lowe contracted malaria and was put out of service for more than a month. The unsuccessful Army of the Potomac was ordered to retreat to Washington, and Lowe's wagons and mules were commandeered for the withdrawal and eventually returned to the Quartermaster. Thus, he was hard pressed to be put any balloons back into service, although he eventually was called to Sharpsburg and Fredericksburg, where his services were used.

The Balloon Corps was now reassigned to the Engineers Corps. Lowe had been paid as a colonel ($10 gold per day), but in March 1863, Captain Comstock was put in charge of the newly reassigned air division and cut Lowe's pay to $6 cash ($3 gold). At the same time, a Congressional assessment was being made of the air division and a disparaging third party report, which Lowe refuted in a lengthy response, gave pause to the Union commanders for further use of balloons. Lowe tendered his resignation in May 1863 and the Allen brothers took charge of the Balloon Corps, but by August, the Corps was disbanded[13].

In a manner that would become common during the introduction of new weapons, senior commanders failed to grasp the significance of the new weapon of war provided to them and eventually disbanded the Balloon Corps. Actually, this was much to the relief of the Confederate Forces, as they understood the application of airborne resources, but did not have the ability to fund development of their own balloonists.

The Invention of the Fixed Wing Airplane

The Wright Brothers' successful powered aircraft flight at Kitty Hawk, NC on December 17, 1903 was the culmination of man's dream of flying. Their work, building on many other explorations and designs, was perhaps the single most influential invention of its time. By necessity, they had to develop and manufacture their own high power-to-weight engine, use innovations such as the wind tunnel to evolve the proper shape of the airfoil for lift, design, build and optimize the propeller for maximum propulsive efficiency, find a way to make coordinated controlled turns, and to solve a staggering array of never previously confronted obstacles. After a series of flights that demonstrated promising increases in capability, the original Wright Flyer was wrecked after it was subjected to a sudden gust, and it was returned to Dayton. The brothers took the opportunity to improve on the breakthrough yet unstable original design.

In 1904 they built a new Flyer II, which appeared to be the same configuration of the original, but incorporated many improvements. When flight-tested at the Huffman Prairie, east of Dayton, it showed the same pitch instability as its predecessor, but the brothers were becoming quite the proficient test pilots, successfully controlling the new ship on over 80 flights, including the first circling flight by an aircraft in history. In 1905 the Wrights built Flyer III, using the engine and propeller from the 1904 machine. This was now considered to be a practical aircraft with upright seating for the pilot and a passenger, and an improved control system in which the rudder was disconnected from the wing warping system so that it could be controlled independently[14].

On October 5, 1905 Wilbur flew 24 miles in 38 mins and 4 secs, circling the field at least 30 times in front of witnesses. After these successful flights of 1905, the brothers did not fly again until 1908, as they set about patenting their inventions. Between 1907 and 1910 the Wrights made seven examples of the Model A—a production aeroplane. Four more were license-built in France[15].

In August 1908 Wilbur Wright demonstrated a US-built Model A to French audiences at a racecourse near Le Mans. Between August and December Wilbur made more than 100 flights, including six of more than 1 hour's duration. The flight demonstrations set a new benchmark for the Europeans, who were galvanized into improving their designs until they could emulate and then exceed the standards they had witnessed—progress thereafter quickly gathered apace throughout Europe. This entrepreneurial bent of the Europeans, and especially the French, accounted for the relative superiority in airpower they enjoyed upon entry into WWI.

U.S. Army Interest in the Use of Aerial Vehicles

Officers in the U.S. Army, and especially in the Signal Corps, had long maintained an interest in the military application of lighter-than-air and heavier-than-air craft but they had to be shown that an aerial vehicle really worked and had military utility. In this regard, one of the most important of the early developments in aviation was the flight of an unmanned, steam-powered "aerodrome" on May 6, 1896, by a team working for Professor Samuel Pierpont Langley, soon to be Secretary of the Smithsonian Institution. The successful flight of this model piqued the Army's interest sufficiently to offer him a contract for a military aerial vehicle. Langley's attempts were unsuccessful for a variety of reasons and he and the Army were severely criticized causing a full scale retreat from the pursuit of other offers. However, by 1907 it was apparent to much of the world powers that they were on the threshold of practical heavier-than-air flight.

It was obvious that if the United States was to maintain its predominant world position as a leader in the Industrial Age, it would have to move forcefully into this burgeoning field. It was not long before War Department officials turned their attention to the airplane once again. To coordinate Army efforts, BrigGen James Allen, the Chief Signal Officer, established an Aeronautical Division on August 1, 1907, making it responsible for "all matters pertaining to military ballooning, air machines, and all kindred subjects."

Understandably, it was probably with mixed emotions that when two obscure bicycle manufacturers from Dayton, Ohio, approached the Army bureaucracy in 1905 with a proposal to deliver a flyable airplane, they were given little encouragement. But by 1908, the events in France turned this reticence around and the Wrights were given the opportunity to demonstrate their Model A[16].

Wright Brothers demo at Fort Myer, VA

Orville Wright demonstrated a Model A to the US Army at Fort Myer in 1908. From 3 September he made 10 flights, but on 17 September he crashed after the starboard wooden propeller blade broke, probably a fatigue failure. His passenger, Lt Thomas Selfridge was fatally injured and Orville suffered a broken hip. Military trials were postponed until the following year, when a replacement aircraft would be available.

The 1909 Signal Corps Flyer successfully completed the Army's acceptance trials and in July became the world's first airplane accepted into military service[17]. The Wright airplane met the contract's flight specifications on July 31, 1909 and it was then moved to a field at College Park, MD, where the Wrights completed the final part of the contract specifications by training two pilots, Lts Frank P. Lahm and Frederic E. Humphreys. Lt. Benjamin D. "Bennie" Foulois also received some instruction, but not enough to solo. Winter weather in Maryland prompted the Army to move the aircraft to Fort Sam Houston, near San Antonio, TX. Lahm and Humphreys, however, did not accompany the airplane; now designated Signal Corps No. 1 and the Army placed the aircraft in the hands of the partially trained Foulois.

Arriving at Fort Sam Houston in February 1910, Foulois and his detachment of seven enlisted men and one civilian built a temporary wooden hangar at one end of the mounted drill ground with materials furnished by the post quartermaster. The detachment was billeted in the hangar, but that was the least of their concerns. Foulois's major logistical problems centered on the airplane. The Wright machine was fragile, its engine crude and unreliable, and it was extremely difficult to fly in the shifting, gusting winds common at Fort Sam Houston. Foulois literally taught himself to fly and by the end of September he had made nearly sixty flights, but rough landings and minor crack-ups were common. One of the innovations that evolved from Foulois' adventures in San Antonio was the replacement of the traditional Wright aircraft skids with pneumatic cushioned wheels, providing great flexibility and ease in the launch and recovery of the aircraft. Today, that might seem to be a somewhat obvious improvement, but such ideas brought quantum leaps to the airplane's capabilities, and were typical of the evolution of the time.

Foulois would go on to be one the pioneers of Army aviation, relying heavily on his experience in San Antonio and subsequently as Commander of the 1st Aero Squadron, and Chief of Aviation, fortunately for the country in the years to come.

The Aerial Vehicle as a Weapon of War

There was no doubt in any military mind that getting an "eye-in-the-sky" was a distinct advantage and would provide intelligence here-to-fore unavailable and critical to the commander mired in the "fog of battle". Once there, the manned vehicle operators could not help but realize what other advantages they had. What if they could lift weapons aloft and rain them down on the enemy?

It has been reported that "bombing" was the first use of an aircraft in armed conflict and it occurred in the 1911 Italo-Turkish War with the Italian Army Air Corps bombing a Turkish camp at Ain Zara, Libya. Italy had been using aircraft to perform in a typical reconnaissance role to monitor enemy troop movements and search for Turkish artillery positions. Italian pilot Lieutenant Giulio Gavotti, realized that the aircraft could be used for more than simple reconnaissance, and harkened back to medieval times and the dropping of "stuff" from the castle walls onto the invaders.

A Note for the Curious

Bomb is ultimately of onomatopoeic (imitative of the sound associated with the thing or action denoted by a word) origin, and can probably be traced back to Greek bómbos, a word for a booming or buzzing sound. This passed into Latin as bombus, the probable source of Italian bomba, which acquired more explosive connotations. English got the word via French bombe. The derivative bombard preceded bomb into English, in the 15th century.

He considered that he had the "ultimate castle wall" in his aircraft, so Lt Gavotti flew his Taube monoplane over the Turkish camp on November 1, 1911 at an altitude of 600 ft. He took four small 4.5 lb grenades from a leather pouch he carried, screwed in the detonators he had taken aboard his aircraft in his pocket, and threw each bomb over the side by hand. Although no one was injured and little damage was done, Lt Gavotti earned his place in history for conducting the first aerial bombing raid ever recorded[18].

Taube Monoplane

The First Balkan War (1912) was the scene for the next use of military aircraft as a weapon of war where the air-dropped bomb was extensively used, including the first ever night bombing on November 7, 1912. The Bulgarian Air Force bombed Turkish positions at Adrianople. Bulgarian Air Force pilot Christo Toprakchiev suggested the use of aircraft to drop "bombs" (called grenades in the Bulgarian army at this time) on Turkish positions. Captain Simeon Petrov expanded on the idea and developed several prototypes by adapting different types of grenades and increasing their payload. On October 16, 1912, observer Prodan Tarakchiev dropped two of those bombs on the Turkish railway station of Karaagac (near the besieged Edirne) from a two-seater Albatross aircraft similar to the version shown below piloted by Radul Milkov. This is deemed to be the first use of an aircraft as a bomber[19].

It became quickly obvious that the effectiveness of bombing enemy forces was not a simple process, and a number of variables entered the solution to enable a "hit". Airspeed, altitude, trajectory of the bomb, and wind effect on aircraft and bomb were just a few of the factors to be considered. After a number of tests, Petrov created his final design, with improved aerodynamics, an X-shaped tail, and an impact detonator which was widely

Albatross DII—The First "Bomber"

used by the Bulgarian Air Force during the siege of Edirne. Later a copy of the plans was sold to Germany, and the bomb, codenamed "Chataldzha" remained in mass production until the end of World War I. The weight of one of these bombs was about three pounds and on impact it created a crater 12 feet wide and about 3 feet deep.

Not all of the action was over land, and the Navies were not blind to the uses of aerial bombing in a naval arena. In 1913, Greek naval aviation forces dropped four bombs on the Ottoman fleet in the Naval Battle of Lemnos. It would not be long before the navy armadas had to seriously consider the threats from the air.

Entering World War I (WWI)

In 1911, Captain Bertram Dickson, the first British military officer to fly, prophesied that the military use of aircraft would first be used for reconnaissance, but this would evolve into each side trying to "hinder or prevent the enemy from obtaining information", which would eventually turn into a battle for control of the skies[20]. He was correct. But in those early pre-WWI years, merely a decade after Wilbur and Orville's first flight, aircraft were still relatively fragile, with construction consisting of shaped hardwoods, covered with canvas. Payloads were limited, weaponry crude and power plants unreliable. But forces were afoot that would bring quantum leaps in improvements so that a new breed of weaponry would be tested in the crucible of war.

In August 1914, Germany had 230 aircraft on paper, but actually only 180 would be of any use[21]. France had conducted military aviation exercises in 1911, 1912, and 1913, and had refined the use of its aircraft with the cavalry for reconnaissance and with the artillery for spotting. Great Britain was able to contribute three squadrons of 30 aircraft each to the Allies efforts, but had to rely on the French aircraft industry, especially for engines. The U.S. Army and Navy aviation resources were virtually non-existent, even in 1917 when the U.S. entered the War, and were totally dependent on the French industry for its combat aircraft[22].

Reconnaissance

It did not take long for the aircraft reconnaissance mission to prove of value. Initially, the war was tabbed as a "war of movement". On August 22, 1914, British Captain L.E.O. Charlton and Lieutenant V.H.N. Wadham reported German General Alexander von Kluck's army was preparing to surround the British Expeditionary Force (BEF), contradicting all other intelligence. The British High Command listened to the report and started a withdrawal toward Mons, saving the lives of 100,000 soldiers.

By late 1914, the lines between the Germans invading France and the Allies stretched from the North Sea to the Alps and the "war of movement" ground to a halt, and the front became static. By March 1915, three forms of short range reconnaissance had emerged:

- Photographic reconnaissance—Despite the fact that Kodak's invention of cellulose film had already arrived on scene, it did not have sufficient resolution for airborne use. Observers used glass plates, and on return, a complete mosaic of the enemy trench system could be developed.
- Artillery "spotting"—The ranging of artillery on targets invisible to the gunners quickly became essential. Radio telephony was not yet practical from an airplane, so a two-seater on "artillery observation" duties was typically equipped with a primitive radio transmitter transmitting in Morse code, but had no receiver. The artillery battery signaled to the aircraft by laying strips of white cloth on the ground in prearranged patterns.

- "Contact patrol"—The aircrew attempted to follow the course of a battle and communicating the information to advancing infantry while flying over the battlefield. The technology of the period did not permit radio contact, and methods of signaling were necessarily crude, and included dropping messages from the aircraft.

Aerial Combat

True to Dickson's predictions, air combat was extremely rare, and definitely subordinate to reconnaissance. There were numerous stories of the crew of rival reconnaissance aircraft exchanging nothing more belligerent than smiles and waves as the knights of the air displayed their chivalry. But as it became clear that air superiority provided distinct advantages for the ground forces, improvised air-to-air weapons were employed, progressing from the throwing of bricks, grenades, and other objects, even rope, which would tangle the enemy aircraft's propeller. The first aircraft brought down by another was an Austrian reconnaissance craft rammed on September 8, 1914, by Russian pilot Pyotr Nesterov in Galicia in the Eastern Front. As might be expected, both planes crashed as the result of the attack, killing all occupants. It did not take long until pilots began carrying handguns aloft, firing at enemy aircraft[23]. Natural escalation continued, and on October 5th 1914, French pilot Louis Quenault opened fire on a German aircraft with a machine gun and reported history's first air to air kill. The era of air combat proper began as more and more aircraft were fitted with machine guns and living legends were created as "Ace" pilots and their derring-do became the focus of wartime publicity.

Early Bombing Attempts

The typical aircraft of 1914 could carry only very small bomb loads, so the bombs themselves, and their carriage, were still very elementary, and effective bomb sights were still to be developed. Nonetheless the beginnings of strategic and tactical bombing date from these earliest days of the WWI war. Of note were the raids by the RNAS on the German airship sheds at Düsseldorf, Cologne and Friedrichshafen in September, October and November 1914, as well as the formation of the Brieftauben Abteilung Ostende (or "Ostend carrier pigeon detachment", cover name for the first German strategic bombing unit), which mounted the first token raid over the English Channel in December.

In January of 1915[24], Germany conducted the first bombing of cities vice enemy forces, opening a whole new concept of warfare. Using two Zeppelins, they dropped 24 fifty-kilogram (110 lbs) high-explosive (HE) bombs and three kilogram (6.6 lbs) incendiary bombs on the English towns of Great Yarmouth, Sheringham, King's Lyn and surrounding villages. Four people were killed and 16 injured. Following the Kaiser's permission for directed bombing of urban centers, London was hit in May and July of 1916, among 23 raids that dropped 125 tons of ordnance, killing 293 people and injuring 691.

England improved its air defensive posture, and only 11 raids were conducted in 1917 and 1918. By the end of the war, the German's could count 51 raids, the dropping of 5,806 bombs, 557 people killed and 1,358 injured. It was argued that the raids were effective far beyond any material damage inflicted, as wartime production was disrupted, precious aerial resources had to be diverted to homeland defense, and the national psyche became depressed.

The U.S. Aviation Ramp-Up to WWI

The Aviation Section, U.S. Signal Corps was created by the 63rd Congress (38 Stat.514) on July 18, 1914, to absorb and replace the Signal Corp's Aeronautical Division after earlier legislation to make the aviation service independent from the Corps died in committee. The new law authorized a significant increase in size of U.S. military aviation to 60 officers and 260 enlisted men, but stipulated that most be volunteers from other branches of the Army than the Signal Corps. (The Signal Corps had previously mandated by regulation that the aviation service be limited to four years away from their regular units.) The first funding appropriation for the Aviation Section was $250,000 for fiscal year 1915[25]. The new law also decreed what today would seem to be ludicrous restrictions, but it must be remembered that aviation was in its infancy and had a "daredevil" aura about it. Among them was a requirement for officers detached to the section to be unmarried and no higher in rank than 1st lieutenant. Additionally, all 24 pilots previously rated as Military Aviators were automatically reduced to Junior Military Aviator (JMA) and therefore incurred a 25% reduction in flight pay. These restrictions created discipline problems in the Aviation Section and in many ways hampered the efforts to expand its roles and influence.

At its creation, the Aviation Section had 19 officers and 101 enlisted men, hardly enough for one squadron. On August 5, 1914, the section was organized into the Aeronautical Department in Washington, DC with three officers and ten men. The 1st Aero Squadron, with the 1st and 2nd Companies of the squadron, totaling 16 officers, 91 enlisted men, seven civilians, and seven aircraft formed the Signal Corps Aviation School in San Diego. While this activity was afoot, most of the air service was still on detached service in Texas for the second time in three years, training to support Army ground forces in a possible war with Mexico over the Tampico Affair. With its defusing, the Aviation Section returned to Texas in April 1915, when the Army massed around Brownsville, TX, in response to civil war between the forces of Pancho Villa and the Carranza government. By December 1914 the Aviation Section consisted of 44 officers, 224 enlisted men, and 23 aircraft.

Beginning in August 1915, the 1st Aero Squadron spent four months at Fort Sill, OK, training at the Field Artillery School with eight newly-delivered Curtiss JN-2s. After a fatal crash on August 12, there was concern amongst the pilots that the JN-2 was unsafe and they met with the squadron commander, Cpt Benjamin D. Foulois. Foulois and Cpt Thomas D. Milling disagreed, and the JN-2 remained operational until a second crashed on September 5. The aircraft were grounded until October 14, when conversions of the JN-2s to the newer JN-3 began, two copies of which the squadron received in early September. Between November 19 and 26, 1915, the six JN-3s of the 1st Aero Squadron at Fort Sill (the other two were on detached duty at Brownsville) made the first cross-country squadron flight of 439 miles (707 km) to a new airfield built near Fort Sam Houston, TX which became the "first permanent aeronautical station" on January 6, 1916, designated as the San Antonio Air Center. (Later, this first "permanent" base was abandoned after several months and its remaining funding allocated to the establishment of the new training

Curtiss JN-3

school at Signal Corps Aviation Station, Mineola (later Hazelhurst Field on Long Island, New York.)

Strength gradually increased towards the authorized numbers, and on January 12, 1916, the strength of the Aviation Section stood at 46 officers (23 pilots) and 243 enlisted men (eight of whom were pilots) organized into four subordinate organizations: The Aeronautical Division in Washington DC, The Signal Corps Aviation School in San Diego, The 1st Aero Squadron, and the 1st Company, 2nd Aero Squadron, in Manila. It had 23 aircraft: four seaplanes based overseas at Manila, two seaplanes and nine trainers at San Diego, and eight JN-3s in Texas. 32 other aircraft had been destroyed or written off since 1909, one was in the Smithsonian Institution, and three were too damaged to repair economically.

The Air Section received an opportunity to display its ability to respond to threats and support the Army following Pancho Villa's raid on Columbus, New Mexico, on March 9, 1916. The 1st Aero Squadron, consisting of 11 pilots, 84 enlisted men (including two medics), a civilian mechanic, and an engineering officer and 14 men and eight Curtiss JN-3s, was attached to General Pershing's Punitive Expedition. The aircraft were disassembled at Fort Sam Houston on March 12th and shipped the next day by rail to Columbus, along with the squadron's twelve trucks, one automobile, and six motorcycles. The JN-3s were reassembled as they were off-loaded on March 15th, the date the first column marched into Mexico. The first observation mission by a JN-3 was flown the next day, lasting 51 minutes. On March 19th, Gen. Pershing telegraphed Foulois and ordered the squadron forward to his base at Colonia Dublán to observe for the 7th and 10th Cavalry Regiments[26].

The ground echelon moved forward by truck, and the eight JN-3s took off at 5:10 pm. None of the eight aircraft made Dublán that evening: one turned back to Columbus because of engine problems, and one was destroyed by scavengers after a forced landing in Mexico. Four that landed together at Ascensión (about halfway to Dublán) flew on to Dublán in the morning, where they were joined by the plane that had returned to Columbus and one that had landed on a road at Janos.

The squadron returned to Columbus on April 22nd, where it expanded to a roster of 16 pilots and 122 enlisted men. At both Dublán and Columbus, the squadron flew a total of 540 liaison and aerial reconnaissance missions, flying 19,553 miles with a flight time of 345 hours 43 minutes. No observations were made of hostile troops but the squadron performed invaluable services maintaining communications between ground units deep inside Mexico and Pershing's headquarters.

Aircraft limitations constantly plagued the deployed elements. Their airplanes did not have sufficient power to fly over the Sierra Madre Mountains nor did they perform well in the turbulence of its passes, and missions averaged only 36 miles from their landing fields. The planes were nearly impossible to maintain because of a lack of parts and environmental conditions (laminated wooden propellers had to be dismounted after each flight and placed in humidors to keep their glue from disintegrating), and after just 30 days service only two were left. Congress voted the Aviation Section an emergency appropriation of $500,000 (twice its previous budget), and although four new Curtiss N-8s (numbers 60-63, and later designated JN-4s) were shipped to Columbus, they were rejected by Foulois after six days of flight testing. Although recommended for condemnation, they were shipped to San Diego, modified, and ultimately became training aircraft. Not an auspicious time for the fledgling Air Section.

A Stab at New Aircraft

Recognizing the woeful state of U.S. Army aviation, the Technical Advisory and Inspection Board was created within the Aviation Section, headed by Cpt Thomas D. Milling, and staffed by pilots who had attended engineering course at the Massachusetts Institute of Technology (MIT) and civilian engineers, including Donald Douglas.

Curtiss R-2

The Board recommended a new squadron be equipped with Curtiss R-2s, which used a 160 horsepower engine. The first two were delivered on May 1, 1916, and the remaining ten (assigned numbers 64-75) by May 25th. The R-2s were equipped with Lewis machine guns, wireless sets, and standard compasses, but their performance proved little better than their predecessors. Pilots were quoted by name in both the New York Times and New York Herald Tribune as condemning their equipment, but Pershing did not pursue the issue, noting they had "already too often risked their lives in old and often useless machines they have patched up and worked over in an effort to do their share of the duty this expedition has been called upon to perform."

As a result of this negative publicity regarding its airplanes in Mexico, the Aviation Section came under severe criticism in the spring of 1916. Maj Billy Mitchell, a General Staff officer acting as its head while its chief was on temporary duty in the office of the chief signal officer, defended the department, insisting that the U.S. firms did not produce better aircraft. The outcry produced several long-term results, including instructing Mitchell in political tactics, participation in which ultimately resulted in his court-martial later at the end of his career.

Revelations of serious mismanagement, disregard for flying safety, favoritism, fraud, and concealment of malfeasance in the Aviation Section's chain of command led to a messy series of charges, countercharges, courts marshal and of course, more reorganization. Senator Joseph T. Robinson immediately brought the matter before the United States Senate, introducing Senate Joint Resolution 65 in January 1916, calling for an investigation of malfeasance in the Aviation Section. He also conducted hearings and released to the public all of the documents held in evidence at the court martial of an Aviation Section Officer. The resolution 65 passed on March 16, 1916, without opposition.

While the Senate hearings were in progress, Chief Signal Officer BrigGen George P. Scriven issued a statement accusing the young aviators of "unmilitary insubordination and disloyal acts" in an attempt to form an air service independent of the Signal Corps. This might have been a direct result of the restrictions placed on aviators mentioned previously. BrigGen Ernest A. Garlington, the Inspector General, was appointed by Army chief of staff Gen Hugh L. Scott to head a board of investigation into the Aviation Section. The Garlington Board confirmed previous allegations and also cited its leaders for failing to supervise the section adequately, holding them responsible for acquiring substandard aircraft. The Garlington Board's report, together with the Senate resolution and public criticism of the equipment used in Mexico, prompted Secretary of War Newton Baker to issue letters of censure to the leaders and they were temporarily replaced by Cpt William Mitchel. LtCol George O. Squier was recalled from duty as military attaché in London and appointed Chief of the Aviation Section on May 20th, with orders to reform it from the ground up.

On April 24, 1916, the General Staff appointed a committee chaired by Col Charles W. Kennedy to make recommendations for reform and reorganization of the Aviation Section. Milling was named the representative from the section, over the objections of Foulois, who believed him to be too close to the previous Signal Corps leadership. The committee took statements from all 23 officers then on flying duty with the Aviation Section and found that 21 favored separation of aviation from the Signal Corps. The Kennedy Committee recommended in July 1916 that aviation be expanded and developed, and that it be removed from the Signal Corps and placed under a central agency, in effect endorsing for the first time a call for a separate air arm. Naturally, this recommendation was quickly attacked by Assistant Army Chief of Staff Gen Tasker Bliss, who branded the air officers supporting separation as having "a spirit of insubordination" and acting out of "self-aggrandizement". The Kennedy Committee's recommendations were rejected by the War Department, but the issue of a separate Air Force had been born and would not die until separation was finally achieved in 1947.

On June 3, 1916, in anticipation of possible U.S. entry in the war in Europe, Congress adopted the National Defense Act of 1916. Included were provisions to increase the size of the Aviation Section to 148 officers and provide the President with the authority to determine the size of the enlisted complement. It also established the first reserve components for aviation, the Signal Officers Reserve Corps (297 officers) and The Signal Enlisted Reserve Corps (2,000 men). On August 29th, Congress followed with an appropriations bill that allocated $13,000,000 (more than 17 times the previous combined allocation) to the military aeronautics in both the Signal Corps and National Guard. Despite these quantum leaps in authorized numbers, by December 7, 1916, the force still consisted of a total of only 503 personnel.

The Aviation Section's poor showing in Mexico also showed that the U.S. aviation industry was not competitive in any respect with European aircraft manufacturers. There were no purpose-built American-manufactured airplanes, none were mounted with weapons, and all were markedly inferior in speed and other performance characteristics. While U.S. companies were distracted by protracted legal battles and in-fighting over licenses and royalties, their European counterparts had been energized by the needs of the battlefield.

When in Doubt, Reorganize

Apparently dissatisfied with the progress being made, Congress once again stepped in six months later and passed the Aviation Act on July 24, 1917. The Act authorized the transfer of aviation support functions from the Aviation Section to several newly established organizations within the Office of Chief Signal Officer (OCSO). Procurement of aviation supplies went to a new Engineering Division. The construction and maintenance of airfields became the province of the Construction Division, renamed the Supply Division on October 1st. On January 24, 1918, the Supply Division itself created a subordinate Material Section to take on the responsibility for procurement from the Engineering Division, while that Division took on the research and design of airplanes They too underwent a name change and were redesignated Science and Research Division on October 22nd. Lumber contracts for materials to build airplanes were the responsibility of the Spruce Production Division.

In its final year as a component of the Signal Corps, from April 1917 to May 1918, the Aviation Section developed into parallel air forces, a training force in the United States and a combat force in Europe. At the time of the declaration of war on Germany by the United States in April 1917, the Aviation Section consisted of 65 regular officers, 66 reserve officers, 1,087 enlisted men, and 55 airplanes (all trainers), with 300 on order. The service had 36 pilots and 51 student pilots. By comparison, the United States Navy's air service had 48 officers, 230 enlisted men, and 54 powered aircraft[27]. Of its seven authorized squadrons, the 1st was in Columbus, New Mexico, the 2nd in the Philippines, the 7th was training to be deployed to the Panama Canal Zone, the 6th was newly formed in Hawaii, and the 3rd, 4th, and 5th were not yet formed. Six reserve squadrons were being organized for coast defense.

Not Ready for Prime Time

It became clear that the Aviation Section was overwhelmed with the problems of rapid expansion to fight a modern war. The recruitment and training of pilots and mechanics, the production of airplanes, the formation and equipping of combat units, and the acquisition of air bases were more than the Section could handle. Overseas a second force, the

Air Service of the American Expeditionary Force (AEF), emerged and absorbed most of the experienced leadership of military aviation and took over much of the expansion responsibilities except aircraft production. The Air Service of the AEF used European-built aircraft and training facilities and became the birthing place for many of the leaders who would successfully prosecute WWII and forced the separation of aviation from the Signal Corps.

Another major contributing factor back home was the inability of the Aviation Section to fulfill its most pressing need, the production of new airplanes. Under pressure from the French, President Wilson's administration set up a production plan to develop a force of 6,000 pursuit planes, 3,000 observation craft, and 2,000 bombers, a ratio established by General John Pershing. Over resistance from the Army General Staff, $640,000,000 was funded by Congress to meet this goal (45 times the budget of the preceding year) when BrigGen George O. Squier, Chief Signal Officer and former head of the Aviation Section, appealed directly to the Secretary of War.

An Aircraft Production Board was set up under the chairmanship of Howard Coffin of the Hudson Motor Car Company, but the mass-production methods of automobile manufacturing were not successfully adapted to the manufacture of the airplanes of World War I. A lack of focus on the provision of spare parts had an adverse impact as well. Although there were bright spots, such as the development and production of the Liberty engine, of which 13,500 were produced, the industry as a whole failed. Attempts to mass-produce European models under license in the U.S. were largely failures.

President Wilson determined that the Chief Signal Officer was too overburdened to supervise the Aviation Section and he removed it from the Signal Corps. An interim organization, the Division of Military Aeronautics, was created April 28, 1917 to replace the Aviation Section on May 20, 1918 and reported directly to the Secretary of War as the administrative headquarters of the air force. However, the Division only lasted four days, and was itself subordinated to the new Army Air Service, created May 24, 1918.

War Grooms Some Aviators for Bigger Things to Come

A number of Air Service pilots served in the AEF and the combat experience gained in the best aircraft of the day provided them with insights into the future of aerial warfare and what the United States needed to do after the Armistice. Among them was 1stLt, later MajGen, Benjamin Foulois. As noted previously, he was one of the first half dozen Army pilots, and he brought to the conflict his experience as the Commander of the 1st Aero Squadron tasked to support Gen John Pershing's Mexican Punitive Expedition to capture Pancho Villa. A strategic thinker, a statement in his thesis included the following prescience vision: "In all future warfare, we can expect to see engagements in the air between hostile aerial fleets. The struggle for supremacy in the air will undoubtedly take place while the opposing armies are maneuvering for position . . .". He also forecasted the replacement of the horse by the airplane in reconnaissance, and wireless air-to-ground communications that included the transmission of photographs. As a result, the staff of the chief signal officer selected him for the aeronautical board designated to conduct the 1908 airship and airplane acceptance trials. In April 1917, America entered World War I, and Foulois was rapidly promoted to temporary Brigadier General. At the Office of the Chief Signal Officer, in Washington, he finished the plans to build an air force to support the three million-man army. Foulois took the $640 million plan and draft legislation to the House Military Affairs Committee and won approval over the Army General Staff's own recommendations.

But all was not well in this time of national emergency and clashes between early pioneers equipped with passionate views over which directions to take were the norm. The fledgling Air Service of the AEF was in turmoil when Foulois was assigned as Air Service Chief in November 1917. Resentment of his staff, with inexperienced and recently commissioned non-flying officers, led to strong criticism from BrigGen William "Billy" Mitchell, who commanded the Air Service Zone of Advance. In May 1918, Pershing appointed BrigGen Mason M. Patrick to replace Foulois, who then became Patrick's assistant. There would be many more bitter clashes between these two strong-willed visionaries. We will explore Foulois' career in greater detail in Chapter III.

Barney M. Giles, later LieutGen, went to Canada when the war broke out to see if he could join the Royal Flying Corps. When the United States entered the war, Barney and his twin brother Benjamin joined The Army Air Corps cadet program. He was commissioned a 1stLt in April 1918 and flew with the 168th Observation Squadron in France for a year. He resigned his commission in September 1919, but returned to active duty one year later.

Caleb V. Haynes, later MajGen, graduated from Wake Forest College in 1917 with a bachelor of Laws degree, attended the School of Military Aeronautic at Georgia Polytechnic Institute, then sailed for France. He served at the Saint-Maixent-l'Ecole, the machine Gun School at Gondrecourt-le-Château and was commissioned a temporary 2nd Lt in the Air Service and sent to Tours as a test pilot. Later in 1918, he became an instructor at the Second Aviation Instructor Center at Issoudun.

Harold L. George, later LieutGen, joined the Army in 1917 as a reserve 2nd Lt in the Cavalry and was assigned to the Cavalry at Fort Myer, VA. Six months later, he resigned his commission so as to become an aviation cadet with the Army Signal Corps Aviation Section. George studied aeronautics at Princeton University and learned to fly at Love Field in Dallas. After receiving his wings, he was assigned to the 7th Aviation Instruction Center in Clermont, then to the 163rd Bomb Squadron, 2nd Day Bombardment Group, where in the one week the squadron saw action when it flew 69 sorties. It was here that he observed that massed formations of bombers swamped enemy defenses and reduced the casualties, later making him a leading member of the "Bomber Mafia".

Robert Olds, later MajGen, and father of the legendary MajGen Robin Olds, enlisted in 1917 in the Aviation Section, Signal Enlisted Reserve Corps, became a sergeant, and entered flight training with the Curtiss Flying School in Newport News, VA. By the time he received his pilot's rating, the U.S. was at war. In a matter of a couple of months, he was promoted to 1stLt and assigned as Commander of the brand new, and untrained, 17th Aero squadron at Kelly Field, TX. The next day the squadron entrained for Toronto, Canada to begin unit training with the Royal Flying Corps.

Frank M. Andrews, later LieutGen, was born in Nashville, TN, and entered the United States Military Academy at West Point in July 1902. Within a month after the United States entered World War I in April 1917, Andrews was transferred, over the objections of his cavalry commander, to the Aviation Section, U.S. Signal Corps. After a short time in Washington, DC, Andrews went to Rockwell Field, California, in April

1918. There, he earned his aviator wings at the age of 34. Andrews never went overseas during the war as a member of the Air Service. Instead, he commanded various airfields around the United States and served in the war plans division of the Army General Staff in Washington, DC Following the war, he replaced BrigGen Billy Mitchell as the air officer assigned to the Army of Occupation in Germany, which his father-in-law, Gen Allen, commanded.

Cpt Carl Andrew Spatz (Changed in 1937 to Spaatz) graduated from West Point in 1914 and served briefly in the infantry, and later assigned to the Aviation Section in October 1915. Spaatz served in the First Aero Squadron which was attached to General John J. Pershing during his expedition to Mexico in 1916. Spaatz was promoted to first lieutenant in July 1916 and to captain in May 1917. Following America's entry into World War I, Spaatz was sent with the AEF in command of the 31st Aero Squadron. He spent most of the war commanding the American Aviation School at Issoudun, France but he saw three weeks of action during the final months of the war. In this brief period, Spaatz shot down three enemy planes and was awarded the Distinguished Service Cross (DSC); during the time he was with the 13th Aero Squadron. Spaatz was given a temporary promotion to major in the Air Service in June 1918.

As we describe more fully in Chapters III-V, these early Army aviation pioneers were destined to play major roles in the United States' ability to successfully prosecute WWII by developing strategic bombing doctrine in the between-the-war years.

1. *First, Lasts & Onlys: Military,* Jeremy Beadle and Ian Harrison,
2. *Science and Polity in France: The Revolutionary and Napoleonic Years,* pp. 372-373, Charles Coulston Gillispie
3. ibid
4. ibid
5. ibid
6. ibid
7. ibid
8. ibid
9. *Military Ballooning During the Early Civil War,* Stansbury Haydon
10. *Thaddeus Lowe America's One-Man Air Corps* pp. 9-10Hoehling, Mary
11. ibid pp. 107-108

12. Lowe's Official report to the Secretary of War
13. Lowe's official report, Part II
14. *The Bishop's Boys : A Life of Wilbur and Orville Wright*, Crouch, Tom
15. Wikipedia; Excerpts from "Wright Brothers "
16. *L'Auto*, August 9 and *L'Aerophile*, August 11, 1908, quoted in Crouch 2003, p. 368.
17. Centennial of Flight Commission *The First Military Flyer*18. ibid
19. Aerospaceweb.com
20. Wikipedia.org/wiki/First_air_dropped_bomb
21. *Knights of the Air* (1980) Ezra Bowen pp. 24-26
22. *White Heat: The New Warfare 1914-1918* p31, Terrain, John
23. ibid p30
24. http://www.wwiaviation.com/earlywar
25. Ward's Book of Days—Interesting Anniversaries
26. *Roots of Military Aviation* 1997, Heindahl, W.C. and Hurley, A.F26. Air Force Historical Study 98, Hennesey, Juliette

CHAPTER
II
AAC Evolution Post WWI

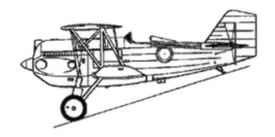

The Beginnings—Organizational Flux

As noted in Chapter One, during the period of 1916—1918, when the U.S. was ramping up its military aviation in a frantic catch-up mode, there was what could be mildly characterized as a time of organization turbulence. The Signal Corps, the General Staff, Congress and the administration all tried their hand at bringing discipline to the organization, increasing aircraft production capabilities and placing a military focus on the fledgling air resources, and organization changes were endemic. Finally, some sense of order came to the Army aviation in 1918 when it was recognized that the AEF Air Service effectively became another air force. LtCol William "Billy" Mitchell was first on scene in Europe and had reported to Gen Pershing his readiness to support him. Never one to shy away from taking charge of a situation, Mitchell became a central figure in the skies and on the ground in Europe.

Established by General Order No. 51 on May 24, 1918 after entry of the U.S. into WWI, the Army Air Service replaced the Aviation Section of the U.S. Signal Corps which had been the nation's air force from 1914 to 1918. No Director of Air Service was appointed until August 28, when President Wilson made John D. Ryan a Second Assistant Secretary of War and civilian Director of the Air Service. But that was short-lived with the November 11th Armistice and the Air Service was again directed by a military officer and remained so until the Air Service was replaced by the Army Air Corps on July 1, 1926.

The Air Service became the first form of the air force to have both its own unique organizational structure and identity with the embroidered badge depicted below, as prior organizational forms were staffed by permanent personnel who were part of the Signal Corps and its pilots were on temporary assignment from other branches of the Army between

**Army Aviator Embroidered Badge
1917-1920**

May 1918 and July 1920, enlisted men were assigned to and new officers commissioned in the Air Service as either war-mobilized National Guard Army or United States Army (Regulars). After July 1, 1920, all personnel retained by the Army and designated as members of the Air Service, received new commissions in the Air Service branch. The cadre was forged and gave the Air Service a cohesion and vision previously denied. The new Air Service's members worked diligently to promote the concept of airpower and an autonomous air force between 1926 and 1941. There were supporters of an independent Service on a par with the Army and Navy and those who preferred a branch of the Army similar to the Signal Corps or Quartermaster Corps and saw the aviation resources deployed with the ground commanders. But forces within the Army and external political pressure mandated that its primary purpose would remain the support of ground forces rather than independent operations. For example:

- The Secretary Of War convened a group of General Staff officers called The Lassiter Board who recommended to the him in 1923 that the Air Service be replaced by a force of bombardment and pursuit units to carry out independent missions under the command of an Army General Headquarters in time of war[1]. In

1925, The Lampert Committee of the House of Representatives, after eleven months of extensive hearings, proposed a unified air force independent of the Army and Navy, plus a department of defense to coordinate the three armed services[2].

- Meanwhile, another board headed by Dwight Morrow, a personal friend of President Calvin Coolidge, had already reached a completely opposite conclusion in only two and one-half months. Appointed in September 1925 by Coolidge, ostensibly to study the "best means of developing and applying aircraft in national defense", it was really formed to minimize the political impact of the pending court-martial of Billy Mitchell (See Chapter Four) and to preempt the findings of the Lampert Committee. The Morrow Board issued its report two weeks before the Lampert Committee's and in consonance with the views of the President, rejected the idea of a department of defense and a separate department of air. Obviously, it was too big a jump for the conservative forces in play in the military at the time. It did, however, recommend that the Air Service be renamed the Air Corps and it be given special representation on the General Staff, and that an Assistant Secretary of War for Aviation be appointed.

- Congress accepted the Morrow Board proposal, and the Air Corps Act was enacted on July 2, 1926 changing the name of the Air Service to the Air Corps, "thereby strengthening the conception of military aviation as an offensive, striking arm rather than an auxiliary service." The act created an additional Assistant Secretary of War to help foster military aeronautics, and it established an air section in each division of the General Staff for a period of three years. Other provisions required that all flying units be commanded by rated personnel and that flight pay be continued. Two additional brigadier generals would serve as assistant chiefs of the Air Corps. The Chief of the Air Service, MajGen Mason Patrick, then became Chief of the Air Corps.

Despite the changes, the position of the air arm within the Department of War remained essentially the same as before[3]. The flying units were under the operational control of the various ground forces corps commands and not the Air Corps, which remained responsible only for procurement of aircraft, maintenance of bases, supply, and training. Even the new position of Assistant Secretary of War for Air, held by F. Trubee Davison from 1926 to 1932, was of little help in promoting autonomy for the air arm.

The Air Corps Act gave authorization to carry out a five-year expansion program. However, the lack of funding caused the beginning of the five-year expansion program to be delayed until July 1, 1927. The goal was to create an inventory of 1,800 airplanes with 1,650 officers and 15,000 enlisted men, to be reached in regular increments over a five-year period. But even this modest increase never came about because adequate funds were never appropriated in the budget and the coming of the Great Depression forced reductions in pay and modernization. Organizationally the Air Corps did double from seven to fifteen groups, as shown in the table below.

Inevitably, as units of the Air Corps increased in number, so did higher command echelons. The 2nd Wing was activated in 1922 as part of the Air Service, and then renamed the 2nd Bombardment Wing in 1929 when the 1st Bombardment Wing was also activated. A third wing, initially called the 3rd Attack Wing, was activated in 1932, at which time the 1st Bomb Wing was redesignated the 1st Pursuit Wing. The three wings became the foundation of General Headquarters (GHQ) Air Force upon its activation in 1935.

NEW AIR CORPS GROUPS ADDED IN DECADE 1927-1937			
ORGANIZATION	LOCATION	DATE	AIRCRAFT
18th Pursuit Group	Wheeler Field, Hawaii	January, 1927	PW-9
7th Bomb Group	Rockwell Field, California	1 June 1928	LB-7, B-3A
12th Observation Group[1]	Brooks Field, Texas	1930	O-19
20th Pursuit Group	Mather Field, California	15 November 1930	P-12
8th Pursuit Group	Langley Field, Virginia	1 April 1931	P-6
17th Pursuit Group[2]	March Field, California	1 July 1931	P-12
19th Bomb Group	Rockwell Field, California	24 June 1932	B-10
16th Pursuit Group	Albrook Field, Canal Zone	1 December 1932	P-12
10th Transport Group	Patterson Field, Ohio	20 May 1937	C-27 C-33

[1]Disbanded on 20 May 1937
[2]Redesignated 17th Attack Group (1935), 17th Bomb Group (1939)
Air Corps Groups added 1927-1937

In 1931, the Air Service "Got its foot in the door" with the agreement on roles and missions between the Army and the Navy. In January 1931, it gained a mission for which only it would have the capability, while at the same time creating a need for technological advancement of its equipment. Chief of Naval Operations Admiral William V. Pratt was desirous of having all naval aviation, including land-based coastal defense aircraft, tied to carrier-based fleet operations. He reached an agreement with new Army Chief of Staff Douglas MacArthur that the Air Corps would assume responsibility for coastal defense beyond the range of the Army's Coast Artillery guns, ending the Navy's role in coastal air operations. It was the touchstone upon which Air Corps leaders would rely on when preaching the "gospel" of air power. The agreement was simple, but encompassed broad responsibilities:

> "The Naval Air Force will be based on the fleet and move with it as an important element in solving the primary missions confronting the fleet. The Army Air Forces will be land-based and employed as an essential element to the Army in the performance of its mission to defend the coasts at home and in our overseas possessions, thus assuring the fleet absolute freedom of action without any responsibility for coast defense."[4]

It did not take long for the Navy to realize that they had ceded a wide-ranging and flexible over-riding mission to the Air Corps, and they tried to repudiate the statement when Adm. Pratt retired in 1934. The Air Corps clung stubbornly to its granted mission, and provided itself with the basis for development of long range bombers and creating new doctrine to employ them.

The Search for Unity of Command

The struggle for a separate air arm continued unabated, pushed by those who saw air power as a strategic weapon of war, and not just a ground support entity. Following the fiasco of the Air Mail operations in the 1930s, which we'll explore later, it was manifestly obvious that Army Aviation had a long way to go if it were to be an effective force in case of war. Stung by the criticism, Secretary of War Dern convened a board chaired by Newton D. Baker to investigate the condition of the Air Corps and make recommendations. The Baker Board convened at the Army War College in 1934 to find and recommend ways to improve the Air Corps and among the many recommendations for pilots were more training in night, instrument, cross-country, radio-beam, and bad-weather flying; and to obtain more ammunition and live bombs for training. The Air Corps should develop better instruments, communications, and armament; strengthen its meteorological setup; and give tactical units training under various conditions in different parts of the country. The board further urged action on a variety of personnel problems-the officer shortage, over age in grade, stagnation of promotion, and rank. Many of the officers testifying before the board recommended that a separate Air Force should be created.

Before the Baker Board had completed its tasks, Congress directed President Roosevelt to convene a Federal Aviation Commission to study aviation in the United States, and that body heard much of the same testimony re: a separate Air Force. It did not recommend a separate Air Force "At that time", but the issue continued to simmer and the War Department announced on December 27, 1934, that Secretary of War Dern had approved of a test of GHQ Air Force.

MajGen Frank M. Andrews and Staff at GHQ

On March 1, 1935, the Army activated the General Headquarters Air Force (GHQ Air Force), a command element conceived in 1924 yet inactive until its creation in 1933, for centralized control of aviation combat units within the continental United States. LtCol Frank M. Andrews was jumped to a temporary rank of BrigGen and assumed GHQ command and reported directly to the Chief of Staff of the Army[5].

The Air Corps commander, MajGen Benjamin D. Foulois, had wanted command over both the Air Corps and the GHQ, a seemingly logical hierarchical arrangement, but others were afraid of his gaining too much power. The separation of the Air Corps from control of its combat units caused many problems of unity of command that became more acute as the Air Corps enlarged in preparation for World War Two. It would be incumbent on the leaders of the two elements to not let this division diminish the accomplishment of the overall goals.

With the establishment of the GHQ Air Force, 40% of the Air Corps migrated to the new command. Organizational competitiveness was inevitable and grew sharper when Andrews was promoted within one year to MajGen. GHQ Air Force had three wings, with the 1st Wing commanded by newly promoted BrigGen Henry H. Arnold. MajGen Oscar Westover succeeded Foulois as Chief of the Air Corps in December 1935, and he clashed frequently with Andrews, as he again attempted to bring the GHQ under the wing of the Air Corps.

On December 28, 1935, BrigGen H.H. Arnold was summoned to Washington by the Chief of Staff, Gen Malin Craig, and over his protests was made Assistant Chief of the Air Corps under the new chief Westover, and placed in charge of procurement and supply. Three years later, Westover was killed in an air crash, and Arnold became Chief of the Air Corps, with an immediate promotion to MajGen. In that position, he was soon directed by President Roosevelt to preside over an expansion of the Air Corps that saw it double in size. However, the continued separation of the combat organization (GHQ Air Force) from the logistics organization (Air Corps) created serious problems in the coordination of efforts. Having been on both sides of the organizational spats, he developed a sympathy and understanding that permitted him a unique insight to work to resolve problems.

When MajGen Delos Emmons relieved MajGen Andrews of the GHQ in March 1939, Arnold was nominally assigned to supervise the tactical forces, but the divisions of responsibilities remained fuzzy at best. Late in 1940, Arnold proposed to create an Air Staff, unifying the entire air arm under one commander. The General Staff rejected the proposal on all counts. But with the war approaching in July of 1940, The Army's organization, fueled by build-up requirements, convulsed once

MajGen Delos C. Emmons again with the activation of the Army GHQ. By November 1940, five years after its formation, GHQ Air Force assumed its war-time role and was assigned to the Army GHQ. The original three wings became the four numbered air forces and Emmons became a LtGen and thus senior to Arnold who, as a MajGen, was Chief of the Air Corps and Deputy Chief of Staff for Air, which was an "awkward situation" by Arnold's account.[6] The organizational machinations and tribulations would unfortunately continue right on through WWII until the establishment of the U.S. Air Force in1947.

1. Mauer (1987) pp. 72-73
2. The Select Committee of Inquiry into the Operations of the U.S. Air service
3. *From the Air service to the Air Corps: The Era of Billy Mitchell. Winged Shield, Winged sword: History of the USAF, Vol I* , Shiner, LtCol J.F. (1997)
4. http://en.wikipedia.org/wiki/United_States_Army_Air_Corps
5. http://en.wikipedia.org/wiki/Frank_Maxwell_Andrews
6. *Air Force Magazine*, September 2008, John T. Correll, Editor

CHAPTER
III

Army Aviation Pioneers

Early Air Power Pioneers

The ability of man to get aloft via a variety of balloon configurations whetted his appetite for aerial warfare for many years. But it was not until the Wright Brothers managed to overcome the numerous obstacles to powered flight, did technology provide the wherewithal for the military to get airborne, carry a payload, have control over his direction and altitude and enter the fray. Even more tantalizing was to be able to control the battlefield by controlling the air over it.

By 1907, it was rapidly becoming apparent to world leaders that air power was going to be a force to be reckoned with, and those who failed to embrace the technology would be left behind. To coordinate U. S. Army efforts, BrigGen James Allen, the Chief Signal Officer, established an Aeronautical Division on August 1, 1907, making it responsible for "all matters pertaining to military ballooning, air machines, and all kindred subjects".[1] It was staffed by one officer and two enlisted personnel. In 1908, the Wright brothers demonstrated the Model A at the Army's Fort

Myer in VA. 10 flights were made, but in what was probably the first case of aeronautical fatigue failure, a propeller broke, and Lt Thomas Selfridge was killed, the first military crash fatality.

Frank P. Lahm[2]

Further demonstrations were delayed until a replacement aircraft returned, and the Army accepted the first military aircraft in 1909. Lts Frank P. Lahm and Frederic E. Humphreys received training as part of the contract, and Lt. Benjamin D. "Bennie" Foulois also received some instruction. Both Lahm and Humphreys soloed, with Humphreys going first. Amazingly, with little more than three hours apiece flying time, they were pronounced pilots on October 26th. It was not long before the inexperience caused the first mishap. When Lahm and Humphreys crashed November 5, the Army lost its entire air force, one plane. Both were uninjured, and the airplane was repaired, but the Signal Corps lost them when they returned to their regular assignments.

Lahm's career took him to France with the AEF, and following the Armistice, Colonel Lahm returned home in August 1919 and studied at the General Staff College in Washington, DC, until August 1920. The Air Corps Training Center was established at San Antonio, TX in August 1920 and Lahm was assigned as Commanding Officer of the school, which

Frank P. Lahm.

included not only primary and advanced flying school, but the School of Aviation Medicine. By 1930, Lahm had been appointed assistant to the chief of the Air Corps with the rank of brigadier general. In 1931, Lahm went to France as assistant military attaché for air. Four years later he was chief of aviation for the First Army at Governors Island, NY followed by duty at the Gulf Coast Air Corps Training Center at Randolph Field, TX where he retired November 20, 1941 in the grade of brigadier general, one of the Army's true aviation pioneers.

Frederic E. Humphreys

Like Lahm, Frederic E. Humphreys was a West Point graduate, and volunteered for assignment to the Aeronautical Division, U.S. Signal Corps and was chosen to replace Benjamin Foulois in pilot training by the Wright brothers. On October 26, 1909, after three hours of instruction by Wilbur Wright, he became the first Army aviator to solo in a heavier-than-air craft. He could be considered the first designated aviator in the long line of Army and Air Force pilots to follow.

Colonel Frederic E. Humphreys, 102nd Engineers, NY National Guard

Following the crash of the only Army aircraft in November 1909, Humphreys resigned his commission in 1910 to attend to his father's business, founded by his grandfather in 1853. He joined the National Guard in 1915, and was called up the following year for the Army's Mexican campaign against Pancho Villa. After initial service with his regiment at the divisional training post at Spartanburg, SC, he was recalled and was transferred to the Air Service in January 1918. After flight training at Rockwell Field in San Diego, CA he was assigned to the first class of the School of Military Aeronautics at the Massachusetts Institute of Technology (MIT) for advanced technical training. Following graduation, he remained at MIT as head of the school's Department of Practical Aircraft Design, and then was made school commander. At about the time of the Armistice, he was assigned to the newly founded Technical Section, Engineering Division, at McCook Field, in Dayton, OH, remaining there until he was demobilized in February 1919. At that time, he returned to New York, and was appointed Colonel of the 102nd

Army Engineers, a position he had until his retirement due to ill health on July 11, 1939. At the time he was the senior Colonel of New York. He was advanced to brigadier general on the State Retired List.[3]

Benjamin D. Foulois

Foulois was not a graduate of West Point, but had enlisted in the infantry in 1898, and by 1901, was commissioned. In 1908, he graduated from Signal School, and his final thesis was "The Tactical and Strategical Value of Dirigible Balloons and Aerodynamical Flying Machines", within which he demonstrated prescience with such statements as: "In all future warfare, we can expect to see engagements in the air between hostile aerial fleets. The struggle for supremacy in the air will undoubtedly take place while the opposing armies are maneuvering for position . . ." He forecast the replacement of the horse by the airplane in reconnaissance, and wireless air-to-ground communications that included the transmission of photographs. He was assigned to the office of the Chief Signal Officer in Washington. He was selected for the aeronautical board designated to conduct the 1908 airship and airplane acceptance trials. During this tour he operated the first dirigible balloon purchased by the U.S. government and as noted above was one of the first three officers in the Army to operate the first military airplane purchased by the government from the Wright Brothers in 1909.

After the November 5 crash of Lahm and Humphreys, it was decided to seek a warmer training climate and Foulois was directed to report to Fort Sam Houston in San Antonio, TX and from there he was directed by the Army chief signal officer, BrigGen James Allen, to "teach yourself to fly." He did so, and at 9:30am on March 2, 1910, on the Arthur MacArthur parade field made four flights on a Type "A" Wright Flyer, which include his first solo takeoff, first solo landing, and first crash. Between November 1909 and April 1911, he was the only pilot, navigator, instructor, observer and commander in the heavier-than-air division of the U.S. Army.

In 1916, Pancho Villa crossed into New Mexico and killed 17 Americans. BrigGen John J. Pershing was directed to pursue Villa back into Mexico, and Foulois in turn was ordered to take eight airplanes to provide reconnaissance and communication. On November 19, 1915, Foulois led the first squadron cross-country flight of six Curtiss JN3s from Post Field, Fort Sill, OK, to Ft Sam Houston, San Antonio, TX, which became the new home of the 1st Aero Squadron.

Foulois and Thomas D. Milling (fourth and fifth from left) In San Antonio

In April 1917, America entered World War I, and Foulois was rapidly promoted to temporary brigadier general and assigned to the Office of the Chief Signal Officer where he finished the plans to build an air force to support the three million-man army. The fledgling Air Service of the American Expeditionary Force (AEF) was in turmoil when Foulois was assigned as Air Service Chief in November 1917. Resentment of Foulois' staff, with inexperienced and recently commissioned non-flying officers, led to strong criticism from BrigGen William "Billy" Mitchell, who commanded the Air Service Zone of Advance in Europe. In May 1918, Pershing appointed BrigGen Mason M. Patrick to replace Foulois, who then became Patrick's assistant. This would not be the last time these two would clash; the patrician Mitchell and the blue-collar Foulois sprang from different sources and approached the day from different aspects. Mitchell tended to work at swaying the public to his theories and opinions while Foulois worked the halls of congress, and both paths were to have an impact on the future of Army aviation.

From March to September 1917, General Foulois was charged with the responsibility for the production, maintenance, organization and operations of all American aeronautical material and personnel in the United States. In October 1917, he was transferred to France, where he assumed the same responsibilities for France, the British Isles and Italy[4]. In November 1917 he was named chief of Air Service, American Expeditionary Forces, and assumed additional duties as a member of the Joint Army and Navy Aircraft Committee in France; representative of the commander in chief, American Expeditionary Forces on the Inter-Allied Expert Committee on Aviation of the Supreme War Council, and commandant of the Army Aeronautical Schools. The arrival of Foulois, with a staff of 112 officers and 300 enlisted men, created an inevitable showdown between Foulois and Mitchell. It ended when Foulois, recognizing Mitchell's ability to lead in combat, recommended to Pershing that Mitchell resume command of the Air Service—Foulois became the assistant chief of the Air Service, Zone of Advance.[5]

After the Armistice of November 11, 1918, Foulois served with the chief of the Air Service on the Supreme War Council, drafting the air clauses of the Treaty of Versailles.[6] Upon his return to the U.S. in July 1919, Foulois was assigned to the Office of the Director of Air Service at Washington, DC, in charge of the Air Service Liquidation Division, responsible for the settlement of war claims against the United States.[7] Just as quickly as he had been promoted from major to brigadier general, he was reduced in rank to permanent captain in the Infantry and temporary rank of major in the Air Service.[8]

In October 1919, as was his wont, Foulois appeared before the Senate Military Affairs Subcommittee, and testified with stinging accusations against the Army General Staff and Franklin D. Roosevelt, the assistant Secretary of the Navy.[9] Having stirred up Washington, Foulois heard that a military attaché was needed in Germany with aviation expertise, and away he went. Foulois gathered the equivalent of a railroad boxcar full of valuable documents, drawings, technical bulletins, magazines, books, blueprints and reports, but to his regret, few paid any attention to what would become the Luftwaffe of WWII fame. After many years, Foulois achieved his desire to command a flying unit, and was assigned command of Mitchel Field, Long Island, NY, in 1925. The same year, Billy Mitchell was convicted in a court-martial, which resulted in his resignation in February 1926.

After stints as assistant Chief of the Air Corps, Chief of the Materiel Division at Wright Field, Dayton, OH, and the Office of the Chief of Air Corps, Washington, DC, on December 19, 1931, he was designated Chief of the Air Corps, and promoted to major general. During the next four years, he maintained constant communication with Congress on the future of the Air Corps, during a time when economic hardships were forcing severe budget cuts.

A compromise reached between the Chief of Naval Operations and Army Chief of Staff General Douglas MacArthur in December 1931 gave the Army land-based air arm the mission of defending the coasts, while the Navy was to defend the fleet. At the same time, the apparent invincibility of long range Martin B-10 bombers against the slower Boeing P-12 pursuit planes led Foulois and the Air Corps leadership to begin the development of long-range bombers in 1933. Without this foresight, the development of the B-17s and B-24s, so essential to winning World War II, would not have taken place.

Mason Patrick

It is perhaps somewhat of a stretch to call Mason Patrick an Air Power visionary, for initially, he was not even a pilot. Graduating from West Point in 1886, a classmate of future leaders such as John J. Pershing and Charles T. Menoher, he became a member of the Corps of Engineers. As a colonel in 1916, he led the First regiment of Engineers against Pancho Villa. As a brigadier general he oversaw the construction of ports, railroads, depots and airfields in Europe supporting the AEF in WWI. In 1918, his friend and classmate Jack Pershing sought out his leadership to assume command of the Air Service where strong personalities were clashing to the detriment of effectiveness. By the end of WWI, he had things under control and he returned to the engineers.

Once again, however, by 1921 the Air Service was suffering from a number of maladies, including severe budget cuts and a crusading BrigGen Billy Mitchell and his naval bombardment demonstrations. Down to only 950 officers and flying obsolete aircraft, the War Department considered Patrick to be the only officer who could control Mitchell and restore the efficacy of the Air Service, and its commander, Menoher, was asked to resign.[10]

Despite his lack of aviation experience, Patrick became a tireless crusader for more funds, and to gain the respect of his men, he earned his pilot wings at age 59, and flew whenever he could. A staunch supporter of airpower, he quickly formed a vision that airplanes were more effective when used in offense and embraced the theory that the military aviation could be divided into an air service attached to ground units and an air force devoted to offensive purposes.

Despite Patrick's attempts to protect Mitchell, he was eventually court martialed with concomitant messy publicity. As a testimony to his administrative and political skills, Patrick introduced a carefully crafted bill that would give the Air Service some autonomy, and eventually, the Army Air Corps Act of 1926 was passed in June.[11]

Rebel with a Cause; William Lendrum "Billy" Mitchell

William Lendrum "Billy" Mitchell is regarded by many as the father of the U.S. Air Force. He is one of the most famous and most controversial figures in the history of American airpower. Mitchell served in France during the First World War and, by the conflict's end, commanded all American air combat units in that country. After the war, he had been expected to head up the Air Service, but found that MajGen Charles T. Menoher, who had commanded the Rainbow Division, and was a classmate of Pershing, was given the command. He was appointed deputy director of the Air Service and began advocating for increased investment in air power, believing that this would prove vital in future wars. He argued particularly for the ability of bombers to sink battleships and organized a series of bombing runs against stationary ships designed to test the idea.

He also ran afoul of Navy civilian leadership in April 1919 when he met with the Secretary of the Navy, Franklyn D. Roosevelt, and a board of admirals to discuss the dissolution of Naval Aviation as an organization earlier in the year. He urged that Naval Aviation be developed because of growing obsolescence of the surface fleet. He opined that a national defense organization of land, sea and air components was essential. He eventually was proven prescient, but his thoughts were far ahead of the curve and he was met with cool hostility.

His strong belief in the ability of bombers to sink the "dreadnaughts" of the day and his constant agitation and strenuous efforts to be given the opportunity to prove it put him at odds with the Navy and many in the War Department. He finally received an "Okay" and formed up the 1st Provisional Air Brigade at Langley Field, staffing it with the experienced personnel he needed and armed with bombs specifically designed for the demonstration. Chapter Seven, Project "B", explores the activities leading up to the dreadnaught bombing and the sensational results.

Mitchell met the like-minded Italian air power theorist Giulio Douhet on a visit to Europe in 1922 and soon afterwards an excerpted translation of Douhet's The Command of the Air began to circulate in the Air Service. Tired of his constant proselytizing for air power, in 1924 his superiors sent him to Hawaii, then to Asia, to get him off the front pages. True to form, Mitchell returned armed with his analysis of the Pacific region, a 324-page report that predicted future war with Japan, including the attack on Pearl Harbor. However, one of his visions proved to be wrong in that he saw no future for aircraft carriers. He discounted their value because of what he saw as the limited number of planes carried and the limited conditions under which they could operate. He believed that an attack on the Hawaiian Islands would be conducted by land-based planes island hopping across the Pacific[12]. He published his report in 1925 titled "Winged Defense".

As noted above, Generals Menoher and Patrick had trouble keeping Mitchell under their thumb and out of trouble, especially after he appeared before the Lampert Committee of the U.S. House of Representatives and sharply castigated Army and Navy leadership. The War Department had already endorsed a proposal to establish a "General Headquarters Air Force" as a vehicle for modernization and expansion of the Air Service, but then backed down because of objections from the Navy, which irritated Mitchell. Mitchell's tireless efforts to extol the virtues of airpower put him at odds with many, particularly his superiors in the Army, Major Generals Charles T. Menoher and later Mason Patrick . By March 1925 he reverted to his permanent rank of colonel and was transferred to San Antonio, TX, as air officer to a ground forces corps a move that was widely seen as punishment and exile, since it had been directed by Secretary of War John Weeks.

Never one to remain silent when convinced of his position, he roundly criticized senior leaders in the Army and Navy and accused them of incompetence and "almost treasonable administration of the national defense, following the loss the Navy dirigible Shenandoah crashing in a storm, killing 14 of the crew, and the loss of three seaplanes on a flight from the West Coast to Hawaii. It was the final straw, and in November 1925 he was court-martialed at the direct order of President Calvin Coolidge.

The animosity that had built up around him apparently was influential in the make-up of the court. The youngest of the judges was MajGen Douglas MacArthur, who later described the order to sit on Mitchell's court-martial as "one of the most distasteful orders I ever received."[13] Of the thirteen judges not a single officer had aviation experience and three (including MajGen Charles Pelot Summerall, the original president of the court) were removed when defense challenges revealed bias against Mitchell. Among those who testified for Mitchell were Edward Rickenbacker, Hap Arnold, Carl Spatz and Fiorello La Guardia. Several Field Grade Officers, including Maj Robert Olds also put their careers on the line and testified in Mitchell's defense.

The trial attracted significant interest, and public opinion supported Mitchell. However, the court found Mitchell guilty of insubordination, and suspended him from active duty for five years without pay. MajGen MacArthur felt "that a senior officer should not be silenced for being at variance with his superiors in rank and with accepted doctrine. The scion of a wealthy Wisconsin family, Mitchell resigned instead, as of February 1, 1926, and spent the next decade writing and preaching air power to all who would listen. However, without the platform of service and rank, his ability to influence military policy and public opinion was reduced.

Thomas D. Milling

Thomas DeWitt Milling was an aviation pioneer of the U.S. Army Air Corps. Indeed, he was its first rated pilot, receiving his flight training from the Wright Brothers and awarded Fédération Aéronautique Internationale (FAI) pilot certificate No. 30 on July 6, 1911. Although not the first U.S. Army aviator, he received Military Aviator Certificate No. 1 on July 5, 1912. Milling also received the first badge awarded to an American military aviator in October 1913.

Graduating from Franklin, LA high school, he was appointed a cadet in the United States Military Academy on June 15, 1905, graduating on June 11, 1909. He reported to the 15th Cavalry at Fort Leavenworth, KS, in September 1909 but his tour of duty was cut short when War Department Special Order 95, dated April 21, 1911, assigned Milling and 2d Lt Henry H. Arnold to "aeronautical duty with the Signal Corps," and instructed them to "proceed to Dayton, OH, for the purpose of undergoing a course of instruction in operating the Wright airplane."

Milling began his training on May 3, 1911, and on May 8, after just one hour and fifty-four minutes of flying time, soloed the aircraft. Six more weeks were spent mastering takeoffs, landings, turns, and rudimentary maneuvers, following which, he and Arnold were transferred to College Park, MD, detailed to the Aeronautical Division, U.S. Signal Corps to instruct the commander of the division flight school, Cpt Charles DeF. Chandler, who had only balloon experience, and his adjutant, 1stLt Roy S. Kirtland, in operating the Wright airplane. The school officially opened on July 3, 1911, and taught ten students, including two members of the National Guard.

Only a few months after learning to fly, Milling entered and won the Tri-State Biplane Race against a field of experienced fliers, flying from Boston, MA to Nashua, NH to Worcester, MA to Providence, RI and back to Boston, a total of 175 miles. The race was the longest of its era. Milling flew a Wright B Flyer without the benefit of a compass, or any other type of instrumentation, and even conducted his first night flight, with several large bonfires providing guidance to the landing field.

As can be imagined with his experience, Milling had a number of subsequent instructor assignments, including the Signals Corps Aviation School at Augusta, GA, training at Texas City, TX, in anticipation of war with Mexico and at San Diego, CA. After duty with the Office of the Chief Signal Officer of the Army in Washington, DC, from July to November 1913, Milling was sent to Europe as an observer. On July 23, 1914, Milling was promoted to first lieutenant and served again as a flying instructor, at Galveston, TX, and San Diego. By August 1917, he had been promoted to LtCol and placed in charge of Air Service Training in Europe. There he remained to succeed Billy Mitchell as chief of the Air Service of the U.S. First Army, American Expeditionary Force, and was promoted to colonel.

Milling returned from France in January 1919 and served in a variety of assignments. Perhaps one of the most influential was as officer in charge of the Air Service Field Officers' School, Langley Field, VA (July 1920 to June 1922) and then as assistant commandant of the renamed Air Service Tactical School, also at Langley (June 1922 to January 1925). After a short stint as operations officer, Second Bombardment Wing, Langley Field (January to June 1925) he attended Air Service Engineering School, McCook Field, Dayton, OH, completing the course in August 1926, and the Command and General Staff School at Fort Leavenworth, graduating in June 1927. He was assigned to the War Plans Section, Office of Chief of the Air Corps in Washington, DC and then in June 1930, Milling was sent to the Colorado National Guard in Denver, CO to serve as an Air Corps instructor. Poor health forced him to be admitted to Fitzsimmons General Hospital in Denver where he was a patient from October 1931 to July 31, 1933, when he retired from active duty. But his service to the country was not done.

Milling was recalled to active duty as a major on March 16, 1942, to serve on the War Department Decorations Board in Washington, DC, and was promoted to lieutenant colonel April 27, 1942 and to colonel September 24, 1942. In December 1942, he served as the air representative on the United States Congress Joint Intelligence Sub-Committee and later was a member of the Joint Intelligence Staff in the office of the Assistant Chief of Staff, Intelligence, until December 1943, when he returned to the War Department Decorations Board, serving until March 1946. He retired once again following the war on July 24, 1946, and was promoted to brigadier general on the retired list.

Henry H. Arnold

Henry H. "Hap" Arnold is the only officer to hold five-star rank in two services as General of the Army and General of the Air Force. He started the rise to the top of military hierarchy as a cadet at West Point, graduating in 1907, and assigned to the infantry. He disliked the infantry and volunteered to assist in a cartography detail with the Signal Corps. His superior on that detail was Cpt Arthur S. Cowan, who later became the first chief of the Aeronautical Division of the Signal Corps. Cowan needed to have two 2ndLts trained as pilots and Arnold applied but heard nothing for two years.

His patience was rewarded and he and 2ndLt Thomas D. Milling received orders to Dayton, OH to receive the coveted training with the Wright brothers. Beginning on May 3, 1911, he received three hours and 48 minutes of flying lessons and soloed, ending instruction in June.

Arnold and Milling under Instruction with the Wright Brothers

He received Fédération Aéronautique Internationale (FAI) pilot certificate number 29 and Military Aviator Certificate number 2. General Order No. 39 of May 27, 1913 recognized him as one of the original 24 military aviators and authorized to wear the suspended eagle military badge. Despite the change to the later "wings", he wore both through his long career.

Arnold and Milling were subsequently involved in virtually every "first" in Army aviation; first instructors, setting altitude records, first flying air mail, first to accept an aircraft with engine mounted at the nose, winning the first MacKay trophy, and unfortunately, crashes. Arnold voluntarily removed himself from aviation as a rash of crashes loomed front and center before him (without stigma, as it was considered an extremely hazardous specialty) and was assigned to the Philippines where he was quartered next to 1stLt George C. Marshall, destined for Chief of Staff and a future mentor.

General of the Air Force
Henry H. "Hap" Arnold

It was another Army friend from his Maryland days, Maj "Billy" Mitchell, who offered him the rank of captain if he returned to aviation. He worked hard to overcome the flying phobia, and in late 1916, soloed again. Banished to Panama by a senior officer he testified against, the tour turned out to be an opportunity when he was tasked to find a suitable location for the new 7th Aero Squadron, and then command it. He was ordered to Washington because of a lack of agreement on the Panama location, and while enroute, the U.S. declared war on Germany and despite his desire to go to France as part of the AEF, he was needed in DC. As the youngest full colonel in the Army, he guided, not always successfully, large aviation appropriations and gathered experience in aircraft acquisition and production and the construction of depots, field and schools while overseeing recruitment and training of personnel.

After a surprise stint at the Industrial College, he was back in DC assigned as Chief of Air Service Information in 1925, and worked closely with BrigGen Mitchell. In this position, he continued to provide propaganda to airpower-friendly journalists in defiance of orders. In 1926, Secretary of War Dwight F. Davis ordered General Mason Patrick to discipline leakers. Patrick chose Arnold and gave him a choice: resign or receive a court martial. Arnold chose a court martial, but burned by the bad publicity resulting from Mitchell's kangaroo court, the Army chose instead to exile him to Fort Riley, KS. While there, he managed to do a great job for MajGen James E. Fechet, who had relieved Patrick and was

Chief of the new Air Corps, and as a reward, he was sent to Command and General Staff School.

From that time on, he performed in exemplary fashion. He commanded March Field, CA, worked with the Civilian Conservation Corps (CCC) and commanded one of the three Air Mail Zones. Although the airmail operations were somewhat of a fiasco, his pilots performed in an exemplary fashion. He was also awarded the Mackay trophy for leading a flight of B-10 bombers on an 8,390 mile flight to Fairbanks, AK and return. When the GHQ was formed in 1935, the commander, MajGen Frank M. Andrews picked Arnold to command the 1st Wing at March Field in California, and was promoted to brigadier general. It was a short-lived command, as he was pulled back into Washington as Asst. Chief of the Air Corps, and three years later, when the Chief, MajGen Westover was killed in a crash, he became the chief and promoted to major general. With the onset of WWII, the Air Corps and GHQ disappeared and the Army Air Forces emerged with General Arnold in command.

Frank M. Andrews

We would be remiss to not include Frank M. Andrews in any list of early Army Aviation pioneers. His later strong advocacy of the four-engine bomber in general and the B-17 in particular was evidenced as he pushed diligently for large purchases of the B-17 and to make it the standard Army long-range aircraft. He succeeded in making progress toward a separate Air Force when others had failed. He became the first head of a centralized air force and the first air officer to serve on the general staff.

Graduating from West Point in 1906, and marrying a MajGen Allen's daughter in 1914, it was thought that the general kept him from his aviation aspirations. However, when the war started in 1917, he managed to gain entrance into the Signal Corps and earned his wings in 1918 at the age of 34. Although he did not go overseas during the war, after the armistice, he replaced BrigGen Mitchell as the air officer in the Army of Occupation under his father-in-law, General Allen.

Returning to the United States in 1923, Andrews marched successfully through a wide ranging series of command, school and staff assignments. In 1927 he attended the Air Corps Tactical School (ACTS), the breeding ground for theorists in both the bomber and pursuit camps. Next year, he went to the Army Command and General Staff School, a prerequisite for promotion to greater responsibilities. In succession, he served as the Chief of the Army Air Corps Training and Operations Division, commanded the 1st Pursuit Group at Selfridge Field, attended Army War College, and by 1934, served on the General Staff.

In 1935, General Douglas MacArthur appointed Andrews the first commander of the General Headquarters (GHQ) Air Force, consolidating all of the Air Corps tactical units under a single commander, promoting him to brigadier general, and less than a year later, major general. From that position, he attempted to influence his superiors that the B-17 was the bomber of choice, despite the crash of the Boeing Model 299 at McCook Field (See Chapters VII and IX). Unfortunately for the bomber interests, General Malin Craig replaced MacArthur in October 1935 and he opposed any Air Corps mission except the support of ground troops. At the same time, the general staff was staunch in its opposition to a separate air force and did not agree with Andrews that the B-17 had proven its superiority. They cut back on purchases of the B-17 in favor of the much cheaper DB-1 (B-18). Andrews was eventually proven correct as the realities of WWII set in and the B10s and B-18s proved woefully inadequate and were retired or relegated to less vulnerable roles.

As was often the case in the pre-WWII days of a small Army and even smaller cadre of aviation officers, the interaction between strong-willed personalities caused ebbs and flows for their careers. Andrews was passed over for the job of Chief of the Air Corps on the death of MajGen Oscar Westover, most likely because of his support of strategic bombing. Yet, the Deputy Chief of Staff, George C. Marshall looked upon Andrews as a trusted air advisor, despite Andrew's continued push for the bombers which did not rest well with seniors. Perhaps his January 1939 speech before the National Aeronautic Association, where he characterized the United States as a "sixth rate-airpower" was the last straw that broke the camel's back as Secretary of War Woodring was assuring the public of the superiority of U.S. airpower.

As with so many other Army Aviation Visionaries of the time, two months later he was "punished" by being reverted to colonel and sent to the same exile "Billy" Mitchell endured. The hierarchy of the day must have thought that they had rid themselves of this pesky irritant and Andrews would retire, but newly appointed Chief of Staff Marshall recalled him to Washington and promoted him to the permanent rank of brigadier general. When that raised howls of protest, Marshall threatened to retire, and Andrews' rank and assignment held.

His superior leadership and command experience were immediately capitalized on with the ramp-up to and outbreak of WWII. Command of the Panama Canal Air Force, Caribbean Defense Command, and all United States forces in the Middle East, and eventually, with joint approval, all United States forces in the European Theater of Operations, replacing Dwight D. Eisenhower were testimony to the respect he earned. Arnold and Marshall both considered him the prime candidate for the role of Supreme Allied Commander, but an Icelandic crash in 1943 brought his life and career to a sad end.[14]

Growing up in Aviation's Golden Age

Aviation arguably experienced the most rapid growth in technology and exploits in what many have called the "Golden Age" stretching from the end of WWI to the early 1940s. Larger than life personalities crossed the world stage on the backs of their ever more capable airborne steeds. Charles Lindbergh, Amelia Earhart, Wiley Post, Roscoe Turner, Jimmy Doolittle, Al Williams, and Howard Hughes among others became household names. Barnstormers, air racers, wing walkers and parachutist thrilled the country with their daring-do. With the advent of "moving pictures", aviation serials for the Saturday morning kids' shows spawned a new generation of enthusiasts. Technology such as monocoque structures of light weight metals, aerodynamic drag reduction, powerplant maturation, and even jet propulsion emerged and created an ever challenging environment for those who could sense how best to apply them to air power. The pioneers and their visionary progeny who followed capitalized on these developments in an exciting period of Army Aviation.

1. http://en.wikipedia.org/wiki/Aeronautical_U.S._Signal_Corps
2. http://en.wikipedia.org/wiki/Frank_Purdy_Lahm
3. http://en.wikipedia.org/wiki/Frederick_Erastus_Humphreys
4. *From The Wright Brothers to the Astronauts, The Memoirs of Benjamin Foulois*, McGraw Hill p 157
5. ibid
6. ibid
7. ibid
8 ibid
9 ibid
10. http://en.wikipedia.org/wiki/Mason_Patrick
11. ibid
12. http://en.wikipedia.org/wiki/ William_Lendrium_Mitchell
13. ibid
14. http://en.wikipedia.org/wiki/Frank_Maxwell_Andrews

CHAPTER IV

The Air Corps Tactical School and Doctrinal Evolution

Developments in strategic roles and missions were evolving along with the organizational changes, and they were closely intertwined, making it difficult to determine which one was the driving force. At the end of World War I, observation remained the main role of the Air Service. However, air combat and limited bombardment operations indicated to veterans of the Air Service, including BrigGen Billy Mitchell, that while ideally the service should be separate from the Army, it at the least should be centralized under an Air Service commander with some missions independent of direct support of troops. How best to employ them riddled arguments of the time. A more erudite approach to the situation was needed.

Almost from the time the United Sates had a military, there was recognition that there was a need for it to be an educated military. The Army's Military Academy at West Point was established on July 4, 1802, followed by the Navy's Annapolis in 1845, and the Coast Guard Academy in 1876. The Army continued to feel the need to provide further specialized training to supplement the Academy's formal education. In 1824, the Artillery School of Practice set the pattern for the 1827 establishment of the Infantry and Cavalry informal school, the 1887 Cavalry and Light Artillery School, and by 1904, there were seven specialty schools.

The Air Service followed the precedent of the other combat arms and began planning for its own service schools. Ohio's McCook Field (later Wright Field) was the natural site for the Air Service School of Application for technical training in aeronautical engineering, similar to the Ordnance School of Application at Sandy Hook, New Jersey. The first class began on November 10, 1919. Following that precedent, Maj. Gen. Charles Menoher, Director of Air Service, wrote the War Department in October 1919 for permission to establish a tactical school at Langley Field, Virginia, to train field grade officers in the operation and tactics of the Air Service as a requirement for higher command or staff work. The War Department authorized the Air Service to establish its own service schools on February 25, 1920. In addition to six pilot and advanced pilot training schools, and two technical training schools, an Air Service School planned to host courses for enlisted personnel as balloon observers, balloon mechanics, and aerial photography, but its main course was to be the Field Officers Course.

Maj Thomas DeWitt Milling, designated the first military aviator on July 5th, 1912, was assigned as officer-in-charge of the Field Officers Course at the new school and sent to Langley in July 1920[1]. Armed with War Department General Order #18 of August 14, 1920 providing authorization of the school, he set to work with what would prove to be an all-important undertaking. The balloon courses were split off into a separate school in a different area of Langley and the Air Service School was renamed the Air Service Field Officers School on February 10, 1921. The Air Service ordered 17 officers to Langley, eight as students and nine as instructors, although several officers swapped roles and some instructors were students as well.

The 1920–1921 class opened on November 1, 1920, and although scheduled to last nine months, was concluded in May when both students and instructors were assigned to the 1st Provisional Air Brigade. This would be the ultimate "education" as they were to be as part of the experimental bombing of captured warships by the Air Service and the United States Navy. (See Chapter VI for more details). 11 officers, including four instructors, graduated the first course[2].

Despite the school's title and function, only six of the first 23 graduates were field grade officers. A board reviewed all service schools of the United States Army and observed that the Air Corps' Field Officers School had a course load that in other branches of the Army was distributed among several schools. Because all other Air Service schools were technical training in nature, the board recommended that the school be opened to all air service officers regardless of rank. With adoption of this recommendation, the school became the Air Service Tactical School on November 8, 1922, and underwent another change with the passage of the Air Corps Act of 1926, becoming the Air Corps Tactical School (ACTS) on July 2, 1926.

ACTS became one of the more influential schools for theorists in the nascent aviation warfare development. Those who attended as students and those who instructed became the leaders that prepared us for war, and then led the men into it. Most of these men had been tested in the crucible of WWI, where the United States found itself significantly behind the air forces of our allies and the enemy. They returned with a burning desire to correct that situation.

Unfortunately, there was precious little in the way of precedence when it came to the question of how best to use the fledgling air power. The school never lost sight of its responsibilities to develop strategy, tactics and deployment of airpower, but it could not dodge the fact that they had no body of doctrine to base their instruction on. Aptly coined in 1929 for this new school was its motto: Proficimus More Irretenti—"We Make Progress Unhindered by Custom."

And so, the School based the good part of instruction on theory, but with a unique vision, they developed an integrated body of concepts. School course standardization in 1922 resulted from an Army Board setting out guidelines for a nine-month course. Of the 1,300 + hours of classroom dictated by the Board, approximately 900 hours covered tactics in general, including those of other services and combined arms tactics, with more than half devoted to air tactics in observation, bombardment, pursuit, and attack aviation.

Approximately 290 hours involved technical subjects, including aeronautical engineering, armament and gunnery, navigation, meteorology, and photography. The remaining 150 hours were devoted to the onerous yet inevitable administrative studies, covering staff duties, combat orders, organization of the Army, military and international law, supply and management. That was changed one year later when classes were moved to mornings only, Air Service History added and an afternoon 126-hour course in practical flying instituted to provide refresher training to pilots and non-aviation students.

The ACTS found infrastructure restrictions at Langley Field hampered its growth, and settled in at Maxwell Field, AL, but the influence did not wane, as courses continued to be revised as aviation evolved. In 1934, Col John F. Curry, ACTS Commandant, reorganized the academic structure of the school along functional lines, creating three principal departments: Air Tactics, Ground Tactics, and Basic and Special Instruction. Flying was a fourth department. The "Air Force", "Attack", "Bombardment", "Pursuit", and "Observation" sections were placed within the Department of Air Tactics. The very next year, these departments became the Department of Air Tactics and Strategy, Department of Ground Tactics, and Department of Command, Staff and Logistics.[3]

Faculty Committees were also formed including the Air Corps Board in 1933, restructured by the Tactical School faculty, who doubled as its members, and was directed by the War Department to formulate Air Corps doctrine. The Board became indistinguishable from the Tactical School and undertook 77 projects between 1935 and 1942, a third of which dealt with tactical doctrine, and the remainder with equipment, armaments, field manuals, and training texts.

The Tactical School, in formulating the doctrine, rejected the idea of attacking civilians. Four former instructors of the school, the core of a group known as the "Bomber Mafia", were eventually grouped together in the Air War Plans Division to produce the two war-winning plans—AWPD-1 and AWPD-42—based on the doctrine of precision daylight bombing that guided the wartime expansion and deployment of the Army Air Forces.

Ascendance of Bomber Theory

The Air Corps Tactical School was notable as the birthplace of the Army Air Forces doctrine of daylight precision bombing. This doctrine held that a campaign of daylight air attacks against critical targets of a potential enemy's industrial infrastructure, using long range bombers heavily armed for self-defense, could defeat an enemy nation even though its army and navy remained intact.

Internal organizational and doctrinal issues were irretrievably entwined, and it is difficult to determine which element of the air power resources should lead the way. Initially, the Tactical School taught that pursuit aviation was the most important of air operations, comparing the importance of pursuit to the Air Service to that of infantry to the Army. By 1926, however, the Tactical School modified this principle by asserting for the first time that airpower could strike at vital points deep inside enemy territory rather than merely targeting an enemy's military forces in a war of attrition that the Allies experienced in the Trench Warfare of WWI. By 1931 the Tactical School was teaching that "a determined air attack, once launched, is most difficult, if not impossible to stop." This shift in emphasis from pursuit to bombardment evolved on the backs of two factors: the air war theories of the time and the state of aviation technology.

Devotees of Billy Mitchell dominated the faculty of the Tactical School at Maxwell. With their students, they developed a theory of warfare that invoked the superiority of the long-range bomber over all other types of aircraft. They de-emphasized balanced forces and support of ground troops in favor of a doctrine that heavily-armed bombers could fight their way to industrial targets in daylight and defeat an enemy by destroying their key industrial war production facilities.

Technical advances in the aeronautical engineering were demonstrating that aircraft could be developed that were capable of being flown over great ranges with large payloads. The advent of the Norden bombsight in 1931 provided for precision bombing from high altitudes. Bomber speeds were in excess of the day's pursuit aircraft, and it was deemed that the bombers could fight their way in unescorted. No longer would it be necessary to engage in costly and prolonged ground campaigns aimed at destroying enemy armies. While the theory was based on tenets of strategic airpower developed by Mitchell, Hugh Trenchard, and Giulio Douhet, it rejected the concept of terror-bombing of civil populations as a means of destroying the morale and coercing the will of an enemy state.

Nine key bomber advocates, all of whom instructed at the Tactical School, became known as the "Bomber Mafia." The unofficial leader of the group was the bombardment section chief and later director of the Department of Air Tactics and Strategy, Maj Harold L. George. Two of the most ardent instructors were Kenneth N. Walker and Robert Olds. Other "members" of the advocacy group included Orvil Anderson,

Max F. Schneider, Arthur W. Vannaman, Heywood S. Hansel, Hoyt S. Vandenberg, Lawrence S. Kuter and Samuel E. Anderson.

An Opposing Viewpoint

This doctrine was not universally held among air officers, however. Claire L. Chennault, chief of the pursuit section between 1931 and 1936,

 justifiably reasoned that the same technology that would increase the performance of the bomber would also eventually enable the single-engine fighter to challenge the bomber at high altitude.[4] Combined with a centralized early warning and control system, defending interceptors would inflict serious losses on unescorted forces.[4] The doctrine also ran counter to the theories of Billy Mitchell, who, despite his advocacy of the bomber, believed that pursuit support was essential for daylight bombing operations.

MajGen Claire Chennault

To test his air defense early warning theories developed in the Pursuit Section of ACTS, Chennault was able to mount an exercise in 1933. Working with the Coast Artillery, the system consisted of a warning system, interceptors, and anti-aircraft guns. A line between Indianapolis, IN to Cincinnati, OH, separated the Blue Force to the north at Patterson Field, OH and the Red to the south at Fort Knox, KY, 160 miles away. The Blues had a bombardment group of B-2s, B-7s and B-9s, and an attack group of A-8s augmented by P-16s. The Reds fielded an array of P-6Es and P-12Es. Three regiments of anti-aircraft artillery placed guns, searchlights and listening devices at Fort Knox. The defensive sector was 120 degrees wide extending toward Dayton divided into subsectors of 10 degrees each and five sections each 25 miles deep. Soldiers from the ground forces manned 69 observation posts, all connected to Headquarters at Fort Knox by phone. Sightings were to be immediately relayed to the headquarters and orders for launch pursuits were sent to Bowman Field. Response times were remarkably short with intercepts being made in as short a time as 12 minutes after takeoff. Most contacts were intercepted in the 25-50 mile sections. Night attempts were also included, but night intercepts were launched only one time.

The joint exercise provided arguments for Chennault and others for warning nets and interceptors. Interestingly, others reviewing the same results drew different conclusions and argued to General Westover that nothing could stop the bomber assault. In the ensuing years, many exercises were conducted on a variety of warning systems and interception techniques, but they never gelled into a coordinated continental U.S. civilian system, nor were the bomber advocates deterred.

Chennault, however, also had a blind spot in his zealous advocacy of fighters as the offensive weapon of the Air Corps and avoided acknowledging the role of accompanying escort fighters as an essential part of an offensive air strike. When his tour at ACTS ended, the fighter-versus-bomber controversy ended, much to the detriment of developing a role and a path for the fielding of escort fighters, so obviously needed in the early raids in WWII Europe.[5]

Thus the "Bomber Mafia" certainly had a "failure of imagination" in not expanding the doctrine to include establishing air superiority as a prerequisite for success and the pursuit fraternity failed to effectively communicate its potential contribution.[5] Their joint "blindness" contributed to the delay in the development of a long-range escort fighter until two years into WWII. The strategic bombing doctrine nonetheless became the foundation for the separation of the Air Force from the Army, and the basis for modern airpower theory. ACTS graduate, instructor, and "Bomber Mafia" member Haywood S. Hansell, concurred that both the theorists and the authors of the AWPD-1 war plan (he was both) made a serious mistake in neglecting long-range fighter escort in their ideas. Hansell wrote:

> "It was recognized that fighter escort was inherently desirable, but no one could quite conceive how a small fighter could have the range of the bomber yet retain its combat maneuverability. Failure to see this issue through proved one of the Air Corps Tactical School's major shortcomings."[6]

Hansell had a unique vantage point, having flown as a member of the "Three Men on a Flying Trapeze" Air Show Acrobatic Team headed by Chennault. He understood the need for air superiority gained through dominance of the skies, yet believed in the offensive capabilities of strategic bombardment. In the crucible of WWII, both camps would be proven essential in achieving success, for without air superiority, massive bombing raids would suffer unacceptable high rates of casualties.

Bomber Theorists Prevail

How did the "Bomber Mafia" change the focus of the Army Aviation so definitively to strategic air warfare? In its first years, the Tactical School taught that pursuit aviation was the most important air operation, which was epitomized by the 1925–1926 class text "Employment of Combined Air Force" that compared the importance of pursuit to the Air Service to that of infantry to the Army. However, in 1926 the Tactical School modified this principle by asserting for the first time that airpower could strike at vital points deep inside enemy territory rather than merely targeting an enemy's military forces in a war of attrition. By 1931 the Tactical School was teaching that "a determined air attack, once launched, is most difficult, if not impossible to stop." This shift in emphasis from pursuit to bombardment was primarily the result of the rapid growth in aviation technology focused on larger aircraft, but also on the evolving world of air war theories of the time[7].

The Billy Mitchell acolytes de-emphasized balanced forces and support of ground troops in favor of a doctrine that heavily-armed bombers could fight their way to industrial targets in daylight, unescorted by fighters, and with precision bombing made possible by the introduction of the Norden bombsight in 1931, defeat an enemy by destroying his key war production targets. In 1932, then 1stLt Kenneth N. Walker, one of BrigGen Mitchell's very capable sidekicks, became an instructor in bombardment aviation, and another of his aides, Cpt Robert Olds joined Walker. Between these two Mitchell acolytes, bombardment strategy and tactics evolved with intense scrutiny and debate.

Despite the fact that these young junior officers viewed war in the abstract and admitted to being unable to offer conclusive proof of their theories, they firmly believed in the dominance of airpower. This doctrine naturally brought them into conflict with the Army General Staff, which did not view airpower as a major striking arm but as an auxiliary to the ground forces. Despite the poor performance of what few bombers the Air Corps possessed, the air theorists persisted in their beliefs, testifying in favor of a separate air force before commissions set up in the wake of the Air Mail scandal. Maj George exhorted his students thusly:

"From today on much that we shall study will require us to start with nothing more than an acknowledged truth and then attempt, by the utilization of common sense and logic, to evolve a formula which we believe will stand up under the crucial test of actual conditions. We shall attempt to develop logically, the role of air power in future war, in the next war. We are not concerned with fighting the past war;-that was done 18 years ago. We are concerned, however, in determining how air power shall be employed in the next war and what constitutes the principles governing its employment, not by journeying into the hinterlands of wild imaginings but by traveling the highway of common sense and logic. In pursuing this purpose, we realize that air power has not proven itself under the actual test of war. We must also realize that neither land power nor sea power has proven itself in the face of modern air power. The question for you to consider from today on war, to have constantly before you as you continue your careers, is substantially this: Has the advent of air power brought into existence a method for the prosecution of war which has revolutionized that art and given to air forces a strategical objective of their own independent of either land or naval forces the attainment of which might, in itself, accomplish the purpose of war; or has air power merely added another weapon to the waging of war which makes it in fact only an auxiliary of the traditional military forces?"

Seldom has a military organization taken such a frank and open approach to defining its future, welcoming debate and a fulmination of dissent in its foremost school. It was painful, but thankfully for future war planning, it was spot on in most of its ultimate conclusions. The most significance on the part of the bomber proponents was their lack of recognition of the need for pursuit/fighter escort.

The School was not maniacally focused on fighters versus bombers, but taught the entire Air Corps officer responsibility spectrum. One of the more famous graduates was Ira Eaker, and he had this student assessment:

> "The course is designed, apparently with two primary purposes: one as a preparatory course to the Command and General Staff School, at Leavenworth; the second for the education of the Air Corps officer in his own arm-the Air Force. During the first half of the school year the student gets the impression that he is attending a service school of one of the other arms or, rather, a combination of all the service schools of the other arms. During this time he is turned over to the tender mercies of Field Artillery, Cavalry, Infantry, and Chemical Warfare officers who teach the precepts of modern warfare as fought by those arms. After Christmas vacation, the student begins to find that this is, after all, an Air school. Bombardment, Attack, Observation, Pursuit and Air Force are then thrown at the student with bewildering rapidity. There is a text for each subject; there are lectures in class, illustrative problems, and the much dreaded map problem."

As the inter-war concepts for the future of warfare evolved, ACTS sought to upgrade the requirements for assignment as an instructor or staff member. Minimum requirements sought were to be a graduate form the school and it was advocated that the instructors be graduates of the Command and General Staff School, and that the Commandant and his assistant be graduates of the Air War College. Steady improvement in the quality of the instructional staff and the attending students led to a discerning focus and an innate curiosity in determine the most effective uses of airpower.

Not only was the staff of the School being upgraded, but the qualifications for entry were made more demanding. By 1935, the requirement for student officers was to be above the grade of second lieutenant, and to have an efficiency rating of not less than excellent;

furthermore, not more than 14 percent of the quota of students was to come from the field officer grades and not more than 60 percent from the grade of captain. All officers of the various eligible grades were placed annually on a list in accordance with their general average efficiency ratings; then within the various percentages in grade, the officers having the highest rating were assigned to the school by the Chief of Air Corps.[7]

By 1926, a completely different approach to the concept of warfare had begun to take form. Up until this time, military doctrine had been based on surface engagements and air power contributions. Now, the bomber enthusiasts proposed using airpower to strike heavily at the vital points of a nation's structure. Maj Donald Wilson was assigned the task of preparing the Air Force course in 1933 and he succinctly reasoned that far more specific targets in the interior of an enemy's country should be designated as the objectives for bomber operations. Wilson saw that it would be effective to select targets whose destruction would disrupt the infrastructure of an enemy's economy and wear away the very foundations of an enemy's ability to function with any degree of normalcy. If airpower could disrupt the population's faith in the military establishment, then public clamor would force the government to sue for peace. From his experience as a civilian with American railroads, Wilson was aware that the destruction of a few vital links would disrupt an entire railroad system.

It did not take long for the airpower advocates to see that if it worked for railroads, it could be extended to other vital links in the enemy's economic structure. For example, if there was a particular highly specialized spring, manufactured by one particular firm and essential to the functioning of the controllable-pitch propellers and selective bombardment could obliterate that production, the enemy's aircraft production could be disrupted.

About this same time, daylight bombing concepts and the desire to bomb from the highest altitudes possible were espoused. The appearance of the B-9, B-10, and B-12 bombers began to lend some credence to the arguments put forth. Most were faster than the pursuits of the time. Instructor Kenneth Walker said "Military airmen of all nations agree that a determined air attack, once launched, is most difficult, if not impossible to stop." With the appearance of the B-17 many bomber enthusiasts declared that nothing could stop the bombers and that escorts were unnecessary. The impact of the B-17 on thought at the Tactical School was profound. Combined with developments in the areas of navigation and sophisticated bombsights, it appeared that the Air Corps had the plane and the bombsight which could accurately place heavy destructive loads on small, distant targets. By 1935 the full-blown theory of high-level, daylight precision bombardment of pinpoint targets was being taught at the Tactical School.

Other Conflicts Abound

Despite the soul-searching open discussions leading to the ACTS conclusions concerning the ability of strategic and tactical bombardment to determine war's outcome, the rest of the military remained to be swayed. The School's concepts and teaching were in direct conflict with the views of the War Department General Staff (WDGS). Throughout the controversy over the development and procurement of heavy, long-range bombers (even after the B-17 was developed, the General Staff hesitated to purchase it in quantity, as is chronicled in later chapters), responsible airmen were careful to avoid the advanced concepts of the ACTS in their arguments for acquisition. Officially, the long-range bomber was couched in phrases that stated it was a defensive weapon. The GHQ Air Force (GHQAF), the WDGS, and the Office of the Chief of the Air Corps (OCAC) were intimately concerned with the problem of how the Air Corps could best assist in the defense of the United States.

In 1935, Training Regulation 440-15, Employment of the Air Forces of the Army governed the use of the air forces of the Army. This regulation clearly indicated that the General Staff still considered airpower to be mainly a valuable means of influencing ground strategy, and admitted that in some minor respects, it was a compromise between air and ground concepts. It correctly noted that the power of air forces had not yet tested, nor had the effect they might produce been determined. Not sure of its foundation of its direction, the regulation also admitted that skillful use of air forces would greatly affect operations in future wars. It also offhandedly admitted to the necessity for counter-air operations by agreeing that such operations were "generally of primary importance."

The regulation openly revealed that the General Staff considered the primary function of the air force still was support of ground operations. In brief, "Air operations, like many other military operations, are governed by the same fundamental principles that have governed warfare in the past," and consequently, "Air Forces constitute a highly mobile and powerful element which conducts the operations required for carrying out the Army mission."

Despite War Department official doctrine, the School continued to expound its own concept of air warfare, based in a large part by the emergence of the B-17. They considered that airpower was the primary weapon of destruction in war and it could efficiently disrupt national life and achieve war's basic purpose—defeat the hostile enemy. Between 1935 and 1940, LtCols Harold L. George and Donald Wilson, Majs Muir S. Fairchild and Robert M. Webster, Lts Haywood S. Hansell and Laurence S. Kuter, and other instructors attempted to determine just what those targets should be. The 1935 text emphasized target selection within the various systems be made on the basis of scientific advice. But selection was a problem as there were no specialists at the Tactical School, nor was money available to hire them. It was assumed, however, that the industrial structure of any great power would parallel that of the United States, and that conclusions drawn from an analysis of American industry might apply to any other highly industrialized nation.

Thus in a unique approach, the School instructors undertook an analysis of our own American industrial structure with a view toward determining the geographic centralization of industry, the component parts of industry, the importance of the various parts, and the vulnerability to air attack of the most critical elements. In their 1935-1940 studies, they determined the points of vulnerability of industrial systems in general and the United States in particular. As a byproduct of their studies, they not only established a method to be used in determining the vulnerability of industrial targets and selecting the critical targets, they also considered the results desired in the light of the capability of available weapons. This approach was significant in the teaching a concept of strategic air warfare and was readily apparent to outside observers. Although, from a practical point of view, American planes did not have sufficient range to reach the vitals of any major industrial nation, careful analysis was given to the whole broad field of strategic airpower. School instructors developed a doctrine of air employment in terms of general capabilities of the air weapon. The successful outcome of WWII can in a large part be contributed to those intrepid instructors of the ACTS refusal to be swayed by the abhorrence of war generated by WWI and the proponents of differing concepts.

It can be easily discerned that the School provided a fertile environment for the advocacy of strategic airpower in the form of long-range bombing of the enemy's industrial nodes. The School staff laid down their personal beliefs, and unfolded a plan for the eventual establishment of airpower as a major element in the prosecution of war. The dedicated followers and avid students took those initial markers and ran with them, becoming visionaries in their own rights.

1. http://en.wikipedia.org/wiki/Thomas_DeWitt_Milling
2. *History of the Air Corps Tactical School*, Finney, Robert T. (1955). USAF Historical Studies No. 100: Center for Air Force History, March 1955 edition,
3. ibid
4. http://en.wikipedia.org/wiki/Claire_L_Chennault
5. *History of the Air Corps Tactical School*, Finney, Robert T. (1955). USAF Historical Studies No. 100: Center for Air Force History, March 1955 edition,
6. Hansell, Haywood S.. "AWPD-1, The Process". Air University, USAF. http://www.au.af.mil/au/awc/awcgate/readings/awpd-1-jfacc/awpdproc.htm#ii
7. *History of the Air Corps Tactical School*, Finney, Robert T. (1955). USAF Historical Studies No. 100: Center for Air Force History, March 1955 edition

CHAPTER
V

Between the Wars Visionaries

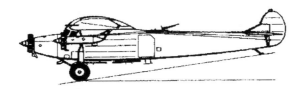

The Air Corps Tactical School (ACTS) cast a wide net over the available talented and skilled Army aviation officers, and the force and passion of the School instructors instilled in their students a bomber mentality. Those students were to figure predominately in the crucibles of WWII. Among them was a veritable galaxy of "stars" of the future.

Harold L. George

In the years just preceding WWI, officers and men were drawn for a number of sources, and not all of the "visionaries" were West Point graduates. Harold L. George was born in 1893 in Somerville, MA and attended George Washington University. On May 21, 1917, he was commissioned a second lieutenant in the cavalry in the Officers Reserve Corps. Within the month, he went on active duty with the Cavalry at Fort Myer, VA, in June but resigned his commission in October in order to take flying training as a cadet.

His unique path found him studying aeronautics at Princeton University in NJ and Flight training at Love Field, Dallas, TX, where he received his wings in March 1918. He went to France in September with

initial assignment to the 7th Aviation Instruction Center at Clermont. Two months later he joined the Argonne front. Two months later he was posted to the Meuse-Argonne front, piloting a bomber with the 163d Bomb Squadron, 2nd Day Bombardment Group.

In the one week that it saw action, the 163nd flew 69 sorties and it was there that George observed that massed bombers, flying in formation, swamped enemy defenses and so reduced the attacker's capabilities to wage the ground war. It was to be a defining moment in his career. [1]

Maj George's close association with bombing continued after the war, when he met and became an adherent of BrigGen "Billy" Mitchell's bombing theories, carrying them forward in a series of important assignments. He next served with the 14th Bombardment Squadron at Langley Field, VA and with the Aberdeen Proving Ground, MD. From 1921 to 1923, George was assigned to Mitchell's 1st Provisional Air Brigade and assisted in his bombing demonstration against old battleships, and helped develop air-to-ship tactics. In August 1925, George went to Washington as chief of the Bombardment Section in the United States Army Air Corps Operations Division. Later that year, still at the rank of first lieutenant, which he stagnated at from 1921 until 1931, he was one of several young air officers to testify at Mitchell's court-martial. After a two-year stint in Hawaii, in 1931, he went to Maxwell Field, Alabama, to study at the Air Corps Tactical School (ACTS) where he helped refine the precision daylight bomber doctrine taught there.

Following his graduation, he became an instructor there, teaching air tactics and precision bombing doctrine, and became the de facto leader of the influential "Bomber Mafia". Along with Haywood S. Hansell, Laurence S. Kuter and Donald Wilson, and others, he was the moving force behind the "Mafia" and believed that daylight bombing would be a war-winning strategy that Wilson termed "industrial web theory". In 1934, George was made director of the Department of Air Tactics and Strategy, and vigorously promoted the doctrine of precision bombing in which massed air fleets of heavy bombers would be commanded independently of naval or ground warfare needs.

Note for the Curious

As a measure of George's dedication and vision, one can point to another of his lesser known accomplishments. 13 years after listening to a Billy Mitchell suggestion to form a fraternal order of Army aviators, a young Lt George formed the Order of Daedalians on March 26, 1934, at Maxwell Field. Virtually all of the more than 14,000 American World War I aviators who were commissioned officers and rated as military pilots no later than the Armistice on November 11, 1918, had Founder Memberships in the Order, even though some did not participate in the Order during their lifetimes. At first, active membership was open only to Founder Members and their descendants, called Hereditary Members. In addition to George, who was the first National Commander, other charter members of the 2nd Bombardment Group (BG) were Vincent J. Meloy, Charles Y. Banfill, and Edwin R. McReynolds. The 2nd BG's Barney Giles was elected National Commander in 1956. Over the ensuing years, membership has been revised and now is open to all military aviators.

Following the coveted path to and graduation from Command and General Staff School, he returned to the 2nd Bombardment Group at Langley Field as commanding officer of the General Headquarters (GHQ) Air Corps 96th Bombardment Squadron. While there, under the tutelage of Andrews and LtCol Robert Olds, George flew as an Y1B-17 aircraft commander on record setting goodwill flights to South America in February 1938 and November 1939. In 1940, George "fleeted up" to take command of the parent 2nd Bombardment Group, and following Air Corps reorganization, filled the position of Executive Officer of the 2nd Bombardment Wing from January 1941. Thus for most of the formative development years of the B-17, he was in the thick of the training and demonstrations of its abilities.

In July 1941, George was appointed assistant chief of staff for Air War Plans Division, a unit of the newly created USAAF Air Staff in Washington. In that capacity he assembled a panel of bombing advocates who prepared AWPD-1, the plan for the air war against Germany. He was promoted to lieutenant colonel in February 1941, to colonel in January 1942, and to brigadier general in April 1942 when he took command of the Air Corps Ferrying Command (ACFC).[1]

His illustrious career was capped in WWII as he took the Ferry Command and formed it into the vitally important Air Transport Command. The Command took on the unheard of logistics responsibilities for moving millions of personnel and massive tonnages of cargo on a worldwide stage in quantities previously unheard of.

Haywood S. Hansell

Haywood S. Hansel was a bit younger than some of the "visionaries" and "bomber mafia" and although an "Army Brat", he also did not follow the typical path to an Army Air Corps, and eventually Army Air Forces, leadership role. Hansell was born in Fort Monroe, VA, on September 28, 1903, the son of First Lieutenant (later Colonel) Haywood S. Hansell, an Army surgeon, and Susan Watts Hansell, both considered members of the "southern aristocracy" from Georgia with a long confederate history tradition and a military lineage of the time. He entered Sewanee Military Academy, in 1916 where as a senior Hansell rose to cadet captain. He developed a reputation as a martinet and his harshness with the Corps of Cadets, combined with other difficulties, led to his reduction to cadet private[2]. Hansell thus declined an appointment to West Point and attended Georgia School of Technology, from which he graduated in 1924 with a Bachelor of Science degree in mechanical engineering. Unable to obtain a position as a civil engineer in California, he decided that aviation was the career field to pursue, and he considered that the quickest way to gain that experience was to join the United States Army Air Corps.[3]

MajGen Haywood S. Hansell

On February 23, 1928, Hansell was appointed a flying cadet and he completed primary and basic flying schools at March Field, California, then advanced flight training in pursuit flying at Kelly Field, Texas. Commissioned as a second lieutenant in the Army Reserve upon graduation on February 28, 1929, he received a regular commission as a second lieutenant, Air Corps, on May 2, 1929.

His first duty assignment took him to the soon-to-be famous 2nd Bombardment Group at Langley Field, testing repaired aircraft. After some temporary duty in 1930, he returned to Langley Field and was detached to the Air Corps Tactical School (ACTS) as armament officer. Due to lack of permanent facilities, the school eventually transferred to Maxwell Field, AL in August 1931, and Hansell went with it, where he became the assistant operations officer, with flying duties in the 54th School Squadron.

During that tour of duty he met Cpt Claire L. Chennault, an instructor at the Tactical School, and joined "The Men on the Flying Trapeze," an Air Corps aerobatic and demonstration team, testifying to his flying acumen as the team performed at the National Air Races at Cleveland, Ohio, in September 1934. Hansell also worked with Cpt Harold L. George, chief of the Tactical School's bombardment section, where his military interest shifted from pursuits to bombers. The friendship that developed from the working relationship led to George becoming both Hansell's mentor and patron. So, at an early stage in his formative years, he was exposed to both the pursuit and bombardment theorists, and found that there was much to be learned from both sides of the doctrinal fence.

Hansell was promoted to 1stLt on October 1, 1934, and entered the ACTS as a student in the comprehensive 845-hour, 36-week course, studying not only air tactics and airpower theory, which comprised more than half of the curriculum, but also tactics of other services, combined (joint) warfare, and a number of associated weapons and administrative subjects. Among his instructors was Cpt George, now director of the Department of Air Tactics and Strategy, whose classes were half lecture, half free discussion and conceptualizing, with George or his assistant Cpt Odas Moon expounding theories and having the students critically examine them for flaws and alternative ideas. Hansell graduated in June 1935, and among his peers were future generals Muir S. Fairchild, Barney Giles, Laurence S. Kuter, and Hoyt S. Vandenberg. He was one of nine in his class invited to become an instructor at the school, the youngest in its history. He served on the faculty from 1935-1938 in the Department of Air Tactic's all-important Air Force Section, first under George, then Maj Donald Wilson (another strategic bombing advocate), and lastly Fairchild. By this time, he was a member of that "bomber mafia", ATCS instructors who were outspoken proponents of daylight precision strategic bombardment and an independent Air Force.

In the instructor role, he had the opportunity to influence the thinking of many of his ACTS students, who included Ira C. Eaker, Elwood R. Quesada, Nathan F. Twining, Earle E. Partridge, Kenneth Wolfe, Orvil Anderson, John K. Cannon, and Newton Longfellow, all of whom became general officers and strategic airpower advocates during World War II.[4] Next came Command and General Staff School, and after graduation and promotion to captain, he was assigned to the Office, Chief of Air Corps (OCAC) under "Hap" Arnold, and then Ira Eaker. His assignments started with Public Relations, and then he worked on establishing the Intelligence Section. After a tour of RAF Intelligence Facilities in London, he returned and played a major role under George in the Air War Plans Division of the newly formed Army Air Forces, establishing the Strategic Planning for WWII.

Robert Olds

Born in Woodside, MD on June 15, 1896, he graduated from Central High School in Washington DC. On January 16, 1917, he enlisted in the Aviation Section, Signal Enlisted Reserve Corps, became a sergeant and entered pilot training at the Curtiss Flying School, Newport News, Virginia. By the time he received his Reserve Military Aviator rating on May 15, 1917, the United States had entered World War I. Like many of his peers, he was anxious to get into the WWI fray and he did not have to wait long. On June 7, 1917, he was commissioned as a 1st

MajGen Robert Olds

lieutenant in the Signal Officers reserve Corps and assigned commander of the newly-organized and untrained 17th Aero Squadron at Kelly Field,

Texas. The next day the squadron entrained for Toronto, Canada, where they arrived August 4 to begin unit training with the Royal Flying Corps. After three weeks of recruit instruction at Leaside Aerodrome, personnel of the 17th were distributed to various locations for specialized training, while Olds and the squadron headquarters were relocated to Camp Borden, Ontario. Olds remained squadron commander until October 15, when he became a flying instructor at Scott Field, Illinois. Following more instructional assignments at Ellington Field, Texas, he was promoted to captain on September 3, 1918, and sent to France.

Cpt Olds was assigned to pursuit training at the instruction center in Issoudun on September 25 and then to the Aviation Instruction Center at Clermont-Ferrand, where he became "Training Officer for Bombardment" and later Officer-In-Charge. On January 14, 1919, during demobilization of the American Expeditionary Force, Olds was assigned to the staff of the U.S. Second Army at Toule as flight examiner, a post he held until April 29, when he returned to Washington, DC

By this time, Olds had decided to make the Army a career, but somehow, he needed to shed his reserve status. In the post-war stand-down, a 50% reduction in forces was taking place, and it was occurring predominately in the reserve personnel ranks. Olds transferred to Fort Ruger at Honolulu, Hawaii, in October 1919, and while there, Air Service commanders submitted three letters of recommendation on his behalf, and on July 1, 1920, Olds received commissions as 1st lieutenant and captain in the Air Service of the Regular Army.[5] Olds married four times and his first marriage, to Eloise Wichman Nott, was in Hawaii on October 22, 1921 and resulted in sons Robert Jr. (Robin Olds), born in 1922 and who would go on to a stellar USAF career of his own, and Stevan, born in 1924. Eloise died in 1926 while Olds was assigned to the headquarters of the Air Service in Washington, D.C.

After more operational commands in the U.S., Olds transferred to the Office of the Chief of Air Service in Washington, DC in 1923, where he worked in the War Plans Division, often as an aide to the Assistant Chief of the Air Service, BrigGen. Billy Mitchell. In October 1925, he assisted Mitchell during the Morrow Board hearings, and the following month at Mitchell's court martial. With his career conceivably in jeopardy, Olds testified on November 10, describing the dangerous conditions under which the Air Service was forced to operate, and a lack of understanding of aviation requirements on the part of non-flying senior staff and commanders. Although mocked, and questioned with both sarcasm and hostility, during cross-examination by the nine ground forces generals comprising the panel, Olds "held his own".[6]

In September 1927 he was assigned to Langley Field, where he would spend eleven of his next thirteen years and further define the theories learned at the knee of BrigGen Mitchell and hone them as a student in the eighth class of the Air Corps Tactical School. Among his 23 classmates were Majs Frank M. Andrews, George H. Brett, and Willis H. Hale, all of whom would become senior leaders of the Army Air Forces, and John F. Curry (one of his sponsors to the Regular Army in 1920), who would become school commandant several years later. Upon graduation, he became an instructor at ACTS, as did 1stLt Kenneth N. Walker, who had also been a Mitchell aide. Together they served as the Bombardment Section of the ACTS faculty and between 1929 and 1931, when the school moved from Langley to Maxwell, they were directly responsible for the ascendancy of bombardment (which then existed mainly in theory and undeveloped technology) over pursuit as the primary emphasis of both the ACTS curriculum and the development of Air Corps doctrine. Haywood S. Hansell, wrote of them:

> "Bob Olds and Ken Walker together were dangerously close to being a "critical mass." Both were almost explosively intense and dynamic. Under them the Bombardment Section forged ahead . . . They had adopted Ken's contention that bombardment was to air power what the infantry was to the Army-the basic arm . . . "A well planned and well conducted bombardment attack, once launched, cannot be stopped." [7]

When ACTS relocated to Alabama, Olds remained at Langley as Operations Officer to the 2nd Bombardment Group from 1931 to 1933 when he then was afforded the career-enhancing opportunity to attend the Command and General Staff School (CGSS). His role as an airpower advocate continued to expand when in November 1934 he was one of six ACTS instructors invited by name to appear before the Federal Aviation Commission. Chaired by Clark Howell, the commission was created by President Franklin D. Roosevelt to review all aspects of U.S. aviation and in these rapidly evolving years, it became the sixteenth board since 1919 to examine the military's role in aviation.

Following completion of CGSS in 1935, Olds was promoted to major (temporary on June 30 and permanent on August 1) and returned to Langley, and joined the GHQ staff as Chief of Inspection Section under commander MajGen Frank Andrews, the driving force behind acquisition of the B-17 Flying Fortress. On March 1, 1937, Olds was promoted to lieutenant colonel and selected to command the 2nd Bombardment Group, which was about to receive the first twelve operational B-17s. He had a task to fulfill a directive from Andrews to build a capability of conducting bombing missions anywhere in the world and in any weather. Not only would the Army Air Corps watch the implementation of B-17 operations with keen interest, but the entire Army was in a formative state of flux and could nix the thrust in the bud if unsuccessful. On top of that relentless internal spotlight, everyone knew the Navy was at odds with the bombing theory, and the War Department was being pummeled from one side and then the other. They could not have selected a leader better-suited to bring the B-17 to operational status than LtCol Robert Olds. Time and again, Olds displayed his superior leadership capabilities in whipping the Group into a shape that would enable them to accomplish here-to-fore unheard of feats of record breaking long range missions.

Kenneth N. Walker

The other half of the Olds/Walker ACTS instructor team that was in a large part responsible for the bomber ascendency was Kenneth. N. Walker. Walker enlisted in the United States Army at Denver, Colorado, on December 15, 1917, and took his flying training at the University of California's School of Military Aeronautics and at the pilot training base at Mather Field, near Sacramento, He received his wings and was commissioned as a temporary second lieutenant in the United States Army Air Service on November 2, 1918. After Flying Instructor's School at Brooks Field in San Antonio, TX, he became an instructor at

BrigGen Kenneth N. Walker

the flight training center at Barron Field in Everman, TX. In March 1919, he was posted to Fort Sill as an instructor at the Air Service Flying School. During 1918, the School for Aerial Observers and the Air Service Flying School were built at nearby Post Field. He remained there for four years as a pilot, instructor, supply officer, and post adjutant; he added combat observer to his command pilot rating in 1922.

In 1925, Walker became a member of the Air Service Board at Langley Field, which was to become a "home" for him as he filled a number of increasingly important assignments there.. He served as adjutant of the 59th Service Squadron, commander of the 11th Bombardment Squadron, and operations officer of the 2nd Bomb Group. He graduated from the Air Corps Tactical School at Langley Field in June 1929 and stayed on as an instructor with Cpt Robert Olds in the Bombardment Section until July 1933, both at Langley and at Maxwell Field, where the school relocated in 1931. The influence they wielded as proponents of strategic bombing was immense. During their tenure, bombardment achieved primacy over pursuit in the development of Air Corps doctrine, despite pursuit champions such as Claire Chennault.

One of Walker's ACTS tasks was to rewrite the bombardment text. In an article entitled "Driving Home the Bombardment Attack", which was published in the Coast Artillery Journal in October 1930, he argued that fighters could not prevent a bombing attack and that "the most efficacious method of stopping a bombardment attack would appear to be an offensive against the bombardment airdrome". The ACTS eventually developed a doctrine that became known as industrial web theory, which called for precision attacks against carefully selected critical industrial targets. In November 1934, Walker and five other Air Corps Tactical School instructors were invited to testify on the military aspects of aviation before the Howell Commission on Federal Aviation, where they presented arguments to support a separate air organization, not subordinate to other military branches

Walker published another professional article, entitled "Bombardment Aviation: Bulwark of National Defense". "Whenever we speak in terms of 'air force' we are thinking of bombardment aviation," he wrote, dismissing other forms of aviation. Such was the orthodox thinking at the Air Corps Tactical School at the time. They taught that every dollar which goes into the building of auxiliary aviation and special types and not essential for the efficient functioning of the striking force can only occur at the expense of that air force's offensive power. Walker's major thesis was that "a determined air attack, once launched, is most difficult, if not impossible to stop when directed against land objectives." At the conclusion of his article, he called for the creation of an air force "as a force with a distinct mission, of importance co-equal to that of the Army and the Navy".

General Walker was posthumously awarded the Congressional Medal of Honor for leading a raid of B-17 and B-24 bombers on a raid designed to prevent the Japanese from reinforcing troops in Lae, New Guinea in 1943[8].

Caleb V. Haynes

Caleb Vance Haynes grew up and went to school in Mount Airy, NC and graduated from Wake Forest College in 1917 with a Bachelor of Laws degree. Two months after receiving his law degree, Haynes entered the United States Army as a flying cadet on August 15, 1917 followed by attendance at the School of Military Aeronautics at Georgia Polytechnic Institute, and then he sailed for France. He served at Saint-Maixent-l'École, and then entered the Machine Gun School at Gondrecourt-le-Château. In May 1918, he was commissioned a temporary second lieutenant in the Air Service, and sent to Tours as a test pilot. In July of that year he became an instructor at the Second Aviation Instructor Center at Issoudun and the following September was transferred to Orly as a test pilot. After the Armistice in November 1918, he served as an aide to President Woodrow Wilson during the Paris Peace Conference.

After a number of interesting inter-war assignments, he entered the Air Corps Tactical School at Maxwell Field in Alabama in 1931 at the rank of first lieutenant. This was precisely the time when ACTS instructors Olds and Walker were espousing the ascendancy of the bomber in the waging of war. Following graduation from the school in June 1932, he went to Langley Field, VA, for duty as engineering officer of the Eighth Pursuit Group, a unit of fighter aircraft at which he attained the rank of

MajGen Caleb V. Haynes, on right

captain. In February 1934, he assumed command of the Second Station, Eastern Zone, for the Army Air Corps mail operations based at Bolling Field, Washington, DC. From July 1934 until January 1935, Haynes was the commanding officer of the 37th Pursuit Squadron at Langley Field. This turned out to be Haynes's last posting to a fighter unit, but he had the relatively unique understanding of Air Corps needs, not just those of the bomber crusaders. Haynes would go on to participate in a number of Langley Field's 2nd Bombardment Group demonstrations promoting the capabilities of the Y1B-17 pioneering the use of aircraft on missions of here-to-fore unheard of ranges. Subsequent chapters will detail many of his accomplishments.

The experience gained on those missions led to his command in June of a single B-24 Liberator to be used to test a northern Atlantic air route to Great Britain. On July 1, 1941, he took off from Washington's Bolling Field and refueled in Montreal, then again at Gander, Newfoundland before arriving in Ayr, Scotland in the first B-24 delivered overseas. A total of 22 round trip flights were made by others in the next three-and-a-half months. Skeptics existed and the northern route did pose weather related problems. So, once again, Haynes was directed to scout another air route across the southern Atlantic from the U.S. to Brazil to Africa, with the terminus in Cairo, Egypt. On August 31 with Maj Curtis LeMay as his co-pilot (See the later chapters to understand why) and Chief of the Air Corps Maj General George H. Brett as a passenger, it was back to Bolling Field to begin a 26,000-mile round trip journey to Egypt and beyond, conveying Brett to Basra, Iraq, on a special mission. Haynes and LeMay retraced their flight to land back in the U.S. on October 7th. With the southern route thus proved satisfactory, the UK agreed to purchase 16 B-24s to be delivered by this method to Cairo.[9]

Laurence S. Kuter

Laurence S. Kuter graduated from the United States Military Academy, West Point, New York on June 14, 1927 and was assigned as a 2nd Lt to Battery D, 2nd Battalion, 76th Field Artillery, Presidio of Monterey, CA. Two years later in May 1929 he was accepted for flying training, graduating from flying schools at Brooks and Kelly Fields, TX, as a bombardment pilot in June 1930. He was brought into the "bomber fold" when he was assigned as operations officer, 49th Bombardment Squadron, 2nd

Bombardment Group at Langley Field. During his assignment at Langley, Lieutenant Kuter placed second in the annual bombing competition of the Army Air Corps.

In August 1933 Lieutenant Kuter moved up as operations officer of the 2nd Bombardment Wing, and assistant base operations officer at Langley. As a testimony to his flying skills, during this period he flew as an alternate wing position with Cpt Claire L. Chennault's acrobatic group, "The Flying Trapeze" along with Haywood Hansell. This was the first recognized aerial acrobatic team in the military service.

He then was given a leading role in the operational development of the Boeing Y1B-9 twin engine bomber which pioneered high altitude bombing techniques and tactics. From February to June 1934, Lieutenant Kuter served as operations officer of the Eastern Zone Army Corps Mail operations where he was thrust into a situation that the Air Corps was in reality ill equipped to handle, but it was a crucible of learning. He was the last officer relieved from this duty being held over to write the final report and history.

General Laurence S. Kuter

At the conclusion of this assignment he was selected for the Air Corps Tactical School, Maxwell Field, Alabama. He graduated at the top of his class in the spring of 1935 and was retained at the school as instructor in bombardment aviation and in the employment of air power. At this time the school was beginning to develop the role of strategic bombing in future warfare. It is not hard to imagine that his 10,000-plane Air Force envisioned in his lectures taxed imaginations at that time. Early in 1941 he was a principal factor in several augmentations of the Air Corps. In August 1941, Kuter was brought into the Air War Plans Division where he was one of the four principal authors of AWPD-1, the basic plan for employment of air power in World War II.[10]

Ira C. Eaker

Technically speaking, Ira Eaker could not be put in the same category as the other members of the "Bomber Mafia", but he had an illustrious career and worked diligently from positions of influence to focus the spotlight on strategic bombing prior to WWII. His initial WWII assignment was as the commander of the VIII Bomber Command in England, which soon became the Eighth Air Force.

Eaker was born in Field Creek, TX, in 1896, the son of a tenant farmer and attended Southeastern State Teachers College in Durant, OK, then joined the United States Army in 1917. Typically for the time, he was appointed a second lieutenant of Infantry in the Officer's Reserve Corps, and assigned to active duty with the 64th Infantry Regiment at Camp Bliss, El Paso, TX and that unit was assigned to the 14th Infantry Brigade on December 20, 1917, to be part of the 7th Infantry Division when it deployed to France. Eaker remained with the 64th Infantry until March 1918, when he was placed on detached service to receive flying

General Ira C. Eaker

instruction at Austin and Kelly Fields in Texas. Upon graduation the following October, he was rated a pilot and assigned to Rockwell Field, CA, and the following year was transferred to the Philippine Islands, where he served with the 2d Aero Squadron at Fort Mills, with the 3d Aero Squadron at Camp Stotsenburg, and as executive officer of the Department Air Office, Department and Assistant Department Air Officer, Philippine Department, and in command of the Philippine Air Depot at Manila until September 1921. As a regular Army captain in the Air Service, he returned to the United States in January 1922, for duty at Mitchel Field, NY, where he commanded the 5th Aero Squadron and later was post adjutant.

Eaker's heretofore relatively routine career took a turn that enabled him to wield influence and gain degrees of fame when he was named executive assistant in the Office of Air Service at Washington, DC. From December 1926, to May 1927, he served as a pilot of one of the planes of the Pan American Flight which made a goodwill trip around South America and, with the others, was awarded the Mackay Trophy. He then became executive officer in the Office of the Assistant Secretary of War at Washington, DC. In September 1926, he was named operations and line maintenance officer at Bolling Field, Washington, DC. While on that duty, he participated as chief pilot on the endurance flight of the Army plane, *Question Mark*, from 1 to January 7, 1929, establishing a new world flight endurance record. For this achievement the entire crew of five, including Eaker and mission commander Carl Spaatz, were awarded the DFC. In 1930, he made the first transcontinental flight entirely with instruments. He was ordered to duty at March Field, CA, where he commanded the 34th Pursuit Squadron and later the 17th Pursuit Squadron. He gained a unique perspective when in the summer of 1935, he was detached for duty with the Navy and participated aboard the aircraft carrier USS *Lexington*, on maneuvers in Hawaii and Guam.

Eaker entered the Air Corps Tactical School at Maxwell Field, Alabama, in August 1935 when the bomber doctrines had been well-established and was suitably "indoctrinated". Upon graduation the following June he entered the Command and General Staff School at Fort Leavenworth, KA, from which he graduated in June 1937. He then became assistant chief of the Information Division in the Office of the Chief of Air Corps at Washington, DC. It was in this position that he played a key role in planning and publicizing the interception of the Italian liner *Rex* at sea[11]. That story is told in full in Chapter IX, Expanding the Envelope.

1. http://en.wikipedia.org/wiki/Harold_L._George#cite_ref-Edkins5_4-0#cite_ref-Edkins5_4-0

2. http://en.wikipedia.org/wiki/Haywood_S._Hansell#cite_ref-0

3. ibid

4. ibid

5. www.wikipedia.org/wiki/Robert_Olds#CITEREFZamzow2008#CITEREFZamzow2008

6. www.wikipedia.org/wiki/Robert_Olds#CITEREFWaller2004#CITEREFWaller2004

7. *AWPD-1, The Process*, Hansell, Haywood S. Air University, USAF. http://www.au.af.mil/au/awc/awcgate/readings/awpd-1-jfacc/awpdproc.htm#ii

8. http://en.wikipedia.org/wiki/Kenneth_Walker

9. http://en.wikipedia.org/wiki/Caleb_V._Haynes

10. http://en.wikipedia.org/wiki/Laurence_S._Kuter

11. http://en.wkikpedia.org/wiki/Ira_C._Eaker

CHAPTER
VI

"Billy" Mitchell and Project "B"

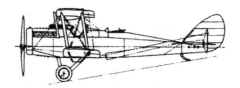

General William Lendrum "Billy" Mitchell

Few would deny that Billy Mitchell was a controversial figure, or that he was considered the father of the U.S. Air Force. Born on December 28, 1879 in Nice, France to wealthy Wisconsin senator John H. Mitchell, he enlisted in the Army in time for the Spanish-American War at age 18. He quickly earned a commission, probably because of his father's influence, and joined the Signal Corps. When the war ended, he remained on active duty, and as early as 1906, while an instructor at the Army's Signal School at Fort Leavenworth, predicted that future wars would be fought in the air. This was a prescient prediction, especially considering that the Wright Brothers had made their first flight only three years previously. His vision(s) would ultimately provide him worldwide recognition and conflict.

Helping to shape that vision, in 1908, Mitchell was one of the Army's observers at Fort Myer, VA when Orville Wright demonstrated the Wright Flyer proposed military model. Mitchell quickly grasped the practical application of his previous visionary theories. After tours in the Philippines and Alaska Territory, Mitchell was assigned to the Army's General Staff—at the time, its youngest member at age 32. He became interested in aviation and was assigned to the Aeronautical Division, U.S. Signal Corps, and a predecessor of the Army Air Service. Demonstrating his determination and focus on achievement, in 1916 at age 38 he took private flying lessons because the Army considered him too old and too high-ranking for flight training.

When the United States declared war on Germany on April 6, 1917, then-LtCol Mitchell was on a trip in Europe, where he had intended to be an observer of the ongoing combat operations. He was immediately deployed to France and set up an office for Army aviation.[1] At the time, U.S. Army Aviation had virtually non-existent resources, so he needed to collaborate extensively with British and French air leaders, studying their strategies as well as their aircraft, and soon had the experience to begin establishing the foundations for American air operations. A daring, flamboyant, and tireless leader, he eventually was elevated to the rank of brigadier general and commanded all American air combat units in France. This action essentially created two parallel U.S. air forces: the training and support functions in the continental U.S., and all of the combat arms under Mitchell. In September 1918 he planned and led nearly 1,500 British, French and Italian aircraft in the air phase of the Battle of Saint-Mihiel, one of the first coordinated air-ground offensives in history.

Considered to be a top American combat airman alongside aces such as Eddie Rickenbacker, he was probably the best-known American in Europe and was awarded the Distinguished Service Cross, the Distinguished Service Medal and several foreign decorations. Despite his superb leadership and his fine combat record, he alienated many of his superiors during and after his 18 months in France. He was a man in a hurry to achieve a superior aeronautical position for the United States, but found himself facing those who still thought that future wars would be fought exclusively on the ground a la the trenches of the past conflict with aircraft providing reconnaissance and artillery spotting.

It had been widely expected throughout the Air Service that Mitchell would receive the post-war assignment of Director of Air Service. Instead, for whatever reasons, Gen Pershing chose an infantryman and West Point classmate, MajGen Charles T. Menoher, surely rankling Mitchell and many others. Mitchell was appointed the deputy director of the Air Service upon his return to the United States in early 1919, retaining his one star rank[2].

Project "B"

Not one to bide his time and wait for more opportune moments to push for more aeronautical funding to upgrade U.S. aviation, his relations with superiors continued to sour as he began to attack both the War and Navy Departments for being nearsighted when it came to the military use of airpower. He advocated the development of an entire panoply of airborne technologies, including bombsights, ski-equipped aircraft, engine superchargers and aerial torpedoes. Additionally, he ordered the use of aircraft in a multiple of new arenas and scenarios, and encouraged Army pilots to challenge speed, endurance and altitude records, doing anything it took to keep Army aviation in the news.

Fearing a warship building "war" that would threaten the tenuous peace of the time, the Naval Powers of the time convened the Washington Naval Conference of 1921 with all of the countries considered to be naval powers in attendance. Great Britain and the United States were granted 500,000 tons, while Japan and Italy were capped at 300,000 tons, with the focus being on dreadnaughts, as battleships were named at the time. Mitchell was concerned that the building of dreadnoughts was taking precious defense dollars away from military aviation. He was convinced that a force of anti-shipping airplanes could defend a coastline with more economy than a combination of coastal guns and naval vessels. He reasoned that a thousand bombers could be built at the same cost as one battleship, and could sink that battleship. He infuriated the Navy by claiming he could sink ships "under war conditions," and boasted he could prove it if he were permitted to bomb captured German battleships.

To counter Mitchell, the Navy brought the old battleship *Indiana* to shallow waters off Tangier Island in Chesapeake Bay near the wreck of the battleship *San Marcos* (ex-*Texas*). The Navy subjected her to aerial bombing tests and she was hit with dummy bombs from aircraft while explosive charges were set off at the positions where the bombs hit. The conclusions drawn by the navy from the experiments conducted on *Indiana* were very different from the claims made by Mitchell. Navy Secretary Daniels had hoped to squelch Mitchell by releasing a report on the results written by Capt (USN) William D. Leahy that stated: "The entire experiment pointed to the improbability of a modern battleship being either destroyed or completely put out of action by aerial bombs." The Navy assigned an accuracy score of 11 percent to the bombs, which limited the explosions set off. Further evidence pointed to accuracy of about 40 percent.[3] However, when *the New York Tribune* revealed that the Navy's "tests" were done with dummy sand bombs and that the ship was actually sunk using high explosives placed on the ship, Congress introduced two resolutions urging new tests and backed the Navy into a corner.

Fortified with this public support, in February 1921, Mitchell was able to persuade Secretary of War Newton Baker and Secretary of the Navy Josephus Daniels to authorize a test of aerial bombing of naval ships of the line to test his theories. They agreed to a series of joint Army-Navy exercises, known as Project "B", to be held that summer in which surplus or captured ships could be used as targets.

Dragging their collective feet, the Navy reluctantly agreed to the demonstration as there was little defense following the leaked news of its own "tests". In the arrangements for these new tests, provisions were made for a news blackout until all data had been analyzed at which point only the official news report would be released. Mitchell correctly felt that the Navy was going to bury the results. Reacting to Navy complaints about Mitchell's criticisms, the Chief of the Air Service attempted to have Mitchell dismissed a week before the tests began, but the new Secretary of War John W. Weeks backed down when it became apparent that Mitchell had widespread public and media support.

BrigGen Mitchell Pointing out features of Martin Bomber to Gen Pershing While Secretary of War Meeks Looks on Provisional Air Brigade

On May 1, 1921, Mitchell assembled the 1st Provisional Air Brigade, an air and ground crew of 125 aircraft and 1,000 men at Langley Field, VA, using six squadrons from the Air Service:

- Air Service Field Officers School, Langley Field, Virginia, (SE-5 fighters)
  - 50th Squadron (later 431st Bomb Squadron)
  - 88th Squadron (later 436th Bomb Squadron)
- 1st Day Bombardment Group (later 2nd Bomb Group), Kelly Field, Texas (SE-5 fighters, Martin NBS-1, Handley-Page O/400, and Caproni CA-5 bombers)
  - 49th Squadron
  - 96th Squadron
- 7th Observation Group/Second Corps Area, Mitchel Field, New York (DH-4 fighters and Douglas O-2 observation planes)
  - 1st Squadron
  - 5th Squadron

Mitchell took command on May 27th after testing bombs, fuzes, and other equipment at Aberdeen Proving Ground, and began training his brigade in anti-ship bombing techniques. Alexander Seversky, a veteran Russian pilot who had bombed German ships in the Great War, joined the effort, suggesting the bombers aim near the ships so that expanding water pressure from the underwater blasts would stave in and separate hull plates. Further discussion with Captain (USN) Alfred Wilkinson Johnson, Commander, Air Force, Atlantic fleet aboard USS *Shawmut*, confirmed that near-miss bombs would inflict more damage than direct hits.

Rules of engagement

Obviously, the Navy and the Air Service were at cross purposes regarding the tests. Strangely supported by Army Gen Pershing, the Navy set rules and conditions that enhanced the survivability of the targets, stating that the purpose of the tests was to determine how much damage ships could withstand. It was immediately apparent that General Mitchell did not agree with the Navy Department's plans for the experiments as he thought the aircraft should bomb the ships with everything they had and sink them as fast as possible. The Navy countered by stating that the primary purpose of the bombing experiments was to learn as much as possible about the effect of the explosives rather than about tactical methods.

U.S. Navy Captain Watts, the conference briefer, explained that the experimental bombing was to ascertain the damage on certain types of naval vessels of certain intensive weapons of different types. The limitations as to the size of the bombs and number of hits required were prescribed after careful study of the material bureaus—not by the operating end of the Navy. He said, "It would be unsatisfactory for instance to drop a 2000 pound bomb on the destroyer and end the thing right there—the experiment would be robbed of its value."

The ships had to be sunk in at least 100 fathoms of water (so as not to become navigational hazards), so the Navy chose an area 50 miles off the mouth of Chesapeake Bay rather than either of two possible closer areas, minimizing the effective time the Army's bombers would have in the target area. The Army bombers were forbidden to use aerial torpedoes, would be permitted only two hits on the battleship using their heaviest bombs, and would have to stop between hits so that a damage assessment party could go aboard. Smaller ships could not be struck by bombs larger than 600 pounds, and also were subject to the same interruptions in attacks. The targets were to be an aged and surplus US battleship and four former German Navy vessels, including the battleship *Ostfriesland*, obtained in the peace settlement after World War I and scheduled for demolition. The attacks on the first four ships were strictly preliminary events. The tests opened the morning of June 21, with press and observers present on the naval transport USS *Henderson*. The air operations would be directed by Navy Captain Alfred W. Johnson, commander of the air force of the Atlantic Fleet, who interestingly was not a pilot.[4]

Mitchell held to the Navy's restrictions for the tests of June 21st, July 13 and July 18. On June 21st, Navy airmen sank the ex-German submarine *U-117* with 12 bombs. On July 13th, the Army airmen made their first appearance. Their Martin bombers (limited to 300-pound bombs by the rules) sank the former German destroyer *G-102* in 19 minutes. On June 29th, Navy airplanes attacked the old US battleship *Iowa* with dummy bombs. Of 80 bombs dropped, only two were scored as direct hits and the battleship advocates took comfort from this round of the testing. On July 18th both Navy and Army airplanes took turns attacking the former German light cruiser *Frankfurt*. No bomb heavier than 600 pounds was allowed. There were frequent intermissions as inspectors dragged out their on-board inspections, but eventually, the Air Service was allowed to strike and sank the vessel with 600-pound bombs. The Navy had figured on using gunfire from ships to finish off *Frankfurt*, and frankly was surprised.[5]

On each of these demonstrations the ships were first attacked by SE-5 fighters strafing and bombing the decks of the ships with 25-pound anti-personnel bombs to simulate suppression of antiaircraft fire, followed by attacks from twin-engined Martin NBS-1 (Martin MB-2) bombers using high explosive demolition bombs. Mitchell observed the attacks from the controls of his own DH-4, nicknamed *The Osprey*.

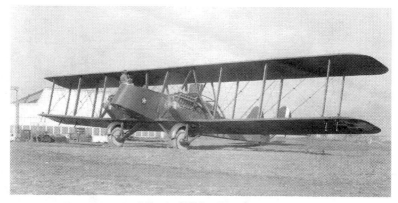

Martin NBS-1 Bomber

Handley Page TypeO/400

SE-5 Fighter

On July 20, 1921, the Navy brought out the ex-German WWI battleship, *Ostfriesland*, considered by some to be unsinkable. Bombardment of *Ostfriesland* was planned in several phases, spread out over two days, July 20th and 21st. A large number of Navy ships had gathered in the target area to watch, and about 300 VIP observers were present aboard the transport ship *Henderson*. Among them were Pershing (who had become Army Chief of Staff on July 1st), Secretary of War Weeks, Secretary of the Navy Edwin Denby, 18 members of Congress, 50 news reporters, and various admirals and generals. Once again Billy Mitchell was flying overhead in his personal airplane, Osprey, with a long blue pennant streamed from the tail for identification. Mitchell was accompanied by Cpt St. Clair Streett, flying in the back seat as navigator.

Mitchell ready to Launch in his DH-4

In one day of scheduled 230, 550 and 600 lb bomb attacks by Marine, Navy and Army aircraft, *Ostfriesland* settled three feet by the stern with a five degree list to port and was taking on water. Further bombing was delayed a day, as the Navy claimed that rough seas prevented their Board of Observers from going aboard. The Air Service complained that as the Army bombers approached, they were ordered not to attack. Mitchell's bombers were forced to circle for 47 minutes, as a result of which they dropped only half their bombs, and none of their larger types of bombs. The *Ostfriesland* was still afloat and the Navy gloated. Clinton Gilbert of *The Washington Post* reported, "On the good ship *Henderson*, Secretary Denby told us how little impression the bombs had made. High naval officers sniggered cheerfully." Sen. Wesley L. Jones of Washington stated that a Navy officer told him "it was a thousand to one that the ship would not be sunk by the bombing."

On the morning of July 21st, in accordance with a strictly orchestrated schedule of attacks, five NBS-1 bombers led by 1stLt Clayton Bissell dropped a single 1,100 lb bomb each, scoring three direct hits. The Navy stopped further drops, although the Army bombers had nine bombs remaining, to assess damage. By noon, *Ostfriesland* had settled two more feet by the stern and one foot by the bow. On the control ship, Johnson, supposedly an objective director of the testing, let his emotions show. "By Jove," he said, "we're not going to sink this ship!"

The last shot at *Ostfriesland* was set for midday July 21st. Cpt W. R. Lawson would lead a flight of six Martins and two Handley Pages, each carrying a 2,000-pound bomb. Although the written agreement had been that the Air Service would be allowed two direct hits with their biggest bombs, as the pilots stood by waiting to take off, Johnson called with a change in rules. The bombers could bring no more than three of their biggest bombs to the target area. To say the least, Mitchell was angered and ordered all eight aircraft to proceed. He fired off a message to the Navy, saying that his bombers were carrying 2,000-pounders and would continue attacking "until we have secured [the] two direct hits [the] Army is authorized to make." He received no reply.

One of the Handley Pages had to drop out of the formation and return to base for mechanical reasons, but the other seven airplanes went on to the target. They had no intention of making two direct hits and stopping the test. Their orders were to aim for near misses to create water hammer shock waves against the hull.

Gone in Twenty-two Minutes

The first bomb fell at 12:18 p.m. and was a near miss, as planned. The other airplanes swept in at spaced intervals and delivered their ordnance. "We could see her rise eight or 10 feet between the terrific blows from under water," Mitchell said. The sixth bomb, at 12:31, sealed *Ostfriesland's* doom. Twenty-two minutes after the first bomb fell, the old battleship sank at 12:40. The seventh airplane, a Handley Page, dropped its unneeded bomb as a final salute at the point where the battleship had gone down. Mitchell followed the bombers back to Langley, jubilantly waggling the wings of Osprey as he flew by *Henderson.*[6]

Martin NBS with 2,000 lb Bomb Under Fuselage, Smaller Bomb Under Wing

Bomb Bursts over the Battleship *Ostfriesland*

The Battleship *Ostfriesland* **Sinking**

The success or failure of the tests depended on who was telling the story, and debates were easily started. Although Mitchell had stressed "war-time conditions", the tests were certainly conducted under static conditions. The sinking of the *Ostfriesland* was accomplished by violating rules agreed upon by Gen Pershing that would have allowed Navy engineers to examine the effects of smaller munitions. Up until this time, little was known about the effect of bombs on naval vessels, and the Navy wanted to progressively build up in the size of munitions with inspections between each mission. The schedule was to be:

Schedule of Bombing Experiments for *Ostfriesland*		
1st attack	14" armor-piercing bombs	Navy planes
2nd attack	230-pound bombs	USMC and Navy planes
3rd attack	550-pound bombs	Navy planes
4th attack	600-pound bombs	Army planes
5th attack	1000-pound bombs	Army planes
6th attack	1000-pound bombs	Navy planes
7th attack	2000-pound bombs	Army planes
8th attack	2000-pound bombs	Navy planes

Bombing Schedule

Transcripts of the admittedly primitive communications of the time indicate that there was more than a modicum of confusion in the coordination of strike missions, but the strong-willed and impatient Mitchell was intent on proving his point, and moved in with the heavy munitions, and sank the battleship.

Later, Navy studies of the wreck of the *Ostfriesland* showed she had suffered little topside damage from bombs and was sunk by progressive flooding that might have been stemmed by fast-acting damage control parties on board who would have maintained water-tight integrity. Mitchell used the sinking for his own publicity purposes, though his results were downplayed in public by Gen Pershing who hoped to smooth Army/Navy relations. Even H.H. Arnold stated:

"Rules or no rules, Billy Mitchell had been out to sink that battleship. His first wave of Martin Bombers was loaded with two 1000-pound bombs apiece, and after a few hits, the ship went down. Within a matter of hours, the Navy had protested against Mitchell's tactics. The protests, however, were drowned in the wave of excited headlines. Billy Mitchell had proved his point. His bombers had done what he said they would do." [7]

Controversy Continues

A Joint Army and Navy Board report on bombing tests, made public on August 19th and reported in The New York Times stated that "The battleship is still the backbone of the fleet and the bulwark of the nation's sea defense, and will so remain so long as the safe navigation of the sea for purposes of trade or transportation is vital to success in war. The airplane, like the submarine, destroyer, and mine has added to the dangers to which battleships are exposed, but has not made the battleship obsolete." General Pershing was the senior member of the board and his signature was the only one on the report, a deliberate expression of solidarity with the Navy and intended to diminish the significance of the tests. [8]

Mitchell made his own report to MajGen Menoher, Chief of the Air Service and it contradicted the Joint Board report signed by Pershing. Menoher filed it away, but it soon fell into the hands of the press. "Had the Army Air Service been permitted to attack as it desired, none of the seacraft attacked would have lasted 10 minutes in a serviceable condition," Mitchell said in a part of the report quoted by The New York Times on September 14th.

Good soldier and classmate of Pershing, Menoher said that either Mitchell went or he would. Perhaps he should not have been so rash, for Secretary Weeks, again consulting the political omens, decided that Menoher would be the one to go. Pershing sent for Mason M. Patrick, a strong officer who had gotten Mitchell under control in France, promoted him to major general and made him Chief of the Air Service.

Patrick was made of sterner stuff than Menoher. When Mitchell threatened to resign if he didn't get his way, Patrick invited him to put in his papers and escorted him to the office where he could do it. Mitchell backed down and did not challenge Patrick again. Patrick, who learned to fly and won his wings as a junior pilot at age 60, gained both the respect and the affection of the force he led.

Regardless, the Project "B" test was highly influential at the time, causing budgets to be redrawn for further air development and forcing the Navy to look more closely at the possibilities of naval airpower. Despite the obvious advantages enjoyed by the bombers in the artificial exercise, Mitchell's report stressed facts that were repeatedly proven later in war.

- Sea craft of all kinds, up to and including the most modern battleships, can be destroyed easily by bombs dropped from aircraft
- Bombs are the most effective means of destruction
- Adequate air forces constitute a positive defense of our country against hostile invasion.

The fact of the sinkings was indisputable, and Mitchell repeated the performance twice in tests conducted with like results on obsolete U.S. pre-dreadnought battleship Alabama in September 1921, and the battleships Virginia and New Jersey in September 1923. The latter two ships were subjected to teargas attacks and hit with specially designed 4,300 lb demolition bombs.

Photo # 80-G-424471 Army bombing tests on the former USS Alabama, in Chesapeake Bay, September 1921

The *Alabama* Takes a Hit in Chesapeake Bay Tests Sept. 1921

Photo # NH 924 Phosphorus bomb strikes the former USS Alabama, during tests in September 1921

Phosphorus Bomb Explodes on *Alabama* as Observer DH-4 Flies By

Dual Bomb Rack with two 1,000 lb Bombs Rigged and Ready

USS *Virginia* Takes a Direct Hit with a 1,100 lb Bomb

The "sea-minded" admirals, or battleship sailors, who were responsible for our naval policy and the Navy's state of readiness for war certainly under-rated the airplane; the "air-minded" generals, on the other hand, over-rated the airplane. Both suffered from a myopic view of global war as they ignored the "big picture". The admirals were more concerned with war on the high seas, and on islands and continents across the seas than they were with the ability of airplanes to sink battleships close to our shores. Yet the generals rightfully considered the airplane to be not only an offensive weapon to reach deep into the enemy's home resources, but one to effectively defend the shores from enemy invasion. Thus the tests were not simply a vindication of the airplane or the battleship, but over the very fundamental philosophies of the conduct of war.

A technical note is worthwhile mentioning at this juncture. All of the tests focused on "pin-point" horizontal bombing exercises from altitude. It has been reported that in WWII, no U.S. Navy underway ship was sunk by the "pin-point" horizontal bombing from altitude. The many that were sunk by Japanese planes were sunk by dive bombers, torpedo bombers and Kamikaze strikes. With the development of electronics, electronic fire control systems, and the perfection of the proximity fuse early in World War II, the picture reversed and anti-aircraft gun fire became a very effective weapon and added new life to the battleship. So it is with the give and take of weapon development, and why proponents of one system or another passionately promote their theories.

Pushing the Point to the Extreme

As noted in Chapter III, Mitchell was passionate in his advocacy for the supremacy of airpower and push for a separate Air Force. Despite the success of his Project B demonstration, he failed to use it to the Army's advantage. If anything, he became more passionate and vociferous, and it led to his ultimate resignation. One may argue the approaches he took, but not with his vision.

1. *American Airpower Biography: Billy Mitchell* Colonel Phillip S. Meilinger, USAF. Maxwell AFB

2. *Mitchell William. Biographical Data on Air Force General Officers*, 1917-1952. AFHRA (USAF).

3. *Billy Mitchell and the Battleships*, John T. Correll, AIR FORCE Magazine, June 2008,.

4. ibid

5. ibid

6. ibid

7. *The Army and Its Air Corps: Army Policy toward Aviation, 1919-1941*, Tate, Dr. James P., Lt Col USAF, Retired (1998).. Air University Press. ISBN 0160613795

8. *Billy Mitchell: Crusader for Air Power*, Hurley, Alfred F.

CHAPTER VII

Proving the Concept

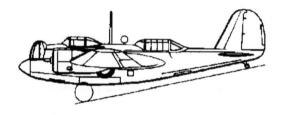

The Quest for Performance

The visionaries were well on their way to establishing the Air Service and eventually the Air Corps as a strategic weapon to be reckoned with following the successful prosecution of the 1st Provisional Air Brigade's performance during Project "B". But doubts remained in the minds of many and debates continued over the rules of engagement and their effect on the outcome. The Army took up the challenge and sought out every opportunity to prove that they had the strategic vision, the tools to effect enemy defeat and the personnel who could make it happen through the exploitation of that airpower.

There were so many seemingly insurmountable obstacles standing in the way of a developing strategic airpower offense, that it is a testimony to the vision, fortitude and aeronautical skills that they succeeded. The range, speed and payloads of existing aircraft such as the NBS-1 made extension of their concepts little more than a dream and the bomber mafia was the first to admit that. The insidious effects of high altitude flight were little understood. Navigation had not gone beyond visual contact with the ground and long range, high altitude navigation at speeds over 200 mph was an unexplored realm. Weather aloft was really an unknown, with such things as frontal phenomena and jet streams yet to be learned. All weather flying and instrument approaches would need to be developed to make airpower effective. Unlike the relatively exact science of Army Artillery and Naval Gunfire solutions, bombing from altitude was fraught with a host of unknowns. One thing that was foremost in their minds was the demand for more performance from their bombing platforms.

The Army visionaries viewed the advances in commercial aviation and in the many promotional air shows and races as proof that given the transformation of that technology to military platforms it would yield the type of platforms they needed.

The Platform Search—Finding the Bomber of the Future

The Project "B" Operation of 1921 showcased a number of "bombers" including the Martin NBS-1, the Handley-Page O/400, and Caproni CA-5. Despite the success of the tests, it was obvious that these fragile, unreliable, wood-structured, fabric-covered relics were not the answer for the future. The Army looked at what was happening in the commercial world, and as was typically the case at that time, private entrepreneurial efforts were leading the way and on the cutting edge of technology. Facing an internal resistance to change, General Mitchell knew that the future of Army aviation would be relegated to merely supporting the ground troops unless the Air Service could demonstrate to the public, and more importantly, to the Congress who held the purse strings, that airpower was to be the predominant weapon in future wars. He encouraged Army aviation to tackle seemingly impossible performances to publicize the capabilities of air power. The Air Service and Air Corps were only too happy to prove his points.

First Aerial Circumnavigation of the World

One of the early efforts to "show-the-flag" and demonstrate global reach capabilities was the Army Air Service's interest in having a squadron of their aircraft make the first "round-the-world" flight. There had been a number of attempts, almost since the time of the Wright Brothers' first flight. In 1922, British Maj W.T. Blake and his team made it from London to Bay of Bengal in fits and starts before crashing. England's Stuart Macmillan also made it as far as Russia with a Vickers Vulture before crashing. The Army Air Service thought that a round-the-world flight success would capture the public's imagination and elevate their status and pave the way for the funding of more capable aircraft.

In the spring of 1923, a group of officers was assigned to find suitable aircraft and to plan the mission. They conducted a review of the Army's inventory of aircraft and it revealed that there were no satisfactory models available for the task. Therefore, they began to look outside the Air Service for an aircraft that could be fitted with either floats or landing gear interchangeably. It must be remembered that in these early days of aviation, there were few acceptable landing fields outside the U.S. and parts of Europe, and the globe had an abundance of its surface covered with water so an ability to change the configuration to floats was almost demanded.

The War Department directed the Air Service to investigate the Fokker F-5 transport and the Douglas *Cloudster* and determine if either would be suitable.[1] When asked for information on the *Cloudster*, Donald Douglas instead submitted the specifications for a modified DT-2 torpedo bomber that was built for the U.S. Navy in 1921 and 1922. A proven aircraft that had demonstrated its ruggedness and durability in naval service, it could be equipped with interchangeable wheels or floats. The clincher for the Army was Douglas' promise to be able to deliver aircraft within 45 days after contract award since it was an existing aircraft. After Air Service agreement, a member of the assigned planning group, Lt Erik Nelson, was dispatched to California to work out the details. The acquisition process then was certainly simpler and more effective than that which exists today!

The DT-2 was modified for the circumnavigation requirements, and foremost of the modifications was the increase in fuel capacity. This was accomplished by removing all of the internal bomb-carrying structures and adding fuel tanks in virtually every available space while maintaining weight and balance. A testimony to their success is the total fuel capacity growing from 115 gallons to 644 gallons. Lt Nelson presented the details to MajGen Mason M. Patrick, Chief of the Air Service. The design was approved on August 1, 1923 and a War Department contract was awarded for one test plane. The test aircraft met all expectations and another contract was let for four more aircraft and the necessary spare parts. The spares included 15 extra Liberty engines, 14 sets of floats and enough replacement parts for two more ships which would be sent ahead along the route the aircraft, now called Douglas World Cruisers, would follow.

The Douglas World Cruiser

The Four planes, now named *Seattle, Chicago, Boston and New Orleans* left Santa Monica for Seattle and the start of their quest. The crews consisted of:

    Seattle—Maj Frederick Martin, pilot and flight commander and SSgt Alva Harvey, flight mechanic (We'll learn a lot more about him later)

    Chicago—Lt Lowell Smith, pilot, and 1stLt Leslie Arnold

    Boston—1stLt Leigh P. Wade, pilot, and SSgt Henry H. Ogden

    New Orleans—Lt Erik Nelson, pilot, and Lt Jack Harding

On April 6th, the ships left for Alaska, leaving the Seattle behind for repairs. When the *Seattle* tried to catch up, it crashed into a mountainside in the dense fog of the Alaskan Peninsula. The crew, Maj Frederick L. Martin and SSgt Alva L. Harvey, survived and made their way through the wilderness to safety. SSgt Harvey was not deterred or done with flying, despite his harrowing ordeal. The Air Corps insisted that pilots be commissioned, but did allow enlisted personnel of SSgt or above to enter flight training as cadets. SSgt Harvey was selected for flight training and

went through the cadet program at Brooks and Kelly Field in 1922 and
was promoted to 2ndLt upon
graduation and given a regular
commission. He continued his storied
career and was a pilot in command of
a B-17 on the Argentina goodwill
flight, described in Chapter Ten.

The other three aircraft continued
on through Asia, the Middle East,
and Europe, relying on a carefully
planned logistics system, including
pre-positioned spare engines, to
keep the aircraft flying. The *Boston*
was forced down while crossing the
Atlantic and damaged beyond repair
while being recovered by the Navy
light cruiser USS *Richmond*.

**Maj Martin and SSgt Harvey after
walking away from Alaskan crash**

Sinking of the *Boston*

The remaining two aircraft
continued across the Atlantic back
to the United States, where they
were joined by the test aircraft,
now christened *Boston II*. The
aircraft returned to their Seattle
starting point on September 28,
1924, 23,942 nm (44,342 km)
and 175 days since departing.
Appendix A details the route, miles covered, and flight time for each leg.[2]

World Cruiser Instruments
(Panel center top row; Compass, Driftmeter, Sextant in middle row;
Flight Indicator and Airspeed Indicator in bottom row)

They had conquered the globe bringing many accolades to the crews and to the Army for it was truly a monumental achievement. Perhaps only the military, and especially the Army Air Service, could have accomplished such a venture at this time given the required logistics and the government financial wherewithal. Typical comments included, "A Tribute to American persistence, skill and resourcefulness." "Other men will fly round-the-earth, but never again will anybody fly around it for the first time." Their round-the world flight has never been duplicated by anyone flying in a single engine, open-cockpit airplane.

Stretching Range with In-flight Refueling

The short range of the existing aircraft severely limited their capabilities of fulfilling the Army's dreams of strategic reach. Adding fuel capacity to increase range the Douglas World Cruiser eliminated any offensive payload. If a method could be found to safely transfer fuel and oil to an in-flight bomber, quantum leaps in range capabilities could be realized.

Perhaps stimulated by the barnstorming stunts such as the always popular wing-walking, the United States Army Air Service accomplished

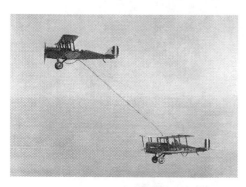

the first mid-air refueling between two planes on June 27, 1923, with two Airco DH-4B biplanes flying over San Diego's Rockwell Field. Later, they would take the skills gained in that accomplishment and set an endurance record with three DH-4Bs (a receiver and two tankers) on August 27–28, 1923. The receiver

1923 Army Air Service In-Flight Refueling

airplane remained aloft for more than 37 hours using nine mid-air refuelings to transfer 687 gallons of aviation gasoline and 38 gallons of engine oil. With the concept proven, the next step was to show how this would translate to increasing range and mission applicability. The same crews demonstrated the utility of the technique on October 25, 1923, when a DH-4 flew from Sumas, WA, on the Canadian border to Tijuana, Mexico, landing in San Diego, using mid-air refuelings at Eugene, OR, and Sacramento, CA. Their records would not stand for long, as a Belgian team set a record of 65 hours in 1928.

2nd Lt. Elwood R. Quesada, an engineer of the U.S. Army Air Corps stationed at Bolling Field in Washington, DC, developed a plan with a U.S. Marine Corps aviator from next door neighbor Anacostia Naval Air Station to break that 65 hour endurance record established by the Belgians. The plan was reviewed by Cpt Ira C. Eaker, an aide to Assistant Secretary of War for Air Forces, Trubee Davison. Both Eaker and Quesada had a personal stake in stretching range through in-flight refueling as they had piloted an aircraft on an April 1928 long-range rescue mission to Labrador, and had nearly run out of fuel. Eaker in turn took the plan to MajGen James E. Fechet, Chief of the United States Army Air Corps (successor to the Air Service in 1926). Both Fechet and Davison approved the project on the condition that it demonstrate a military application and not just as a publicity stunt. Overall command of the project was given to Maj Carl A. Spaatz (who then spelled his named "Spatz"), the Assistant G-3 for Training and Operations in Fechet's office.

A new Atlantic-Fokker C-2A transport, serial number 28-120, assigned to the 14th Bombardment Squadron at Bolling Field, was flown to Middletown Air Depot, PA, and modified for the project. The C-2A was an American-built military version of the Fokker F.VIIa-3m trimotor, a high-wing monoplane with a gross weight of 10,395 pounds, re-engined with three Wright R-790 motors producing 220 HP each. The C-2A had an internal fuel capacity of 192 gallons in a pair of wing tanks, and for the project, two 150-gallon tanks were installed in the cargo cabin. A hatch was cut in the upper fuselage of the C-2 behind the wing for transfer of the fuel hose and passage of supplies from the tanker to the receiver. 72-octane aviation gasoline would be received in 100-gallon increments of approximately 90-seconds duration.[3]

The *Question Mark* being Refueled

A 45-gallon tank was used to provide engine oil to the three motors, replenished by in-flight deliveries of 5-gallon cans of Pennzoil® triple-extra-heavy oil lowered on slings. Radial engines of the time were notorious for valve failure due to lack of rocker arm lubrication, so copper tubing system was installed in an attempt to adequately lubricate the rocker arms of the engines in-flight. Doorways were cut on each side of the cockpit and catwalks built on the wings to enable mechanic Roy Hooe to access the engines for emergency maintenance. To reduce propeller noise, in a revolutionary move for the time, the two wing engines were mounted with Westinghouse twin-blade Micarta® propellers. Micarta® was developed by George Westinghouse at least as early as 1910 using phenolic resins invented by Dr. Leo Baekeland. Originally used in electrical and decorative applications, it is still in use today in many similar industrial applications. The nose engine continued with the Standard three-blade steel propeller.

As a result of the overwhelming number of questions on the endurance expectations, a question mark was painted on each side of the fuselage to provoke interest in the endurance record attempt. The ship was appropriately christened *Question Mark.*

Two Douglas C-1 single-engine transports, a design evolving from the previously described World Cruisers, were modified to deliver the fuel to the C-2A. The pilots were seated side-by-side in an open cockpit forward of the wing and two 150-gallon tanks were installed in its cargo compartment attached to a lead-weighted 50-foot length of 2.5-inch fire hose. The hose had a quick-closing valve on the tanker's end and was tightly wrapped with copper wire; one end of which could be attached to a corresponding copper plate mounted in *Question Mark* to ground the hose, a very important step to eliminate the potential for a static electricity spark igniting transferring fuel. The C-1's would each carry a third crewman in the cargo compartment to reel out the hose or lower a supply rope, and to work the shutoff valve.

The operation was planned to begin January 1, 1929, at Los Angeles, CA, both to take advantage of weather conditions and to generate publicity by overflying the 1929 Rose Bowl football game played that day in Pasadena. The equivalent of today's Super Bowl, it was a chance not to be missed. The C-2A would fly a 110 mile long race track oval between Rockwell Field in San Diego and Metropolitan Airport, now Van Nuys Airport, with refueling planes situated at each end. The flight would originate and terminate at Metropolitan in order for any endurance record to be officially recognized by the Fédération Aéronautique Internationale (FAI).

The crew of *Question Mark* consisted of Maj Spaatz, Cpt Eaker, 1stLt Harry A. Halverson, 2ndLt Quesada, (A star-studded cast, as they all would eventually become generals) and future Hall of Famer, Sgt Roy W. Hooe. Refueling Airplane No. 1 (at Rockwell) was crewed by pilots Cpt Ross G. Hoyt and 1stLt Auby C. Strickland (also destined to reach general rank), with 2ndLt Irwin A. Woodring reeling the hose. Refueling Airplane No. 2 (at Van Nuys) was crewed by pilots 1stLt Odas Moon and 2ndLt Joseph G. Hopkins, and hose handler 2ndLt Andrew F. Solter. Four pilots of the 95th Pursuit Squadron, based at Rockwell Field, flew the PW-9 "blackboard planes" (The Fokker's radios had been removed to save weight, so messages were written on the large blackboards of the PW-9s): 1stLt Archie F. Roth, and 2ndLts Homer W. Kiefer, Norman H. Ives, and Roger V. Williams.

During the first night-time refueling, Spaatz was drenched with fuel when turbulence caused the hose to pull out of the receptacle. Fearing that chemical burns from the gasoline might force him to parachute from the airplane to seek medical treatment, Spaatz ordered Eaker to continue the flight regardless and he shed all his clothing and was wiped off with oil-soaked rags. Although he directed at least one refueling without his clothing[4], replacements were soon delivered. Quesada was briefly overcome by the same accident but quickly revived. Spaatz experienced two other fuel spills without injury, using oil to wipe his skin and zinc oxide to protect his eyes.

Question Mark Crew (left to right: Cpt Ross G. Hoyt, refueling plane No, 1 pilot, Cpt Ira C. Eaker, Chief Pilot, MajGen James E. Fechet, Chief Air Corps, Maj Carl Spaatz, Project Commander, Lt Elwood R. (Pete) Quesada and Master Sgt R. W. Hooe

Despite deliberate flight at slow cruising speeds to nurse the engines, they eventually became overworked from their extended use. The left engine began losing power as early as the third day. Sgt Hooe, taping down his trouser cuffs, wearing a parachute, and connected by a lifeline, attempted to service them from the makeshift catwalks but the in-flight lubricating systems only delayed and could not prevent engine wear. Eaker found that he was able to clear fouled spark plugs by completely opening the throttles.

On the afternoon of January 7th, the left wing engine quit and Hooe went out on the catwalk to attempt repairs, immobilizing the wind milling propeller with a rubber hook. Eaker eased on throttle on the remaining two engines to maintain flight while repairs were attempted, but they too began to strain. The plane lost altitude from 5,000 to 2,550 feet before Hooe was called back inside and the decision made to land. The *Question Mark* landed under power at Metropolitan Airport at 2:06 pm; 150 hours, 40 minutes, and 14 seconds after takeoff. The left engine had seized because of a pushrod failure, and the others all suffered severe rocker arm wear.

In the course of the operation, the tankers made 43 takeoffs and landings, in both day and night, a real challenge for the day. Hoyt flew 27 sorties, ten of them at night while Moon flew 16 sorties, two at night. Altogether, they refueled the *Question Mark* 37 times, delivered 5,660 gallons of fuel (33,960 pounds), 245 gallons of engine oil (1,838 pounds delivered in 49 five-gallon cans that had to be physically muscled aboard), and storage batteries, spare parts, tools, food, clothing, mail, and congratulatory telegrams to the five man crew. In all, the flight broke existing world records for sustained flight (heavier-than-air), refueled flight, sustained flight (lighter-than-air), and distance. [5]

Later examination of two of the *Question Mark's* three engines showed that they had been reduced almost to junk after the 150 hours and 40 minutes of continuous flight time. The ultimate unreliability of the engines resulted from having no adequate means for lubricating their rocker arms, the linkage that operated the engines' valves.

In a ceremony at Bolling Field on January 26, 1929, the Air Corps decorated each member of the *Question Mark's* crew with the Distinguished Flying Cross (DFC). Those who flew the tankers had to console themselves with the Biblical assurance that it is more blessed to give than to receive. At some later date letters of commendation were slipped quietly into their 201 files. 47 years after the event, in a small ceremony in the Pentagon on May 26, 1976, Hoyt and Hopkins finally were awarded the DFC for their refueling labors of 1929; the four other refuelers of 1929 were deceased[6].

Eaker was involved in a second attempt at aerial refueling in September 1929. Piloting a Boeing Model 95 mail plane nicknamed the *Boeing Hornet Shuttle* on a transcontinental endurance flight eastbound from Oakland, California, he was refueled in flight by C-1s and Boeing Model 40 aircraft. Over Cleveland, Ohio, a Boeing refueling crew accidentally dropped a five-gallon can of oil through his upper wing, ending the first attempt. On a second attempt westbound, his engine quit over Utah when dirt clogged the fuel line, forcing him to crash-land in the mountains near Salt Lake City.

The Air Corps followed up the flight of the *Question Mark* with a mission to demonstrate its applicability in combat. On May 21, 1929, during annual maneuvers, a Keystone LB-7 piloted by Lt. Moon took off from Fairfield Air Depot in Dayton, OH, on a simulated mission to New York City via Washington, DC. Plans were for the bomber to be refueled in flight several times, drop a flash bomb over New York harbor, then return to Dayton non-stop, again by way of Washington. Moon had 1stLt John Paul Richter, who had been a hose handler on the first-ever refueling aerial refueling mission on May 28, 1923, as a member of his five-man crew. The C-1 tanker employed to refuel the LB-7 was flown by Cpt Hoyt and two enlisted men. While it performed a premature air refueling enroute from Dayton to Washington, icing forced the tanker to land in Uniontown, PA, where it got stuck in mud. After flying to New York, the LB-7 was forced to land at Washington's Bolling Field. The next day the tanker joined the bomber and both flew to New York, where they made a public demonstration of air refueling and four dry runs.

As noted above, of the 16 Army aviators involved in the project, six later became general officers. Spaatz, Eaker and Quesada played important roles in the United States Army Air Forces during World War II. Spaatz rose to commanding general of the Army Air Forces and became the first Chief of Staff of the United States Air Force. Eaker commanded the Eighth and Mediterranean Allied Air Forces. Quesada commanded the IX Tactical Air Command in France. After retirement, he became the first head of the Federal Aviation Administration (FAA). Although not a member of the "Bomber Mafia" nor what we have called the Visionaries, Quesada certainly made a mark for himself:

> Elwood Quesada, son of a Spanish banker and an Irish immigrant, was working as a lifeguard at Washington's Tidal Basin on June 11, 1924, when Millard "Tiny" Harmon, seeking football players for the Army Air Service's team, suggested to Quesada that he join the Air Service. Quesada, a Washington native, was fascinated by the feats of Eddie Rickenbacker and Hap Arnold and went to Bolling Field, and was taken on a flight by Harmon. Quesada was hooked and enlisted in September 1924 as

a flying cadet and received his wings and commission in the Air Reserve one year later. He was inactive for one and a half years, but in September 1927 he went on duty as an engineering officer at Bolling Field, Washington, DC, where he served until June 1928. He became aide to Maj General James Fechet, then chief of the Air Corps.

Perhaps it was Quesada's familiarity with the Washington scene or just his personality, but he lived a most unusual life as a junior officer, serving as the personal pilot for the Chief of the Air Corps, Assistant Secretary of War, Secretary of War, George Marshall when the future five-star general was a colonel at Fort Benning, and the Ambassador to Cuba. Such activities made him unusually politically well-connected and served him in good stead in the years ahead. In addition, in 1929 he joined Carl Spaatz and Ira Eaker on the famous *Question Mark* flight over San Diego.

Quesada went to Cuba as assistant military attaché from October 1930 until April 1932. He returned to Bolling Field and was promoted to first lieutenant in November and became aide to F. Trubee Davison who was Assistant Secretary of War for Air. Lieutenant Quesada flew Davison and explorer Martin Johnson all over Africa on a mission to collect animals for the New York Museum of Natural History in the summer of 1933.

Soon thereafter, Quesada was assigned as chief pilot on the New York-Cleveland route when the Army men flew the airmail in 1934. One year later he became commanding officer of Headquarters at Langley Field, VA. He was promoted to captain in April 1935. Quesada served as aide to General Hugh Johnson, administrator of the NRA, and then Secretary of War Dern. Quesada completed the Command and General School course at Fort Leavenworth, KA., in June 1937 and went to Mitchel

Field, NY, as commanding officer of the 1st Bomb Squadron. That tour ended in June 1938 when he went to Argentina for two and a half years as technical advisor to Argentina's air force. He was assigned to intelligence in the Office of the Chief of Air Corps in October 1940 with promotion to Maj in February 1941. Quesada returned to Mitchel Field in July 1941 as commanding officer of the 33d Pursuit Group. He was promoted to lieutenant colonel in January 1942 and continued a distinguished career in WWII, retiring as a lieutenant general.

Strickland, Hoyt and Hopkins all became brigadier generals in the United States Air Force and the Brigadier General Ross G. Hoyt Award is issued annually for the best air refueling crew in the Air Force. Halverson, though he rose only

Consolidated Y1P-15

to colonel, led the HAL-PRO ("Halverson Project") detachment, 12 B-24 Liberators that bombed the Ploeşti oil refineries in 1942, and was the first commander of the Tenth Air Force.

Moon, a bomber pilot, became an influential member of the "Bomber Mafia" at the Air Corps Tactical School from 1933 to 1936, but died on November 19, 1937, awaiting retirement from the service at the age of 45. Solter, a pursuit pilot, was killed in a flying accident at Randolph Field, TX, in 1936. Elmendorf, while not having a flying role in the project, was an accomplished test pilot and was killed on January 13, 1933, testing the Y1P-25 at Wright Field, OH. Elemendorf AFB, Alaska, commemorates his service.

These pioneering efforts proved that the concept of in-flight refueling was viable and it has evolved into the sophisticated systems in use today. Allowing deployment of airpower resources anywhere in the world at virtually a moment's notice is a hallmark of USAF operations and provides for the global reach of airpower.

1927 Pan-American Goodwill Flights

To improve relations with Latin American countries, to encourage commercial aviation, and to provide valuable training for Air Corps personnel, the Army planned the historic Pan-American Goodwill Flight of 1926 and 1927 through Mexico and Central and South America. Ten Army pilots were assigned to fly five Loening OA-1A amphibian aircraft on an ambitious circumnavigation of Central and South America. The challenge was enormous, for aircraft were uncommon there, and services and facilities were non-existent. To stimulate public interest, each airplane was named, a la the World Cruisers, after a major U.S. city-the *New York, San Antonio, San Francisco, Detroit,* and *St. Louis.* The 22,000 mile flight began on December 21, 1926, from San Antonio, TX. The journey took 59 flying days, interspersed with 74 days for scheduled maintenance and diplomatic meetings and ceremonies.

Loening OA-1A Amphibian
San Francisco

As can well be imagined, the trek was fraught with perils, and less than enthusiastic responses from some local populaces, although official welcomes were warm. After a ceremony in Buenos Aires, Argentina, the flyers left for an overnight stay at a flying field in nearby Palomar. Due to damage to the *Detroit's* landing gear, it could not be cranked down by the pilot, so as the aircraft prepared for landing, Lt Benton went out on the wing to lower the landing gear by hand. To increase his freedom of movement, Benton chose not to wear a bulky parachute.

As the formation descended to 1,500 feet, the *Detroit* accidentally drifted into the *New York*, and the aircraft locked together and spun out of control. Maj Dargue and Lt Whitehead of the *New York* parachuted to safety. Rather than use his own parachute, Cpt Woolsley chose to stay with the helpless Lt Benton, and they both perished when the *Detroit* hit the ground. The remaining aircraft and crews gamely continued on.[7]

The flight concluded at Bolling Field in Washington, DC, on May 2, 1927. Within three weeks, however, the impressive achievement was eclipsed by Lindbergh's solo trans-Atlantic flight in the Spirit of St. Louis, and the exploit soon faded from the public's eye.

The Air Mail Fiasco

Otto Praeger, Second Assistant Postmaster General, was the impetus behind the birth of air mail. He was a non-flyer and just sought methods to improve the delivery of mail on intercity transfers. Oblivious to the limitations of 1918 aircraft technology and performance, he convinced his boss, Postmaster General Burleson, to suggest to the President that the Secretary of War could order the Army Air Service to assume this new role, starting in just a matter of several days! And so the executive orders were quickly passed to War Secretary Newton D. Baker, thence to Chief of the Army Air Service Col "Hap" Arnold, who promptly summoned Maj Reuben H. Fleet, his Executive Officer. The orders were dated May 3, 1918, and they read to initiate daily air mail service between Washington and New York on May 15, 1918. Hap Arnold and Reuben Fleet were professional soldier-pilots who knew all too well that you didn't say "No" to the President, and they had to salute and carry out the orders as best they could, given no suitable airplanes, and no pilots with adequate cross-country navigational training in good weather or bad.

Maj Fleet had "Jenny" aircraft modified to carry more fuel and provide space for the mail. He hand-picked the best Army instructor pilots who could at least read a road map and do dead-reckoning navigations. The Army Air Service continued to operate one trip per day from DC to NY along this 218 mile route using the mail-configured JN-4Hs on a 6-day week, with Sundays off (for the pilots, not the ground crews) up until August 12, 1918, when the Post Office Department determined that it was best for the department to have control of the airmail operations.

For nine years, using mostly war-surplus de Havilland DH-4 biplanes, the Post Office built and flew a nationwide network. In the beginning the work was extremely dangerous; of the initial 40 pilots, three died in crashes in 1919 and nine more in 1920. It was 1922 before an entire year ensued without a fatal crash.[8]

Operational safety and efficiency improved, and soon transcontinental flights were underway. To encourage commercial aviation, the Kelly Act (or Contract Air Mail Act) was enacted in 1925 authorizing the Post office to contract with private airlines for feeder routes to the main transcontinental system. By 1927, the transition to entirely commercial transport of air mail had taken place at a cost of $1.10 per mile. But soon subsidies for carrying mail exceeded the cost of the mail itself, and some carriers abused their contracts by flooding the system with junk mail at 100% profit or hauling heavy freight as air mail.

A scandal quickly developed, and the Air Mail Act of 1930 ensued, with its main provision changing the way payments were calculated, but it eventually devolved into long-range contracts with only three airlines, prompting an investigation into this practice and eventually leading to a cancellation of the contracts. The investigation revealed fraudulent activities were routine, and President Roosevelt ordered cancellation of contracts on February 7, 1934, but that date would slip.

At the time of the scandal, the Air Corps was in the midst of lobbying for a more centralized control of air operations in the form of an establishment of a General Headquarters (GHQ), Air Force. On February 9, 1934, Secretary of War George H. Dern assured President Roosevelt that the Air Corps could deliver the mail. Strangely, he failed to consult with either Army Chief of Staff Douglas MacArthur or Chief of the Air Corps MajGen Benjamin D. Foulois. Shortly after the cabinet meeting that same morning, second assistant postmaster general Harllee Branch called Foulois to his office. When asked if the Air Corps could deliver the mail in winter, Foulois assured Branch that the Air Corps could be ready in a week or ten days.[9]

At 4 o'clock that afternoon President Roosevelt suspended the airmail contracts effective at midnight February 19. He issued Executive Order 6591 ordering the War Department to place at the disposal of the Postmaster General "such airplanes, landing fields, pilots and other employees and equipment of the Army of the United States needed or required for the transportation of mail during the present emergency, by air over routes and schedules prescribed by the Postmaster General."

In 1933, the airlines had carried millions of pounds of mail on 26 routes covering almost 25,000 miles in well-equipped modern aircraft using ground-based beam transmitters along routes with established maintenance facilities The Air Corps stated that it had selected its most experienced pilots and that it had the requisite experience at flying at night and in bad weather, but in most aspects they were ill-prepared for the rigors of regular air mail operations. In actuality, of the 262 pilots selected, more than half were Reserve junior officers with less than two years flying experience. Only 48 of those selected had logged at least 25 hours of flight time in bad weather, only 31 had 50 hours or more of night flying, and only 2 had 50 hours of instrument time.

Its level of inexperience was not surprising, as the Air Corps was hampered during the Great Depression by pay cuts and a reduction of flight time, and operated almost entirely in daylight and good weather. Experience levels were limited by obsolete aircraft, most of them single-engine and open cockpit planes. Because of a high turnover-rate policy in the War Department, most of the Reserve pilots were unfamiliar with the civilian airmail routes.

The Army Air Corps Mail Operation (AACMO) was placed under the supervision of BrigGen. Oscar Westover, assistant chief of the Air Corps. He created three geographic zones and appointed LtCol Henry H. Arnold to command the Western Zone, LtCol Horace Meek Hickam the Central Zone, and Maj. Byron Q. Jones the Eastern Zone. Personnel and planes were immediately deployed, but problems began immediately with a lack of proper facilities (and in some instances, no facilities at all) for maintenance of aircraft and quartering of enlisted men, and a failure of tools to arrive where needed. Sixty Air Corps pilots took oaths as postal employees in preparation for the service and began training.

On February 16, three pilots on familiarization flights—Lts Jean D. Grenier, Edwin D. White and James Eastman—were killed in crashes attributed to bad weather. This presaged some of the worst and most persistent late winter weather in history. A veritable olio of crashes and deaths and concomitant non-delivery of air mail was the death knell for the latest version of the Army's Air Mail Service. On March 10 President Roosevelt called Foulois and Army Chief of Staff General Douglas MacArthur to the White House, asking them to fly only in completely safe conditions. Foulois had now recognized the folly of precipitously attempting to operate the air mail system and honestly replied that to ensure complete safety the Air Corps would have to end the flights, and Roosevelt suspended airmail service on March 11, 1934.

The immediate results of the operation were disastrous for the image of the Air Corps. Speaker of the House Henry T. Rainey, echoing comments made by BrigGen Billy Mitchell, criticized: "If we are unfortunate enough to be drawn into another war, the Air Corps wouldn't amount to much. If it is not equal to carrying the mail, I would like to know what it would do in carrying bombs." The Air Corps took the criticism to heart and, despite its public humiliation, the Air Mail Fiasco resulted in a number of improvements. On April 17, 1934, Secretary Dern convened a special committee chaired by former Secretary of War Newton D. Baker, to closely examine the program and the overall condition of the Air Corps. Known as the Baker Board, it included all five military members of an earlier board chaired by General Hugh A. Drum, four of them senior Army ground force officers, who tightly controlled the agenda and scope of the board's investigation to prevent it from becoming a platform for advocating an independent air arm. Of the 11 members, only three were Air Corps advocates.

The Baker Board endorsed earlier findings of the Drum Board, supporting the status quo that the Air Corps was an auxiliary force of the Army and opposed to the Air Corps being a separate service equal to the Army and Navy. It did call for the immediate establishment of a GHQ Air Force, placing all air combat units within the continental United States under its command. This provided another, limited step toward an autonomous air force, but also kept authority divided by maintaining control of supply, doctrine, training and recruitment under the Chief of the Air Corps, and airfields in the control of corps area commanders.

Within the Air Corps itself, instrument training was upgraded, radio communications were greatly improved into a nationwide system that included navigation aids, and budget appropriations were increased. The Air Corps acquired the first six Link Trainer flight simulators of a fleet that would ultimately number more than 10,000.

The Boeing Y1B-9

Stung by the Air Mail Fiasco, it was obvious that the Air Corps needed upgrades in many areas, and the obsolete aircraft in the inventory needed to be replaced with new platforms that could capitalize on the strides made in the commercial aviation arena. One of the first truly modern bombers was the Boeing B-9.

In May 1930, Boeing had flown its Model 200 *Monomail* single-engined mailplane. It was a radical design for the time, being

Boeing Model 200 *Monomail*

a semi-monocoque, stressed skin cantilever monoplane with a retractable landing gear. In what would then be a typical daring leap of faith for Boeing, they decided to design and build a twin-engined bomber using the same techniques developed for the *Monomail* to re-equip the Air Corps. Using its own money, Boeing built two prototypes of its new bomber design as a private venture. The two aircraft differed only in the engines used, with the Model 214 to be powered by two liquid-cooled Curtiss V-1570-29 *Conqueror* engines while the Model 215 had two Pratt & Whitney R-1860 *Hornet* radial engines. Both aircraft were low winged cantilever monoplanes with a slim, oval cross-section fuselage accommodating a crew of five. The pilot and co-pilot sat in separate open cockpits, with the co-pilot, who doubled as the bombardier sitting forward of the pilot. Two gunners, each armed with a single machine gun sat in nose and dorsal positions, while

Boeing Model 215, or Y1B-9 with the Retractable Gear Down

a radio operator sat inside the fuselage. Like the *Monomail*, a retractable landing gear system was used. The first of the two prototypes to fly was the radial powered Model 215 which, carrying civil markings and the aircraft registration X-10633, made its maiden flight on April 13, 1931. Boeing leased the aircraft to the Air Corps for testing under the designation XB-901, demonstrating a speed of 163 mph. The testing turned out to be a success and both the XB-901 and the as-yet incomplete Model 214 were purchased as the YB-9 and Y1B-9 respectively on August 13 1931, with an order for a further five for service testing following shortly. The performance was encouraging.

The Y1B-9 (Y1 indicating funding outside normal fiscal year procurement), powered by two liquid-cooled Curtiss V-1570-29 *Conqueror* engines, first flew on November 5 1931. The increased power from these engines, combined with increased streamlining of the engine nacelles, increased its top speed to 173 mph. The YB-9, meanwhile, had been re-engined with more powerful *Hornets*, demonstrating slightly better performance than the Y1B-9, which was therefore also re-engined with *Hornets*. The British RAF eventually fielded a number of successful bombers powered by in-line liquid cooled powerplants, however, the Air Corps stayed with the radial designs for its bombers, With the exception of the B-2 *Condor*, liquid-cooled engines were never used on production bombers for the United States military. The air-cooled radial engine was lighter and more reliable than the liquid-cooled engine, and less vulnerable to enemy damage.

The five Y1B-9A service test aircraft featured the R-1860-11 *Hornet* engines which powered the re-engined YB-9 and Y1B-9 and a redesigned vertical stabilizer. While enclosed canopies were considered and designed, the B-9 was never fitted with them. The first of the five Y1B-9As entered service with the 20th Bomb Group on September 14, 1932, with the rest delivered by the end of March 1933. The new bomber proved impossible to intercept during air exercises, strengthening calls for improved air defense warning systems.

- Maximum speed: 188 mph (163 kts) at 6,000 ft
- Cruise speed: 165 mph (143 kts,)
- Range: 540 mi (470 nmi,)
- Service ceiling: 20,750 ft
- Rate of climb: 900 ft/min
- Guns: 2× .30 in (7.62 mm) machine guns
- Bombs: 2,260 lb bombs

Two of the B-9s were destroyed during crashes in 1933, one of the accidents being fatal, while the remaining aircraft were gradually phased out over the next two years, with the last being withdrawn on April 26, 1935. Although it equaled the speed of all existing American fighter aircraft, no further aircraft were built, as the Glenn L. Martin Company had flown a prototype of a more advanced bomber, the XB-907, which was ordered into production as the Martin B-10.

The Martin B-10

Correctly assessing the Air Corps need to upgrade its bomber fleet, the B-10 started its life as the Martin Model 123, also a private venture, this one from the Glenn L. Martin Company of Baltimore MD. The Army designated the Model 123 the XB-907 when it accepted it for testing. It had a crew of four housed in open cockpits, the trend of the day for bombers, as noted in the Boeing Y1B-9. There were a number of design innovations that set it apart and made existing bombers obsolete: the first use of a powered gun turret in a military aircraft; a deep belly fuselage to carry the bomb load in an internal bomb bay, and retractable landing gear. Powered by Wright *Cyclone* SR-1820-E engines producing 600 HP, it possessed more than enough power to leave current pursuit ships in trail. It started a revolution in bomber design.

Martin Model 123, XB-907

It was returned to Martin for some improvements and returned as the XB-907A with full rather than NACA cowlings, closed cockpits, more powerful engines, and an eight foot increase in wingspan.

The XB-907A became the XB-10 when delivered to the Army and quickly established its superiority in flight tests in June 1932, recording a speed of 197 mph at 6,000 ft. Impressive performance for its day.[10] Following the tests, the Army ordered 48 of these aircraft, slightly modified with a reduction to a three-man crew seated within closed canopies.

The first 14 aircraft were designated YB-10 and delivered to Wright Field. LtCol Henry H. "Hap" Arnold was so impressed with the aircraft that he described it as "the airpower wonder of its day". In 1932, Martin received the Collier Trophy for designing the XB-10. (The Collier trophy is awarded annually by the National Aeronautical Association "for the greatest achievement in aeronautics or astronautics in America, with respect to improving the performance, efficiency, and safety of air or space vehicles, the value of which has been thoroughly demonstrated by actual use during the preceding year.")

B-10B, A Revolution in the Design of Bombers

By 1935, the Air Corps had ordered 103 additional aircraft designated the B-10B, with only minor changes from the YB-10, and first shipments were made to the 2nd Bomb Group at Langley Field, the 9th Bomb Group at Mitchel Field, the 19th Bomb Group at March Field, and the 4th Composite Group in the Philippines.

Not only was the aircraft a breakthrough in its configuration and aerodynamic shape with the resulting performance, a considerable attention to interior detail provided crewmembers with crew stations that were comfortable and ergonomically laid out. The latest available instrumentation and radios were provided.

B-10B Cockpit Left and Right

General characteristics

- Crew: 3
- Length: 44 ft 9 in
- Wingspan: 70 ft 6 in
- Height: 15 ft 5 in
- Wing area: 678 ft²
- Empty weight: 9,681 lb
- Loaded weight: 14,700 lb
- Max takeoff weight: 16,400 lb
- Powerplant: 2×Wright R-1820-33 (G-102) *Cyclone* radials, 775 hp each

Performance

- Maximum speed: 213 mph (185 kts)
- Cruise speed: 193 mph (168 kts)
- Range: 1,240 mi (1,078 nmi)

- Service ceiling: 24,200 ft
- Rate of climb: 1,380 ft/min
- Wing loading: 21.7 lb/ft²
- Power/mass: 0.105 hp/lb

Armament
- Guns: 3 × .30 in (7.62 mm) Browning machine guns
- Bombs: 2,260 lb

The B-10 would figure prominently in a number of aerial demonstrations showing its superiority over virtually every military aircraft then flying. As was typically the case in the between-the-war years when inter-service competition for weapons funding was particularly keen, the Air Corps wanted to showcase the capabilities of this latest bomber introduced to its inventory. In 1934, the Air Corps established a project for a mass flight to Alaska of this new type all-metal monoplane bomber. The successful completion of such a flight would prove the feasibility of sending an aerial force to Alaska in an emergency and not inconsequentially, provide excellent training for personnel flying across isolated and uninhabited areas sans navigational aids.

Ten B-10s, under the command of LtCol H.H. Arnold, left Washington, DC's Bolling Field on July 19th and wound their way to Fairbanks, AK via Winnipeg and Edmonton, Canada, arriving on July 24th. They had covered 4,000 miles in 25 hrs. and 30 min of flying. For the next month they conducted numerous exploratory flights over Alaska, including missions for aerial photography of some 23,000 square miles, generally along lines from Fairbanks to Nome, Whitehorse Canada, Anchorage and Juneau.

The planes took off from Fairbanks on Aug. 16 and returned to Washington, DC, by way of Seattle, WA, and Omaha, NE. They landed at Bolling Field on Aug. 20, completing a round trip of more than 7,000 miles, much of it over uncharted wilderness. For commanding this flight, Arnold won the 1934 Mackay Trophy. (The Mackay Trophy was first presented by Clarence Mackay in 1912 and was later deeded to the National Aeronautic Association. The trophy is awarded for the "most meritorious flight of the year" by an Air Force person, persons, or organization.) All was not accolades, as his route over the water to Seattle angered Army Chief of Staff Gen Douglas MacArthur when the Navy complained to him about

Arnold's grandstanding in the face of previous delicate coastal defense responsibility negotiations. Arnold's detour ensured that no medals were given out for the Alaska flight as long as MacArthur was Chief of Staff.

Despite the general feeling that the Army Air Corps possessed the premier bomber of the day, there was recognition that it was vulnerable to concentrated fighter attack and did not have the "legs" or the payload for the strategic missions the Air Corps considered essential for future combat. Air Corps leaders considered it a tactical bomber, and they were seeking the strategic weapon.

The 1934 Tender of Proposals for a New Bomber

Thus it was on August 8, 1934, that the U.S. Army Air Corps tendered a proposal for a multi-engined bomber to replace the Martin B-10. Requirements were that it would carry a "useful bombload" at an altitude of 10,000 feet for ten hours with a top speed of at least 200 miles per hour. They also desired, but did not require, a range of 2,000 miles and a speed of 250 miles per hour. The Air Corps was looking for a bomber capable of reinforcing the air forces in Hawaii, Panama, and Alaska. The competition would be decided by a "fly-off" at Dayton's Wright Field in. The Boeing competed its Model 299; Douglas with the DB-1; and Martin with its Model 146 for the Air Corps contract.

The Douglas DB-1

The Douglas DB-1 design was essentially that of the DC-2, with several modifications. The wingspan was 4.5 ft greater, the fuselage was deeper to accommodate bombs and the six-member crew with wings fixed in the middle of the cross-section rather than to the bottom. Armament included nose, dorsal, and ventral gun turrets.

Douglas DB-1 (Later Designated B-18A Bolo)

General Characteristics

- Crew: 6
- Length: 57 ft 10 in
- Wingspan: 89 ft 6 in
- Height: 15 ft 2 in
- Wing area: 959 ft²
- Empty wt. 16,320 lb
- Loaded wt. 24,000 lb
- Max TO wt. 27,673 lb
- Powerplant: 2×Wright R-1820-53 radial engines, 1,000 hp each

Performance

- Maximum speed: 216 mph (188 kts) at 10,000 ft
- Cruise speed: 167 mph (145 kts)
- Range: 900 mi
- Ferry range: 2,100 mi (1,826 nm)
- Service ceiling: 23,900 ft
- Climb to 10,000 ft :9.9 min

Armament

- Guns: 3 × .30 in (7.62 mm) machine guns
- Bombs: 4,400 lb

The Martin 146

The Martin Model 146 was a modified B-10A, and as such offered little improvement over the previous model. Despite its place upon introduction as the most modern bomber in existence, 1.5 times more

capable than any other bomber and faster than any contemporary pursuit aircraft, it quickly became obsolete in the rapid technology advances of the 1930s. The 146 could not hope to meet the Air Corps needs.

Figure 7-19
Martin Model 146 (Modified B-10A) at the Baltimore Plant (USAF Photo)

The Boeing Model 299

Seattle's Boeing Aircraft Company was fast becoming one of the most respected and powerful aeronautical firms of the post-WWI years. Building on its early successes following its founding in 1917, a series of acquisitions created a giant of its time. In 1927 Boeing created an airline named Boeing Air Transport, which merged a year later with Pacific Air Transport and the Boeing Airplane Company. In 1929, the company changed its name to United Aircraft and Transport Corporation and acquired Pratt & Whitney, Hamilton Standard Propeller Company, and Chance Vought. United Aircraft then purchased National Air Transport in 1930.

In 1933 they introduced the revolutionary Boeing 247, the first truly modern airliner. It was much faster, safer, and easier to fly than any other passenger aircraft of the day. For example, it was the first twin engine passenger aircraft that could fly on one engine. In an era of unreliable engines, this vastly improved flight safety. Boeing built the first sixty aircraft exclusively for its own airline operations thereby stymieing competing airlines, and was typical of the anti-competitive corporate behavior that the US government sought to prohibit at the time. (It did prompt Donald Douglas to enter the field, resulting ultimately with the legendary DC-3, so one could claim that Boeing's intransigence birthed one of the best airliners of all time.) The Air Mail Act of 1934 prohibited airlines and manufacturers from being under the same corporate umbrella, so the company split into three smaller companies—Boeing Airplane Company, United Airlines, and United Aircraft Corporation, the precursor to United Technologies.

The prototype B-17, designated Model 299, was designed by a team of engineers led by E. Gifford Emery and Edward Curtis Wells and built at Boeing's own expense. It combined features of the huge one-of-a-kind experimental Boeing XB-15 bomber with the technically advanced and very successful Boeing 247. The B-17 could carry a significantly increased number of bombs—up to 4,800 pounds on two racks in the bomb bay behind the cockpit—and sported a defensive weaponry suite of five 0.30 inches (7.62 mm) machine guns, and was powered by four Pratt & Whitney R-1690 *Hornet* radial engines each producing 750 horsepower at 7,000 feet.

In a testimony to the engineering resources at Boeing, and to those translating the design to flight hardware, the first flight of the Model 299 was on July 28, 1935, less than one year after issuance of the request for proposals, with Boeing chief test-pilot Leslie Tower at the controls. Richard Williams, a reporter for the Seattle Times coined the name "Flying Fortress" when the Model 299 was rolled out, bristling with multiple machine gun installations.[11] Boeing was quick to see the value of the name and had it trademarked for use, a name that heard today immediately conjures up a vision of the aircraft.

On August 20, 1935, the prototype flew from Seattle to Wright Field in nine hours and three minutes at an average cruising speed of 252 miles per hour, much faster than the competition.

The Model 299 at Wright Field
(National Archives)

At the fly-off, the four-engine Boeing design's performance was far superior to those of the twin-engine DB-1 and Model 146. Then-MajGen Frank Maxwell Andrews of the GHQ Air Force believed that the long-range capabilities of this large four-engine aircraft were more efficient than shorter-ranged twin-engined airplanes, and that the Model 299 was better suited to their doctrine.

Model 299 Interior Arrangement

His opinions were shared by the Air Corps procurement officers, and even before the competition was finished they suggested buying 65 of the aircraft. The aircraft embodied all that the Air Corps sought.

Boeing Model 299 Cockpit

Developmental testing continued on the Boeing Model 299 at Wright Field, and on October 30, 1935 Army Air Corps test-pilot Maj Ployer Peter Hill and his co-pilot 1stLt Donald L. Putt took off on a second evaluation flight. Also aboard in the rear were engineer John B. Cutting and mechanic Mark H. Koogler. Boeing's chief test pilot Les Tower was standing behind the two pilots in the commodious cockpit.

Boeing Model 299 Crash at Wright Field

Unfortunately, the crew overlooked the requirement to disengage the airplane's "gust lock," a device that held the bomber's movable control surfaces in place while the plane was parked on the ground, and after off, the aircraft became uncontrollable and entered a steep climb, stalled, nosed over and crashed, killing Hill and Tower.

Note to the Curious

Check lists, as we know them now, were nonexistent in the 1930s. If there was to be some good to evolve from this accident, it was the introduction of the use of a check list. The example below depicts a portion of the Y1B-17 Check List of 1937 that evolved as a direct result of this accident.

```
            PILOT'S CHECK LIST
    (To be in pilot's cockpit at all times)

BEFORE TAXIING FROM LINE:
  1. BALLAST - Check combat crew - Loading - Exits.
  2. AUTOMATIC PILOT - Oil pressure and pilot off.
  3. FLIGHT CONTROL LOCKS - Unlock.
  4. TAIL WHEEL - Unlock.
  5. BRAKES - Air pressure (175 - 200) switch on.
  6. WARNING LIGHTS - Test.
  7. SUPERCHARGER - Low Blower.
  8. ALTIMETER - Check for altitude.
  9. MIXTURE CONTROLS - Full rich and lock.
 10. CARBURETOR AIR - Cold, unless icing.
 11. FUEL COCKS - Check position.
 12. MAIN LINE SWITCHES - On.
 13. INSTRUMENTS - Check all instruments.
 14. WING FLAPS - Normally up.
 15. TRIM TABS -Set for take off.
 16. PROPELLER CONTROLS - Maximum automatic RPM - Lock.
 17. ENGINES - Run up, check RPM, ignition, fuel & oil press.
 18. WHEEL BLOCKS - Remove.

BEFORE TAKE-OFF:
  1. ENGINES - Run up individually.
  2. TAIL WHEEL - Lock for take-off.

AFTER TAKE-OFF:
  1. LANDING GEAR AND TAIL WHEEL - Raise and check oleo.
  2. CONTROLS - Adjust (1) Props; (2) Throttles for cruis.
  3. AUTOMATIC PILOT - Adjust before engaging.
  4. INSTRUMENTS - Record periodically.
```

1937 Post-Crash YB1-17 Pilot's Check List (Portion)

The crashed Model 299 was unable to finish the evaluation, and although the Air Corps was still enthusiastic about the aircraft's potential, Army officials were forced to select one of the other competitors. Not the least of the concerns was the much greater expense of the Model 299. Douglas had quoted a unit price of $58,200 based on a production order of 220 aircraft, compared with a price of $99,620 from Boeing. Boeing was legally disqualified from the consideration for the contract and Army Chief of Staff Malin Craig cancelled the order for 65 YB-17s, and ordered 133 of the twin-engine Douglas B-18 Bolo instead.[12]

Boeing was in dire straits before committing to build the 299 from its own funds, and was now in extremis and seemed perilously close to folding. Fortunately, a legal loophole and a concerted plea by MajGen Frank M. Andrews, commander of the GHQ Air Force, allowed the Air Corps to buy a small number of test aircraft—13 to be precise—which was enough to equip one squadron. Could this tiny step forward prove to be prophetic?

Chapter Nine traces the Boeing Company's path leading to the design and production of the soon-to-be legendary B-17. The path was not a smooth one, as the ebbs and flows of the airplane business that were endemic of the times threw many obstacles in their course. The following chapters will detail the valiant efforts of the AAC to show their superiors and the world just what a formidable strategic weapon was now in their hands. Their path too was not without its perils.

1. www.centennialofflight.gov/essay/Aerospace/Douglas_World_Trip/Aero27.htm
2. http://www.seattleworldcruiser.org/historic.htm
3. National Aviation Hall of Fame, Carl A. Spaatz biography
4. *Question Mark*, Walter J. Boyne, Air Force magazine, March 2003
5. http://afehri.maxwell.af.mil/Documents/pdf/75yrs%20in-flight%20refueling.pdf
6. *Air Force Magazine*, Vol 59 (Jul 1976), 22.
7. http://www.nationalmuseum.af.mil/factsheets/factsheet.asp?id=741
8. *The Air Mail Fiasco*. Correll, John T. Air Force magazine, March 2008.
9. *Aviation in the U.S. Army, 1919-1939*, Dr. Maurer Maurer, p. 301.
10. *The Complete Encyclopedia of World Aircraft*. Eden, Paul and Soph Moeng, eds London: Amber Books Ltd., 2002. ISBN 0-7607-3432-1.
11. *B-17 at War*. Yenne, Bill , St Paul, Minnesota: Zenith Imprint, 2006. ISBN 0-7603-2522-7.
12. *Ambassador of American Airpower: Maj General Robert Olds*. Zamzow, Maj (USAF) S. L. (2008). Maxwell Air Force Base, Alabama: Air University.

CHAPTER
VIII

Developing the Bombing Skills

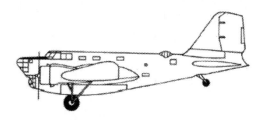

The Army Aviation visionaries readily admitted that their theories and concepts of offensive strategic bombardment were untested and strove hard to prove their worth. While the Army Air Service and its successor, the Air Corps, were seeking the platforms and techniques to further the capabilities of carrying the war to potential enemies, they ran into the realities of long distant, high altitude flight.

Recall that in 1923, the Post Office began erecting the first of some 2,000 lighted beacons that were taking the place of fires for night time mail flights. The Civil Aeronautics Administration took over the establishment of lighted airways in 1926[1].Wiley Post could not find a pressurized aircraft to prove his theories for high speed, high altitude flight, so he found it necessary to develop his own pressure suit with the help of B.F Goodrich. Howard Hughes had to rely on a makeshift oxygen mask to set his transcontinental speed record in his H-1 in 1935. It was also Wiley Post who used new inventions such as the Sperry gyroscope and the radio direction finder to fly around the world solo in seven days in 1933. One could find a superlatively performing platform, but there were still obstacles to identify and overcome.

Long Range Navigation

As the art of navigation moved from the well-established nautical venue to the newly-explored three-dimensional aeronautical scene, there obviously were a number of innovations, or at best, techniques that had to be invented or applied. Not the least of the questions was what type of charts would be most appropriate. Should the perspective presented to the aeronaut look as he might see it from the air? What projections would be most useful to the airborne navigator? How would polar navigation be simplified from ice-bound ship to high-speed aircraft? If the horizon was not visible, how could a celestial sight be taken? How to account for the airplane speed while celestial or other observations were being taken? Was there a way to simplify the celestial calculations? How is the wind effect determined? What kind of compass would work?

Developing the Tools of Long Range Navigation

During the decade following WWI, developments in navigation within the Air Service centered on one individual; Albert F. Hegenberger. Although not a member of the "Bomber Mafia", he certainly could be classed as one of the pioneers that turned their ideas into reality. Hegenberger had left the Massachusetts Institute of Technology (MIT) to enter Air Service flight training during WWI. He subsequently returned to MIT where he received his degree in aeronautical engineering. In 1919 he reported to Ohio's McCook Field (subsequently Wright Field, then Wright-Patterson AFB), the Army's flight test and development center there. 2ndLt Hegenberger established what would become the Instrument and Navigation Branch. He and his associates worked to perfect the art of airborne navigation, investigating the rapidly evolving new developments in compasses, airspeed indicators, drift meters, sextants and charts. He taught a week-long course in air navigation for the Engineering School covering subjects such as star identification and use of the sextant. Because the Navy was consistently flying over vast expanses of the open seas, they had already developed techniques that the Air Service could use. During this period, Hegenberger attended a special course with the Navy at Naval Air Station (NAS) Pensacola that included actual flights over the Gulf to practice dead reckoning (DR) and obtaining celestial sights.

In June 1927, Lieutenants Hegenberger and Lester J. Maitland flew their Fokker trimotor *Bird of Paradise* from California to Hawaii to demonstrate advancements achieved at McCook. Actually, the successful flight was due in a large part to Hegenberger's accurate dead reckoning (DR) calculations using the compass and drift meter, supplemented by celestial observations. The newer earth induction compass had failed, and the radio compasses proved to be unreliable, but wisely, he had pre-computed azimuth and altitude for the sun and some stars for several waypoints along the route. When he took his final morning observations, he calculated that they were far north of course. Persuading Maitland to follow his request for a left turn, they landed safely at Oahu's Wheeler Field. For this first flight from the mainland to Hawaii, the two Air Corps pilots received the McKay Trophy for 1927.[2]

U.S. Army Fokker Trimotor *Bird of Paradise*

Upon return to Wright Field, Hegenberger established a new navigation school that included flights over the Gulf in the *Bird of Paradise*. The school eventually closed, and he focused his attention on blind, or instrument only, flying. After developing a blind flight system at Wright Field, Hegenberger accomplished the first official solo blind flight on May 9th, 1932. This remarkable achievement earned him the 1934 Collier Trophy. Later Hegenberger invented a fully automatic flight system, a testimony to his strong background both as a pilot and engineer.[3]

As transport, and more importantly bomber, aircraft increased their speed, range, and payload performance and strategic force projection became a vital element of warfare, further improvements in navigation were mandated. At this point, there were no designated navigators, as the responsibilities were considered part of a pilot's responsibilities, and the activities were accomplished in primitive conditions. The Martin B-10 was a classic example of the quantum leaps in performance being experienced. When it entered service in 1934, it was the first mass-produced bomber whose performance exceeded that of the Army's pursuit airplanes. It was so revolutionary, that it won the Collier Trophy for the Martin Company in 1932. It was also among the first airplanes to provide for a navigator's position, albeit a rudimentary one. A few essentials were installed in the rear cockpit, and it was usually manned by a pilot who had yet to achieve the 1,000 hours of flight time necessary to move up to become a B-10 pilot.

Powered Bubble Sextant, NASM Inventory

Ever the navigational proselytizer, in 1932 Hegenberger urged the Air Corps to bring civilian Harold Gatty to Washington to become an advisor on navigation.

Gatty had learned maritime navigation at the Royal Australian Naval Academy and had proven himself in air navigation, having done so for Wiley Post on his successful 8-day around the world venture. Gatty is credited with inventing an air sextant which used a spirit level to provide an artificial horizon. A brief explanation of the process of taking a celestial observation with the sextant is contained in Appendix B.

He also invented the "aerochronometer", which offset inaccuracies introduced into observations taken in a moving aircraft. The most important invention of his career was the Gatty drift sight. This optical device was pointed at the ground, or the tops of clouds, and used to determine the rate and direction of an airplane's drift, or movement away from its heading. The device was also used as a ground speed indicator.

He worked with an experimental unit at Bolling Field stressing the importance of a system built on DR navigation and the rigorous, religious use of a log form.

The Gatty Drift Meter, NASM Inventory

Early Production Drift Meter

This group spent much time in creating procedures for calibrating instruments and installing new types of instruments. They developed a protected hatch for the sextant and pelorus (For obtaining relative bearings) as well as periscopic drift and groundspeed instruments.

Later Gyro Stabilized Periscopic Drift Meter Head (Periscope Protruded Beneath the Aircraft)

At the same time, the Naval Observatory published the Air Almanac, a simplified version of the Nautical Almanac as a bow to the airborne navigator who needed to quickly "reduce his observations" to a Line of Position (LOP) at his vastly higher speeds.

Courses for the instruction of air navigation were opened at Langley Field, VA and Rockwell Field in CA and Gatty alternated between the two as chief instructor in celestial navigation. One of the first students at Rockwell was 1stLt Thomas L. Thurlow, a former student of astrology at Stanford, who eventually authored the Air Corps Celestial Air Navigation manual in 1934. Gatty and Thurlow jointly developed a table that simplified calculations of the double drift method, or "Wind Star", that yielded groundspeed information. Students were rated pilots who received 50 hours of air work as a navigator along with instrument flying training.

Gatty eventually resigned his position in 1935 to assist Pan American Airlines pioneer their Pacific routes. That left Rockwell Field's Thurlow as the Army's recognized leader in the celestial navigation field. He moved back to Ohio and joined the Instrument and Navigation Laboratory, the successor to Hegenberger's branch. There he continued to contribute to the air navigation community. Amongst his numerous projects was the reformulation of the Air Almanac which had been abandoned since 1934. He then served as the navigator for Howard Hughes' round-the-world journey in 1938.

One of Gatty's students in the 1933 Langley Field School was an energetic 2ndLt by the name of Curtis E. LeMay. Following the school instruction, he was assigned to Hawaii, where he was directed to organize a navigation school in his unit. His fate in being schooled in the elements of air navigation combined with the special requirements of being an instructor and a desire to always excel at any endeavor placed him in a number of situations that would test his mettle and provide springboards for greater responsibilities.

These four men—Hegenberger, Gatty, Thurlow, and LeMay—were the moving forces behind the thrust of all of the important developments in air navigation prior to the nation's entry into WWII. As we will learn later, LeMay's navigation skills were subsequently given several ultimate tests, and he was not found wanting. They were heralded by another giant in the field, Norris B "Skippy" Harbold, whose career was entwined with them. Harbold joined the Harold Gatty research group as a young 2ndLt four years out of West Point and was instrumental in interpreting of Gatty's astonishing grasp of the details. He served on a committee formed in 1940 to organize the training programs for the anticipated torrent of inputs of navigator, bombardier, and gunnery students ramping up for the looming WWII. Another contributor was P.V.H. Weems, a retired Naval Officer and inventor of the Weems Plotter, who assisted the Air Corps for many years.

Until a separate navigator specialty rating was created in 1941, pilots staffed all of the navigation instructor positions, and once certified in celestial navigation, manned the aircraft of this period.

The Astrocompass

At high latitudes, where magnetic variation can be erratic and the angle of magnetic dip can be steep, the magnetic compass is essentially useless. As the need for flights at high latitudes and/or near the magnetic pole, attention was directed towards perfecting sun compasses incorporating a clock running on solar time. In the mid 1920's, Albert Bumstead, of the National Geographic Society, devised one for Byrd's use on his northern flights in 1925. At the same time, Goerz, a German firm, developed a similar compass for use by Amundsen and Ellsworth in the arctic in 1925. Throughout the 1920's and 1930's, up to W.W.II, one or the other of the sun compasses was used on high latitude flights.

The astrocompass was developed to solve the problem for the military as their aircraft ventured into previously unknown areas indicating true north when pointed at a known star. The astrocompass was not very popular with the airborne navigator as he relied on the bubble sextant for most celestial position computations. The astrocompass could be useful in certain circumstances of erratic compass operations or in going direct to course information.

Astrocompass Mk II, Mounted in a B-25

Since the Earth's axis of rotation remains essentially stationary throughout the year, knowledge of the current time and geographical position in the form of latitude and longitude, which are set on the instrument using dials, an astrocompass can be sighted on any astronomical object with a known position to give an extremely accurate reading. An equatorial drum is mounted on a base plate marked with the points of the compass. On this drum there are a set of adjustable sights and a scale of declination. More advanced versions may have built-in chronometers or default settings for bodies such as the Sun.

To use the compass, the base plate is first leveled with the horizon then pointed roughly to what the user believes to be north. The equatorial drum is then tilted in relation to this base according to the local latitude. The sights are then set using the local hour angle and the declination of whatever astronomical body is being used. Once all these settings have been made, the astrocompass is simply turned until the astronomical body is visible in the sights: it will then be precisely aligned to the points of the compass. Because of this procedure, an astrocompass requires its user to be in possession of a nautical almanac or similar astronomical tables, one of its chief disadvantages.

The old gouge for applying magnetic variation:

+ **W** Variation

Can **D**ead **M**en **V**ote **T**wice

+ **E** Variation

Where **C**=Compass Heading, **D**=Compass Deviation, **M**=Magnetic Heading, **V**=Variation, and **T**=True Heading can then be used to go from true to compass reading for aircraft use.

Using the Navigation Tools

The equipment developed by these air navigation pioneers enabled the aviators of the era to reach here-to-fore unexplored areas such as the earth's poles and span distances unheard of just a few years earlier. But equipment alone was not the panacea, for it took more than a little instruction to learn how to use them, and the discipline to stay on top of the progress as speeds increased. One could get lost faster than at any other previous time! There were some minor tools that evolved and their mastery was just as important as the newly developed hardware.

The Navigator's Bag

To utilize the charts that were evolving for air use, plotters that could be easily handled in the unfriendly aircraft environment were needed. One of the most useful, yet simplest, was the Weems plotter. Courses and distances on any chart were easily determined with this plotter, still in use today in essentially the same form.

The World Aeronautical Chart (WAC) Plotter, Type B-2, was another useful item in the navigators gear bag, but keyed to the WAC Chart use only. Versions of it too are still in use today, testifying to the soundness of their basic design. A pair of dividers, and perhaps a compass (drafting) were needed to step off distances, plot radii, and not to be forgotten was a good supply of lead pencils, erasers and a small pencil sharpener. Masking tape would hold the chart on the table (and could be used to tape a paper cup upside down on the table and pierce the bottom with pencils and divider!)

He needed a computer of considerable capability to calculate true air speed, time x distance calculations, density altitude, etc. Fortunately, the circular slide rule was invented, and in a single hand-held, hand-powered device, the navigator had one of his most versatile tools. The DR Computer, Type E6B, AN5834-1, was foundation for all of the navigation DR solutions.

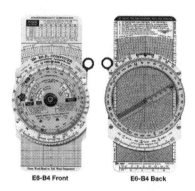

E6-B4 Front   E6-B4 Back

DR Computer, Type E6-B4

The front, or computer, face performed all of the necessary calculations for time, distance, density altitude, statute/nautical mile conversions and compressibility conversions. The rear, or wind calculation, face provided for the calculation of wind and groundspeed calculations.

If the navigator expected to take any celestial observations, timing was critical and errors of a few minutes could translate to miles of position error. A ship's chronometer, in its gimbaled mahogany case, was certainly not the timepiece to take aloft because of its size and inability to withstand the rigors of high altitude and wide temperature ranges. An accurate portable timepiece such as the navigator's watch could be substituted, but had to be calibrated against the standard times, usually broadcast over WWV on a variety of worldwide frequencies. Once synchronized, it could be counted on keeping accurate enough time for the flight duration. With all of that paraphernalia, there was still more: the navigator needed a Hydrographic Office (H.O.)

publication designated H.O. 249, Air Almanac, to compute his line of position (LOP). The bag was filling.

Presumably, the navigator was well-briefed before flight and knew the basic route of flight, and had drawn the charts needed to track the mission. If he was lucky, there would be aeronautical charts with terrain features, radio aids to navigation and airdrome information depicted. Going where aircraft had not been routinely flying forced the use of Coast and Geodetic coastal charts designed for the mariner. When all else failed, the navigator would be required to take a blank chart and actually plot the latitude and longitude of departure, destination and way-points and any significant aids that might exist such as broadcast stations.

Where to put it all? As noted previously, the B-10 was the first bomber to provide a navigator's position in the rear fuselage station, and that as an afterthought. The Y1B-17 had a relatively spacious area just behind the bomb bay, but it too was impractical in that there was no astrodome for sextant sights, only a left side window to take bearings on terrain features, and no viable place for a drift meter. That was corrected in the B-17B, when the position was moved forward into the nose section with the bombardier, where he stayed in all future configurations.

Bombardier and Navigator Positions in Later Model B-17

Typical Underway Tasks—Determining Wind

On-board instrumentation available to the navigator gave him all he needed to know his progress through the air—indicated airspeed, barometric altitude, compass heading, clock, and free air temperature

(FAT). But what if the body of air was in fact moving in a situation analogous to a ship in a current? What effect did that have on the ground track and ground speed? The drift meter would come in to play and the vector solution calculated on the E6B.

Example: True Course to Destination—240°
    True Airspeed from Front Face Calculation—115 Kts
    Wind Speed at Altitude—290° 35 Kts

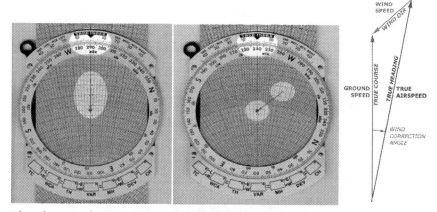

Plot the Wind Vector ,Rotate to the True Course = Ground Speed 93 Kts
Tail of WV on TAS

The Vector Wind Solution

In the days of the Y1B-17 long range missions, there were no constellations of Global Positioning Satellites (GPS), Long Range (LORAN) Radio aids, or super accurate Inertial Navigation Systems (INS) to enable the navigator to quickly and accurately fix his position. RADAR was still years away. If unable to take visual bearings on charted terrain features, radio compass bearings on broadcast stations or be able to view the surface through the drift meter, it was dead reckoning (DR) confirmed with celestial observations, if meteorological conditions permitted.

During the daytime, usually the only celestial body visible was the sun (the moon was sometimes visible during daylight) and sights, or observations, of it were made at frequent intervals and the lines of positions advanced along the predicted track to obtain "running fixes". In the twilight, planets and stars could be seen and more accurate fixes could be made through multiple sights. The telling of these tasks makes it appear that the processes were simple and easily mastered. The reader can easily perceive of a very busy crewmember at the navigation station in the capsule called an aircraft cruising along at 200 + mph!

Celestial Navigation Still in Use

Comtech Miniature Star Tracker

Today, the ubiquitous Global Positioning System (GPS) serves as the sole navigational aid for many a weapon and a primary role aboard aircraft. But what happens if the radio signals from the satellite are jammed or otherwise unavailable? Automated star trackers were used in the B-58 Hustler and the modern B-2 bomber uses a gimbaled telescope for celestial tracking. Miniature star trackers are available today that weigh less than a pound and some are even able to track 6.3 magnitude stars in the daylight. The basic premises of celestial navigation fortunately still hold true and modern techniques solve the celestial triangle automatically.

Creation of the Strategic Bombing Weapon

Great leaps in technology during the golden age of aviation had provided the airframes and propulsion to launch aircraft on long range missions with heavy payloads and the internal systems for physiological comfort. Reduction in communications equipment size and weight made for practical use aboard aircraft, and navigation skills had developed to insure mission route execution accuracy. The development of the weapons of war adapted for aeronautical use made similar parallel progress.

The Aircraft Bombsight

The study of land-based artillery and naval gun battery ballistics had developed into an intricate but computationally solvable science. Just as with the basic tenets of marine navigation were easily transferred to the air, so too would it be with free-fall weapons launched from aircraft.

An American Coast Artillery officer, Lt Riley E. Scott, built a bombsight of his own design in 1911 and it took account of speed and altitude in determining bomb release point and he tested it at College Park, MD. To aim the sight, Lieutenant Scott lay prone on the wing of the aircraft and using hastily prepared bombing tables to make his bombsight settings, was able to place two 18-pound bombs within 10 feet of a four-by-five-foot target from a height of 400 feet. The United States had no corner on the interest in aerial dropped bombs as the world crept inexorably toward WWI. In January 1912, Scott and his bombsight won first place and $5,000 in the Michelin bombing competition at Villacoublay Airdrome in France by scoring 12 hits on a 125-by-375-foot target with 15 bombs dropped from 800 meters.

Later that same year in Hammondsport, NY, 19-year-old Lawrence Sperry built and successfully flight tested an aircraft gyroscopic stabilizer designed especially for one of Glenn Curtiss' early experimental flying boats. Actually, it was a simple autopilot. In June 1914, just before the outbreak of World War I, Sperry won 50,000 francs from the French War Department by demonstrating a "stable aircraft" which he flew without touching the controls and with a mechanic walking on one wing.

The advantage of such stabilization was quickly recognized, and after 1917, Sperry stabilizers were installed in all Allied heavy bombers to keep the aircraft steady on bombing runs, but the idea of gyroscopically stabilizing the bombsight itself did not gain currency until some ten years later. When this idea did catch hold, amazing progress was made in increasing bomb dropping precision.

A Number of Promising Concepts

As it was with the level of aircraft design and manufacturing, the sophisticated aeronautical equipment being developed on the European scene outpaced anything taking place in the Army or the Navy. On December 7, 1917, drawings and models of a British Mark I bombsight were sent to the United States and the joint Army-Navy Aircraft Board at McCook Field, Dayton, OH. The Board was authorized by the Signal Corps Air Service to procure both Mark Is and Mark I-As. The Mark I saw extensive American service during the war and in the 1921 and 1923 Project "B" tests, where General Mitchell's Martin bombers successfully sank three capital ships with 2,000 and 4,000 pound bombs from about 10,000 feet altitude.

There were three prominent bombsight developments during the 1920s and 1930s. They were the Sperry Gyroscope Company "C-Series," the Georges Estoppey "D-Series," and the C. L. Norden "M-Series".

The "C-Series" bombsights were designed by Alexander P. Seversky (or de Seversky). The Sperry Gyroscope Company received a development contract in 1921 for the equipment and Seversky agreed to assist the Sperry organization in developing the C-1. One model was built and tested at McCook Field beginning in 1922. This was the first precision type bombsight to incorporate both the synchronous principle and gyro stabilization. In the synchronous system, the bombardier merely kept the crosshair on the target or aiming point until compensating motors within the system held them. When the crosshairs were thus "synchronized" with the apparent motion of the target, the computer could determine the correct release point presuming that the correct allowances for bomb ballistics had been made prior to synchronization.

The Norden instrument's developments were under the aegis of the Navy and did not receive Army attention until the early 1930's, when their design had almost fully matured. The "C-Series" sights had gyroscopic stabilization while the "D-Series" sights were stabilized by pendulums. Although the ultimate choice of the Engineering Division was to fall on gyroscopes, the Sperry sights generally took a back seat to the Estoppey series for at least ten years following World War I.

While the Air Service had been devoting effort to the Sperry gyroscopically stabilized sight models and variations, the bombers of the period were generally equipped with the "D-Series" pendulum stabilized sights designed by Georges Estoppey. Estoppey came to McCook Field in July 1921 and immediately began work on what soon became the D-1 sight. At the time, only the improved Wimperis Mark I sight was available, and it was rapidly approaching obsolescence; procurement of an improved bombsight was imperative and the Estoppey D-1 was chosen; it was more accurate than the Mark I, was very light, simple to operate, and quite inexpensive: average cost of the early models was about $300 each. The "D-Series" sights were time-of-fall devices using a separate synchronous means for determining ground speed, and providing impact location based on the groundspeed observation. This series went through a great number of modifications and improvements, and the incremental accuracy achieved was applauded.

As noted above, the Norden "M" Series instruments were developed under the aegis of the Navy. Carl L. Norden had begun to study bombing problem as a consultant to the Navy for a number of projects dating back to 1915. Interestingly, for the four years prior to that, he was an engineer working for the newly formed Sperry Gyroscope Co., and continued as a consultant through WWI.[4]

In 1923 Norden went into partnership with another Navy consultant, a former Army colonel named Theodore H. Barth, who provided valuable know-how in sales. Over the next five years, Norden designed bombsights, and Barth built and tested prototypes from Norden's top secret drawings. In 1928, Norden and Barth received their first order from the Navy for 40 bombsights. At that point the two incorporated as Carl L. Norden Inc. The Norden Company delivered its first prototype of its Mark XV bombsight to the Navy in 1931.

Norden's Demonstration Impresses the Army

Army observers witnessed the October 1931 Navy demonstration of the Norden Mark XV sight, and were so impressed that the chief of the Air Corps asked the Navy to furnish 25 of the sights for testing. The first was delivered in April 1933 and tests revealed that the Mark XV performed far better than any bombsight known to that time, and was far superior to anything the Army had either in production or development. The Air Corps then purchased 78 more Norden sights with negotiations with the Norden firm through the Navy Department.

The Norden sights (called the "M-Series" by the Air Corps) operated on the synchronous principle, had effective gyro stabilization, and were relatively easy to use; some models could be connected mechanically to a special automatic pilot—dubbed the Automatic Flight Control Equipment (AFCE)—also developed by the Norden firm. By January 1936, a total of 100 bombsights had been delivered to the Army.

If properly set and operated, the Norden equipment was capable of generating the correct range and course for bombing irrespective of wind, target, motion, altitude, or airspeed. Before range and course could be determined, however, the amount of trail for a given bomb shape, aircraft altitude and airspeed, the actual time of fall of the bomb, and crosswind had to be equated in the bombing solution. Additionally, a new variable added to the bombing problem by drift was called "cross trail." This was the least distance from the point of bomb impact to the ground projection of the aircraft's true heading line. Cross trail depended on the amount of trail and the magnitude of the drift angle.[5]

Since the bomb left the aircraft in the direction of flight, the course problem solution produced the aircraft <u>heading</u> required to score a target hit, while the range solution determined a <u>release point</u> far enough back from the target to allow correct bomb impact.

The Norden system was essentially divided into two primary parts, the stabilizer and the sight head. The stabilizer was a gyroscopically leveled platform that provided a stable base for the sight head's use. The stabilizer was also electrically attached to the aircraft autopilot, permitting it to direct the aircraft to the same level point as the sight head. Alignment between the sight head and the stabilizer was important to insure that the sight head was indeed looking in the same direction as the aircraft heading.

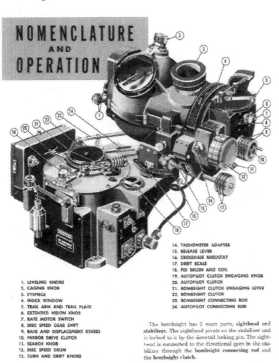

NOMENCLATURE
AND
OPERATION

1. LEVELING KNOBS
2. CAGING KNOB
3. EYEPIECE
4. INDEX WINDOW
5. TRAIL ARM AND TRAIL PLATE
6. EXTENDED VISION KNOB
7. RATE MOTOR SWITCH
8. DISC SPEED GEAR SHIFT
9. RATE AND DISPLACEMENT KNOBS
10. MIRROR DRIVE CLUTCH
11. SEARCH KNOB
12. DISC SPEED DRUM
13. TURN AND DRIFT KNOBS

14. TACHOMETER ADAPTER
15. RELEASE LEVER
16. CROSSHAIR RHEOSTAT
17. DRIFT SCALE
18. PDI BRUSH AND COIL
19. AUTOPILOT CLUTCH ENGAGING KNOB
20. AUTOPILOT CLUTCH
21. BOMBSIGHT CLUTCH ENGAGING LEVER
22. BOMBSIGHT CLUTCH
23. BOMBSIGHT CONNECTING ROD
24. AUTOPILOT CONNECTING ROD

The bombsight has 2 main parts, sighthead and stabilizer. The sighthead pivots on the stabilizer and is locked to it by the dovetail locking pin. The sighthead is connected to the directional gyro in the stabilizer through the bombsight connecting rod and the bombsight clutch.

The Legendary Norden Bombsight

The sight head contained a mechanical analog computer to calculate the impact point of the bombs relative to the aircraft, the sighting telescope and electric motors and gyros that moved the sighting telescope so that a single point on the ground remained stationary in the sight.

As the aircraft approached the target, the bombardier pointed the telescope in front of the aircraft to acquire the target, and the motors and gyros would maintain the target image, rotating the telescope toward the vertical. The rate of change of the telescope angle rotation was a function of the distance to the target and the speed of approach. Facilities were provided for the bombardier to dial in his estimates for airspeed and altitude information on which was available from aircraft instruments. Accurate groundspeed was the key ingredient for accuracy, however, and early aircraft had no way to directly measure groundspeed.

The Norden sight could be used to determine wind speed by selecting an easily visible target and turn on the Norden with its default settings. The selected target would drift across the eyepiece, and the bombardier would use a separate set of fine tuning dials to zero out the drift and the wind speed could then be read from the dials. Once on final approach, the system was turned on and the Norden took control of the aircraft and automatically triggered off the bombs.

Procurement Politics and Sperry versus Norden

Contrary to popular belief, the Norden sight was not the only WWII bombsight used. The Army wanted the sights to be calibrated for higher speeds and altitudes and the autopilot equipment simplified to reduce maintenance difficulties and eventually undertook to have the improvements separately incorporated in the bombsight. Cooperation with the Navy was typically lacking, and turmoil resulted. The Army approached the Victor Adding Machine Company and the Minneapolis-Honeywell Regulator Company for the fabrication of the C-1 electrical autopilot containing the desired (simplified) maintenance features.

In January 1936, the Navy suspended all deliveries of the Norden sight to the Army Air Corps until the Navy's own requirements were satisfied. At that point, the commander of the GHQ Air Force, MajGen Frank M. Andrews, expressed his concern in a memo to the Chief of the Air Corps and to the Navy. He then openly encouraged the Sperry Gyroscope Co. to develop the O-1 bombsight to meet Air Corps specifications.

By 1937 a new type of gyroscope had been developed by Orland E. Esval, one of Sperry's foremost electrical engineers. Since the gyroscopic effect is due to the moment of inertia of the wheel, the greatest effect is obtained by a massive gyro spinning fast. Esval's new gyro had twice the mass of the one used in the then-current Sperry O-1 bombsight, and about the same weight as the vertical gyro in the Norden Mark XV.

However, Esval's gyro was designed to spin at 30,000 rpm, nearly four times faster than the Norden's gyros. The increased gyroscopic effect overcame friction in the gimbals' bearings that was a source of precession (a slow gyration of the rotation axis) and failure. In addition to this technical feature, they made the gyro self-erecting to the vertical, eliminating the necessity for a pilot and bombardier to spend time in a bombing run aligning liquid levels.

Sperry turned a second gyro wheel assembly on its side to make an azimuth gyro and treated it as a sensor only, to eliminate the physical linkage that in the Norden bombsight was a source of friction. When aircraft movements caused the slightest angular deviation of the gyro's from the plane's axes, it generated electric signals that, when amplified, controlled a servomechanism that compensated for the plane's movement and thus stabilized the bombsight optics in azimuth. The new gyros were self-lubricating and induction-powered, eliminating the dc brushes that caused carbon dust. This innovation, however, required the new gyro to have its own ac power source, because in the late 1930s, U.S. airborne instrumentation ran only on dc power or on vacuum suction generated through venturi tubes mounted outside the cockpit.

The Army Air Corps was so inspired by the performance of the Sperry bombsight that it soon adopted induction electrical systems for aircraft, which later facilitated radio instrumentation settling on a 400-hertz electrical system. In 1940 and 1941, the Norden XV bombsight was installed in Air Corps B-17 bombers while the Sperry S-1 was installed in B-24Es used by the 15th Air Force in the Mediterranean area and in lend lease B-24s supplied to the British Royal Air Force (RAF), since the Navy refused to release Norden sights to foreign governments.[6]

The First All-electronic Autopilot

The precision targeting made possible by the bombsights demanded a higher level of precision in maintaining a plane's course, attitude, altitude, and trim—far beyond what could be attained with a bombardier-pilot team or commercial autopilot. Boeing equipped some of the early B-17s in the late 1930s with a Sperry A-3 commercial autopilot. The gyros in the A-3 sensed only simple angular displacement of the aircraft from the desired course. It used pneumatic hydraulic servo systems that were sluggish, and since there was no measure of velocity or acceleration, the system tended to overcompensate in rough air and thus oscillate. The Norden company developed an autopilot called the stabilized bombing approach equipment (SBAE), also based upon the earlier displacement only signal technology of commercial auto pilots. The Norden SBAE's mechanically sliding trolley contact electric servos resulted in flight control no better than that of the Sperry A-3 commercial autopilot.

For the new Sperry S-1 bombsight, Sperry invented the first all-electronic autopilot, the A-5. It was based on three dual element vacuum tube amplifiers, each corresponding to a different axis in the aircraft's control system: roll, pitch, and yaw. More importantly, in addition to the displacement-error signal, the A-5 autopilot adjusted for the first and second time derivatives (the velocity and acceleration with which the aircraft departed from the base reference signal). The amplified signals controlled independent electro hydraulic servomechanisms, providing fast response for stabilizing the aircraft. This resulted in a system that was critically damped, and was much more responsive than the electromechanical technology to wind gusts and command signals from the bombsight.[7]

The Army was so impressed with the performance of the A-5 autopilot and the S-1 Bombsight, that contracts were immediately let for the manufacture of both. A directive was issued that all aircraft should be equipped with the A-5 Autopilot, and provisions made for the aircraft to accept either the Norden or the Sperry Bombsight. Norden balked over such an arrangement, and after a series of negotiations, the Army was able to have Honeywell develop and build a C-1 Autopilot that used Norden gyros, but the rate circuits and servos from Sperry.

That did not sit well with the Norden Company, and they pulled out all the stops to point out that they were a dedicated American Company vice a "multi-national company with ties to Germany and Japan". The Air Corps ultimately cancelled all of the Sperry work and Norden held sway.

1. ttp://www.centennialofflight.gov/essay/Government_Role/navigation/POL13.htm
2. http://www.nationalmuseum.af.mil/factsheets/factsheet.asp?id=3239
3. http://www.nationalaviation.org/hegenberger-albert/
4. The Bombsight Wars, http://thevaluesell.com/images/LSearle_bombsight.pdf
5. ibid
6. ibid
7. ibid

CHAPTER
IX

Boeing and the Development of the Y1B-17

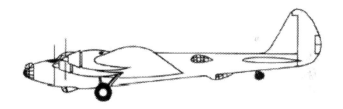

Wilhelm Edward Boeing was born in Detroit, MI to wealthy mining engineer Wilhelm Böing. When he returned from his education in Switzerland in 1900, he changed his name to William and entered Yale University in New Haven, CT. In 1903, the same year the Wright brothers made their first flight at Kitty Hawk, NC, 22-year old William Boeing left Yale engineering college for the West Coast. In a few years, he had made a fortune trading forest lands around Gray's Harbor, WA and moved to Seattle. Although he was an avid leisure-time sailor and had acquired a small yacht building shipyard on the Duwamish River, he became enamored with the field of aviation. But for the next few years, the closest he came to the world of aeronautics was in discussions with Commander George C. Westervelt, a Navy engineer who had taken courses in aeronautics at MIT. After getting a ride in a Curtis biplane, the two were convinced they could build a "better mousetrap". Boeing took flight training with the legendary

Glenn Curtis in Los Angeles in 1915 leaving Westervelt home in Seattle to start designing a biplane, the B & W (For Boeing and Westervelt). They built a special building for its construction just offshore on Seattle's Union Lake.

Replica Boeing B&W Biplane, the First of a Long Line

Unfortunately, the Navy reassigned Westervelt to the East, but Boeing pressed on and completed two B&Ws, making the first flight himself when his pilot failed to arrive on time. He offered the aircraft to the Navy, but the sale was not completed and the aircraft were eventually sold to New Zealand, where one set an altitude record of 6,500 ft. Not to be discouraged, on July 15, 1916, Boeing incorporated his airplane manufacturing business as Pacific Aero Products Co. and a year later, twenty days after the U.S. Declaration of War, he changed the name to the Boeing Airplane Co. Success came quickly when Boeing recognized that the Navy would need to train a large number of pilots for WWI and designed the model C.

The Navy Trainer That Launched Boeing into Manufacturing

After flying two of the aircraft for the Navy at Pensacola, FL, the Navy was impressed enough to order 50 of the model.[1]

Like most companies tied to the production of war materials, the Boeing Co. struggled after WWI, striking off into any direction that might capitalize on their talents and resources. To keep his factory open, Boeing diverted his labor force to furniture and boat production, or anything else where spruce wood could be profitably used.[2]

The Government held the design rights for aircraft it procured and aggressively sought out lowest bids for production of existing designs. Boeing's low cost tenders for modifying and updating 300 DH-4s and to build 200 Thomas-Morse pursuit ships kept the company afloat during the hard post-war times[3]. They

Boeing PW-9; the First of Many Boeing Fighters

were also contracted with to build 25 Curtis HS-2Ls, but knew that they had to design and build their own aircraft to be successful. They did that, and when competing against Curtis, they garnered a contract for their PW-9 pursuit ship, which led to a series of renowned pursuits for the Army and the Navy.

They broke into the air mail business with the Model 40 and 40A. The Boeing Model 40 was a United States mail plane that became the first aircraft built by Boeing to carry passengers. The accommodations were less than comfortable, for the primary purpose was to carry mail. Two passengers could be accommodated in the small cabin through access in a port side door after climbing on the wing. The mail compartment was in the fuselage just forward of the wing, balanced off by the pilot seated well aft of the wing in an open cockpit. Originally designed to compete for a US Mail contract in 1925, it was rejected in favor of the Douglas M-2.

Boeing Model 40A

The design was revived in 1927 as part of Boeing's tender for newly-privatized airmail routes. Designated the Model 40A, this variant was powered by an air-cooled Pratt & Whitney Wasp radial engine, which offered a 200 lb weight saving over the water-cooled Liberty specified by the postal service in 1925. Boeing successfully bid on the San Francisco-Chicago route, and Boeing Air Transport commenced operations on 1 July 1927 with 24 Model 40As.[4]

Boeing made a quantum jump ahead in the transport arena with the introduction of the Model 80. It first flew in August 1928 and was working along Boeing Air Transport's route two weeks later. The 12-passenger Model 80 and the more-powerful 18-passenger 80A (re-designated 80A-1s when the tail surfaces were modified in 1930) stayed in-service until 1933, when replaced by the all-metal Boeing Model 247.

Boeing Model 80 at the Seattle Museum of Flight

Unlike many of the transport aircraft of the day, the Model 80 was the first to be designed for passenger comfort and convenience. A steel truss fuselage covered with fabric provided an enclosed capacious passenger cabin with leather seating. An enclosed cockpit was not universally accepted by pilots, but became the norm as aircraft size increased. A closed lavatory with hot and cold running water was available.

In 1930, Miss Ellen Church, a student pilot and registered nurse, convinced Boeing management to hire female cabin attendants for their Model 80 flights. Until then, it had been the co-pilot's duty to pass out box lunches, serve coffee, and tend to the passenger's needs. Church reasoned that the sight of women working aboard the Boeing 80s would alleviate the passenger's fear of air travel. She and seven others, all nurses, became America's first stewardesses. Serving on a trial basis, they were very popular and became a permanent part of American commercial aviation. Ellen and her compatriots serving aboard the Model 80A became aviation's first female flight attendants, earning $125 for flying 100 hours a month.[5] By this time, Boeing had become one of the largest aircraft manufacturers.

Boeing Aircraft in the 1930s

The Boeing P-26 "Peashooter" and the B-9

The aviation industry was making quantum jumps in materials, power plants and production techniques in the late 1920s and early 1930s. Wooden construction had given way to metal, light weight air-cooled engines produced ever higher power, and the biplane became obsolete. Boeing was quick to capitalize on this transition, and its first all metal aircraft, the Model 200 Monomail was rolled out in 1930.

The Monomail was revolutionary, perhaps too much so, as it needed a variable pitch propeller which had not reached a practical point at the time. By the time one became available, the Boeing 247 airliner was underway. The Monomail did pave the way, however, for the Army's B-9.

The Boeing Model 247

One of the first modern airliners was the Boeing Model 247 which introduced a host of aerodynamic and technical features, eclipsing the products offered by other manufacturers. Among the many "firsts" incorporated were advances such as all-metal anodized aluminum semi-monocoque construction, a fully cantilevered wing, retractable landing gear, control surface trim tabs, an autopilot and deicing boots for the wings and tailplane.[6] This advanced design, which was a progression from earlier Monomail (Models 200, 221, 221A) and B-9 bomber designs, combined speed and safety. The Boeing 247 was faster than the U.S. premier fighter aircraft of its day, the Boeing P-12, which was a biplane. Yet its flight envelope included a rather docile 62 mph landing speed which precluded the need for flaps. The main landing gear did not fully retract into the nacelles leaving a portion of the wheel exposed. This was a fairly common design feature of the time that would preclude serious damage in the case of a wheels-up landing. The tail wheel was not retractable. While the Model 247 and 247A had speed-ring engine cowlings and fixed-pitch propellers, the Model 247D incorporated NACA cowlings and variable pitch propellers.

Boeing refused to sell the 247 to any other airline than their own United Air Transport, thinking that it would place them in a superior position, but that was not to be the case. Stymied by this exclusivity, TWA and American airlines looked elsewhere and Donald Douglas would respond with the DC-1, -2 and ultimately DC-3, perhaps the most widely used transport of its time. However, the 247 did provide the Boeing Company with the design and production skills to move yet again to be on the leading edge of bomber development.[7]

Boeing 247D with Nose Baggage Door Open. Note Full NACA Cowls

Changes at the Helm of the Boeing Company

Emanating from the investigation into the Air Mail scandals, anti-trust legislation of 1934 broke up the conglomerate that was the Boeing Company by preventing aircraft manufacturers from owning airline companies. The break-up resulted in the Boeing owned United Aircraft and Transport Corp becoming United Airlines, United Aircraft, and the Boeing Aircraft Company. Unhappy with this direction, William Boeing resigned his chairmanship of the corporation and left to raise horses. Philip Johnson resigned his presidency of United Aircraft and Transport and went to Canada to help establish Trans Canada Airlines. Claire Egtvedt, took over the helm of the Boeing Airplane Company and pointed the manufacturer toward larger aircraft and directed efforts to building the "Big Boeings."[8] He believed that the company's future lay in large bombers developed in tandem with equally large passenger airplanes. His vision coincided with that of the Army Air Corps' "Bomber Mafia" and it would prove to be a synergistic relationship.

Response to the February 1934 Army Air Corps Project "A"

Despite the formal role of supporting ground forces detailed for Army aviation, there were many who espoused the strategic use of air power. McCook/Wright Field Test and Experimental Center released a requirement for a "long range airplane suitable for military purposes" on April 14, 1934. Boeing, Douglas and Martin submitted responses. The evaluation panel deemed the Boeing Model 294 to be worth pursuing and inked a contract for design data and wind tunnel tests. Based on a favorable review of this data, Boeing was authorized to construct a single experimental prototype, originally designated the XBLR-1 (experimental bomber, long range), it eventually became the XB-15.

Martin's proposed design was dubbed the XB-16. The Martin XB-16 was to use four Allison V-1710 liquid-cooled inline engines, a choice that did not provide the desired performance. In 1935, Martin revised the XB-16 design and the wing span was increased from 140 ft to 173 ft and another set of V-1710 engines added to the trailing edge. This version had a wingspan 20% greater than that of the B-29 Super Fortress, the first operational bomber that would fill the role intended for the XB-16, but it was cancelled for essentially the same reason the B-15 project was: it wasn't fast enough to meet the requirements set by the Army. Since both were cancelled around the same time, Martin did not have time to produce an XB-16.

Proposed Martin XB-16

One-Off Douglas XB-19

Douglas' gargantuan submittal was deemed too far a reach, and eventually delayed until the Wright Cyclone R-3350 engines could be matured. It did not fly until June 27, 1941, and despite the huge engines or their replacement with the Allison V-3420, it lacked the performance needed and only one was built.

The evaluation panel deemed the Boeing Model 294 to be worth pursuing and inked a contract for design data and wind tunnel tests. Based on a favorable review of this data, Boeing was authorized to construct a single experimental prototype, originally designated the XBLR-1 (experimental bomber, long range), it eventually became the XB-15.

One-Off Boeing XLRB-1 (B-15) Bomber

Impressive as its size was, it was far too slow for a combat environment, so the project was terminated and the single prototype aircraft was assigned to the 2nd Bombardment Group at Langley Field, VA. There, it flew a number of significant missions. Commanded by Maj Caleb V. Haynes, it flew an earthquake relief mission, carrying medical supplies to

Chile in February 1939, earning its crew the MacKay Trophy. On June 10th, Haynes piloted the XB-15 to return home the body of Mexican flier Francisco Sarabia who had died in a crash in the Potomac River.

After flying back from Mexico City, Haynes and his copilot William D. Old undertook a series of flight tests at Fairfield, Ohio, lifting very heavy loads. They used the XB-15 to lift 22,046 lbs to 8,228 ft, and 31,164 lbs to 6,561.6 ft, setting two world records for which Haynes was awarded certificates issued by the National Aeronautics Association (NAA). The following month he received certificates from NAA for the establishment of an international 5,000 kilometers (3,100 mi) speed record with a 2,000 kilograms (4,400 lb) payload. The latter performance also established a national closed circuit distance record of 3,129.241 miles (5,036.025 km).

The Army Air Forces converted the only prototype into a transport, designated XC-105, which carried freight around the Caribbean during World War II. In service for eight years, the airplane carried more than 5,200 passengers, 440,000 lbs of cargo and 94,000 lbs of mail. It flew 70 cargo trips and 60 missions including antisubmarine patrol. Unfortunately for the aviation historical restoration community, the XC-105 was scrapped at Howard Air Force Base in Panama in 1945[9].

The Army Air Corps May 1934 Request

The Army apparently realized that it had attempted to stretch the envelope a little too far for the technology of the time. Because of the slow development of the XB-15 and its obvious shortcomings, not six weeks after signing the contract for the huge aircraft, on 8 August 1934, the Army Air Corps tendered a proposal (Army Circular Proposal 35-356) for a multi-engine bomber to replace the Martin B-10. Requirements were that it would carry a useful bomb load at an altitude of 10,000 ft for ten hours with a top speed of at least 200 mph. Desired, but not required, was a range of 2,000 miles and a speed of 250 mph. The competition would be decided by a "fly-off" at Wright Field in Dayton, Ohio between the Boeing Model 299, the Douglas DB-1 and the Martin Model 146 for the Air Corps contract.

The Boeing Model 299

The Boeing Model 299 was designed by a team of engineers led by E. Gifford Emery, Edward C. Wells and a nine man team of specialists.

After quietly consulting with the Army concerning acceptability of a four engine configuration to target the "multi-engine" requirement, the team called upon the features of the experimental Boeing XB-15 bomber and melded them with the Boeing 247 transport airplane. Amazingly, within three weeks, the basic drawings were available for review by the Board of Directors. On September 26, 1934, the Board authorized $275,000 to press on with refining the design. However, as the design progressed, it became obvious that more funding was required, and Boeing was dipping low into what reserves existed. If an order for the aircraft was not forthcoming, the very being of the company was in jeopardy.

The size of this new plane was not too different from existing large airplanes of the day, but with four engines, it was hoped that the performance would be the weighted factor as it translated to increased speed, range and payload capabilities. Otherwise the basic structural design would not be foreign to any designer of the day as the engineers fell on proven structures. In this case, it was a square-sectioned spars with corrugated dural beneath the skins, welded wing fuel tanks, wheels that retracted into the nacelles and a monocoque frame and stringer fuselage. Recent advances in control techniques led to the use of flaps and control surface trim tabs. The relatively recent development of controllable pitch propellers was incorporated as were fully cowled engines and reduced drag techniques at every opportunity.

Actual construction of the prototype, and the genesis of a family tree of an unbelievable number of branches, began in December of 1934. The fuselage was fabricated in four sections: the nose section forward of the cockpit, the main section, with a navigator behind (later to be changed), a vertical stack bomb bay and radio operator's station, and tail. The wing sections were in two sections: the center with the engine nacelles and tanks, and the outer, all joined with taper pins at the attach points at the spars. Aluminum was the basic material of choice, but fabric-covered rudder and elevators were a touch of the past.

On July 16, 1935, the airplane was rolled out after a company-funded investment of 153,000 man-hours and $400,000 of their reserve funds. It was important that good publicity surround the entire scene as failure to obtain a production follow-on contract could mean the end of Boeing as a viable corporate entity. On viewing the roll-out, Richard L. Williams, a journalist for the *Seattle Times,* helped hype the image of the Model 299 when he coined the phrase "Flying Fortress" after seeing the armament installed. The name would resonate and stick, and Boeing would trademark it. A mere 12 days later, the wonder ship would make its maiden flight, actually two years ahead of the XB-15. Boeing's Chief pilot Leslie Tower responded in typical test pilot manner, that the first flight was "just like a little ship, only a little bigger."

The resulting aircraft was capable of hauling up to 4,800 pounds of bombs on two racks in the bomb bay behind the cockpit and five 0.30 inches (7.62 mm) machine guns, and was powered by Pratt & Whitney R-1690 "Hornet" radial engines each producing 750 horsepower at 7,000 feet. As noted above, Boeing chief test-pilot Leslie Tower was at the controls for the first flight of the Model 299 on July 28, 1935, and less than one month later on August 20, 1935, the prototype flew from Seattle to Wright Field in nine hours and three minutes at an average cruising speed of 232 miles per hour, faster than virtually anything in the air at the time. Boeing seemed to have hit the "sweet spot" of bomber performance.

**The Boeing Model 299 at Seattle
(The Museum of Flight, and
National Archives)**

Boeing Model 299 in Flight
(The Museum of Flight, and
National Archives)

Boeing Model 299 Arrival at Dayton
(National Archives)

At the fly-off, the four-engine Boeing design's performance was decidedly superior to those of the twin-engine Douglas DB-1 and Martin Model 146. It was faster than the Martin 146 by about 30 mph, and the Douglas DB-1 by about 20 mph. Its range at 2,000 miles was twice that of the competition. Then-MajGen Frank M. Andrews of the GHQ Air

Force believed that the long-range capabilities of four-engine large aircraft were more efficient than shorter-ranged twin-engined airplanes, and that the B-17 was better suited to their doctrine. His opinions were shared by the Air Corps procurement officers, and even before the competition was finished they suggested buying 65 B-17s. The simple following chart was a graphic presentation of the capabilities of the competing AAC bombers.

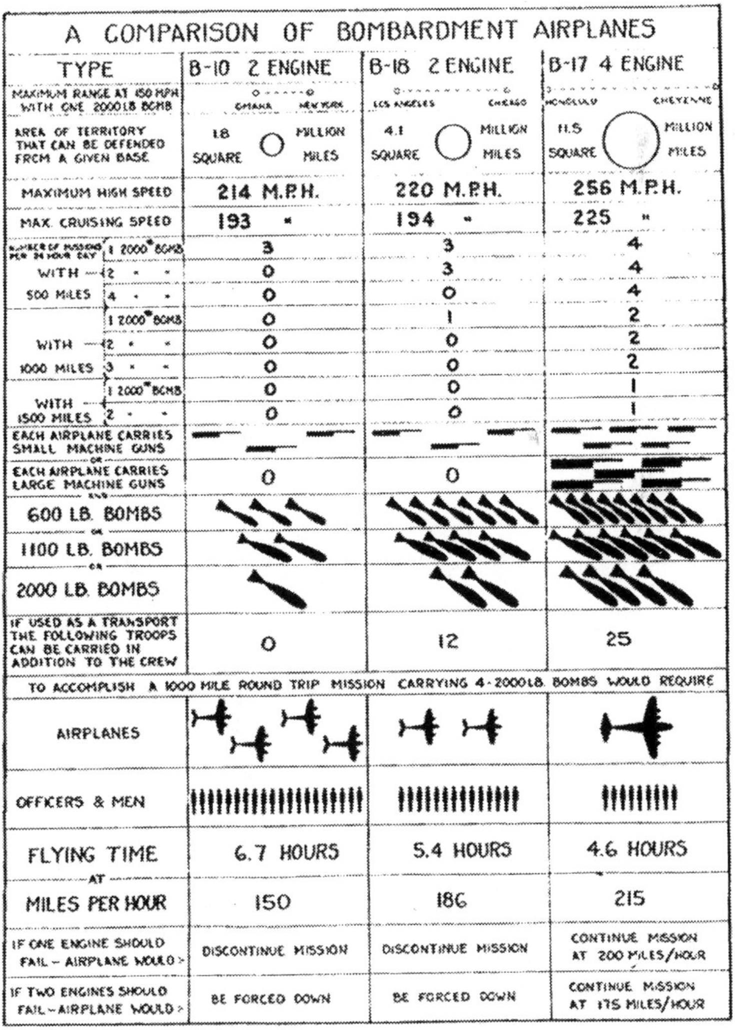

Bomber Capability Comparison Chart
(July 20, 1937 B-17 Suitability Report, 2nd Bomb Group)

Development continued on the Boeing Model 299, and on October 30, 1935 the Army Air Corps test-pilot Maj Ployer Peter Hill and his co-pilot 1stLt Donald L. Putt took off on a second evaluation flight. Also aboard in the rear were engineer John B. Cutting and mechanic Mark H. Koogler. Boeing's chief test pilot Les Tower was standing behind the two pilots in the commodious cockpit. In a classic case of cockpit procedural omission, the crew forgot to disengage the airplane's "gust lock," a device that held the bomber's movable control surfaces in place while the plane was parked on the ground. On takeoff, the aircraft entered a steep climb, the pilots discovered the error, but the aircraft stalled, nosed over and crashed, killing Hill and Tower. The crashed Model 299 could not finish the evaluation, and while the Air Corps was still enthusiastic about its potential, Army officials were faced with a competition that could not be completed by the Model 299. Another major consideration was the much greater expense per aircraft, with Douglas quoting a unit price of $58,200 based on a production order of 220 aircraft, compared with a price of $99,620 from Boeing. The crash legally disqualified Boeing from the consideration for the contract and Army Chief of Staff Malin Craig cancelled the order for 65 YB-17s, and ordered 133 of the twin-engine Douglas B-18 Bolo instead.[10]

Delivery of the First Thirteen Y1B-17s

Despite the turn of events leading to contract award to Douglas for the B-18 Bolo, the Model 299 was such an impressive performer that GHQ's MajGen Frank Andrews went to bat and was successful in gaining approval for an order of at least another 13 aircraft, now designated the Y1B-17.

Note for the Curious

During the years 1928—present day, the letter "Y" in the designation signified a Service Test aircraft. From 1931—1936, the "Y1" signified Service Test aircraft purchased with "F-1" funds instead of USAAC appropriations.

These aircraft were significantly improved over the Model 299 with more powerful Wright R-1820-39 government-furnished[10] engines. Since the original Model 299 was company owned and never received such a designation, it was retroactively given the designation XB-17. A 14th Y1B-17 (37-369), was constructed for ground testing of the airframe's strength at Wright Field. However, when one of the Y1B-17s suffered a departure from normal flight, entered a spin, recovered and subsequently was inspected with no damage detected, the Wright Field ship became a flying test bed and designated the Y1B-17A. One of the significant tests was the installation of exhaust driven turbo superchargers, eventually located under the nacelles, a configuration carried on to all subsequent models, vastly increasing high altitude capability. The service ceiling increased from 31,000 ft to 38,000 ft and the maximum speed increased from 256 mph to 311 mph.

Once service testing was complete, the Y1B-17s and Y1B-17A were redesignated B-17 and B-17A respectively to signify the change to operational status. In February 1937, Maj Barney M. Giles took a crew up to Seattle to bring back the first Y1B-17. Giles delivered the airplane to the 2nd Bombardment Group, Langley Field, VA.—the very field from which Billy Mitchell's open cockpit biplane bombers had flown out to sea to sink *Ostfriesland* in 1921. By August 1937, the Air Corps had its 13 new bombers and all eyes would be on the 2nd Bombardment Group as it developed the operational procedures and demonstrated that the theories could be turned into reality.

Y1B-17 Delivery dates, 2nd Bombardment Group Squadron and side number assigned:

36-149: 1 MAR 1937—49th BS
36-150: 11 MAR 1937—96th BS—Aircraft Number **60**
36-151: 28 MAR 1937—49th BS—Aircraft Number **80**
36-152: 27 MAR 1937—20th BS—Aircraft Number **50**
36-153: 10 MAY 1937—2nd BG
36-154: 16 MAY 1937—49th BS—Aircraft Number **81**
36-155: 1 JUN 1937—2nd BG HQ—Aircraft Number **10**
36:156: 17 JUN 1937—20th BS—Aircraft Number **51**
36-157: 6 JUN 1937—2nd BG
36-158: 30 JUN 1937—49th BS—Aircraft Number **82**

36-159: 14 SEP 1937—20th BS—Aircraft Number **52**
36-160: 28 JUL 1937—2nd BG
36-161: 8 AUG 1937—49th BS—Aircraft Number **89**

Note to the Curious

Naming aircraft was a common occurrence and there was some sentiment to name the first 13 Y1B-17s after the first 13 states. The large squadron/HQ side numbering source or the numbering rationale is unknown.

Arrival and Formal Welcome of the 1ˢᵗ Y1B-17, Langley Field March 1, 1937

2nd Bomb Group Early Operations

Coinciding with the first delivery, Maj Robert Olds was assigned to command the 2nd Bomb Group on March 1, 1937, and promoted to the rank of lieutenant colonel. It was his enviable lot yet extremely demanding responsibility to train the group in operating the most advanced aircraft of its day, develop entirely new techniques and demonstrate how the Y1B-17's performance was critical to the Army's, and the War Department's, success. Not only did he have these crushing tasks, they would have to perform under the watchful and critical eyes of General Andrews and his entire Air Corps GHQ, co-located with him at Langley Field. Fortunately, there was probably no one in the Air Corps better prepared or personally equipped for the job.

Design Synergism at Boeing

The Army's orders for the XB-15 and the Y1B-17 provided a much-needed boost to Boeing's financial well-being. Claire Egtvedt's direction for Boeing to become the manufacturer of larger bombers developed in tandem with equally large passenger airplanes was to pay off. Both bomber aircraft contributed not only valuable design experience, but also actual transfer of structures and other features to transport designs.

Despite being called the "Golden Age" of aviation, the 1930s were still characterized by a lack of acceptable airfields in many parts of the world. A number of manufacturers such as Consolidated, Martin and Short provided seaplanes and amphibians to capitalize on the vast availability of water virtually world-wide. The Boeing 314 was a response to Pan American's request for a flying boat with unprecedented range capability that could augment the airline's trans-Pacific Martin M-130.

Boeing Model 314 with the XB-15 Wing and More Powerful Engines

Boeing's bid was successful and on July 21, 1936, Pan American signed a contract for six. Boeing engineers adapted the cancelled XB-15's 149 feet wing, and replaced the original 850 horsepower Pratt & Whitney Twin Wasp radial engines with the more powerful 1,600 horsepower Wright Twin Cyclone. Its first flight took place with a single, conventional tail before experiments with twin tail and triple tail configurations led to the choice of a triple tail to provide more rudder area for controllability. Pan Am ordered an additional six aircraft with increased engine power and a larger carrying capacity of 77 daytime passengers as the Boeing 314A. The first prototype of the series flew on March 20, 1941.

In a similar fashion, Boeing adapted many of the Model 299 (Y1B-17) structures and features and created the Model 307 Stratoliner. In 1935, Boeing combined the wings, tail, undercarriage and engines of the B-17C with a new, circular section fuselage designed to allow pressurization. The Boeing Model 307 Stratoliner was the first fully pressurized airliner to enter service anywhere in the world and was able to fly 20,000 feet higher than the 5,000 to 10,000 foot-altitude unpressurized airplanes of that time. It carried five crew members and 33 passengers and had a nearly 12-foot wide cabin for overnight berths. The Stratoliner was also the first land-based airplane to have a flight engineer as a member of the crew.

The Boeing Model 307 Stratoliner with "Borrowed" B-17C Wing, Engines, Undercarraige, and Tailplanes.

Its first flight took place on December 31, 1938 with the first delivery to a customer made to multi-millionaire Howard Hughes, who purchased one to carry out a round-the-world flight, hoping to break his own record of 91 hours 14 minutes set between July 10–14, 1938 in a Lockheed 14. Hughes' Boeing 307 was fitted with extra fuel tanks and was ready to set out on the first leg of the round-the-world attempt when Nazi Germany invaded Poland on September 1, 1939, causing the attempt to be abandoned. It later had the extra fuel tanks removed, was fitted with much more powerful Wright R-2600 engines, and was transformed into a luxurious "flying penthouse" for Hughes, although it was little used, being sold to oil tycoon Glenn McCarthy in 1949.

1. http://www.boeing.com/history/narrative/n004boe.html
2. *The B-17 Flying Fortress Story* Roger A. Freeman and David Osborne
3. http://www.boeing.com/history/boeing/40a.html
4. http://www.acepilots.com/pioneer/boeing_247.html
5. *The National Air and Space Museum* Bryan, C.D.B. New York: Harry N. Abrams, Inc., 1979.
6. *Boeing (Business in Action)* Gould, William Bath, Avon, UK: Cherrytree Books, 1995
7. *The B-17 Flying Fortress Story* Roger A. Freeman and David Osborne
8. http://en.wikipedia.org/wiki/Boeing_XB-15
9. *Ambassador of American Airpower: Maj General Robert Olds*, Zamzow, Maj (USAF) S. L. (2008).
10. *The B-17 Flying Fortress Story*, Roger A. Freeman and David Osborne

CHAPTER X

Langley Field

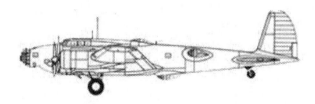

Establishment and the Signal Corps Aviation Section Years

Langley Air Force Base, VA., is among the oldest continuously active air bases in the United States. In 1916, the National Advisory Council for Aeronautics (NACA), predecessor to National Air and Space Administration (NASA), established the need for a joint airfield and proving ground for Army, Navy and NACA aircraft. They determined that the site must be near water for over-water flying, be flat and relatively clear for expansion and the landing and take-off of aircraft and near an Army post. The Army appointed a board of officers who searched for a location sometimes posing as hunters and fishermen to avoid potential land speculation which would arise if the government's interest in purchasing land were revealed.

Fifteen locations were scouted before the site near Hampton, VA was selected. In December 1916 the land that became Langley Field was the first property ever purchased by the United States for aviation purposes. The War Department bought the site for the Army's young air "arm" to build an Aeronautical Experimental Station and Proving Ground, an airfield for aeronautical research, experiments, and flight tests. It would contend with the Air Service's McCook Field in Dayton, OH for the lead in Army aviation development. In 1917, the new proving ground was designated Langley Field for one of America's early air pioneers, Samuel Pierpont Langley. By late 1918, several buildings had been constructed on the field.

The Army and NACA would continue to grow on the storied field sharing the geographic location, moving along different paths, yet sharing some of the most exciting times in the history of aeronautical development. As Langley's military aviators developed their skills and deployed to the far reaches of the world, the scientists and engineers of NACA's Langley Memorial Aeronautical Laboratory advanced aeronautical technology. The Army would field a new generation of aircraft in the late 1930s such as the B-17, B-24, P-36, P-40, and the P-47, based on the engineering work done at the NACA laboratory here.

Lab engineers were active in every area of aeronautics, seeking improvements in propulsion, structures, stability, and aerodynamics. Their wind tunnels were the most advanced in the world, making it world leader in the field well into the 1930s. Work started using a five-foot wind tunnel built in 1920. A variable-density tunnel, built in 1922 by the Newport News Shipyard, was a technical breakthrough that overcame problems with scaling by using air at 20 times atmospheric pressure. A 20-foot propeller research tunnel, complete in 1927, enabled engineers to study the performance of full-size propellers and large aircraft components such as wings, tail surfaces, and landing gear. Finally, they built a full-scale tunnel in 1931, largest in the world at the time, with a test section measuring 30 feet by 60 feet allowing tests of actual small aircraft. In 1936, addition of a high-speed eight-foot tunnel allowed engineers to study stability and control issues at speeds above 500 miles an hour. The 1931 NACA covered water-filled tank allowed engineers to analyze seaplane hull configurations. Perhaps the two best-known advances were development of the NACA cowling and research into laminar flow.[1]

Post WWI Formative Years

Demobilization

As can be easily imagined, the immediate post WWI years were chaotic for the military, and the Army Air Corps struggled with keeping a cohesive force together, and Langley Field was in the thick of the downsizing. With personnel strength of 228 officers and 1,936 enlisted men on December 31, 1918, the drawdown resulted in a drop to 77 officers and 693 enlisted men on December 31, 1920. Although formally instituted as a combat arm of the Army in June 1920, recruitment moved at a snail's pace as Langley tried to fill 168 heavier-than-air positions and 206 in the lighter-than-air disciplines. Despite an estimated six million people being out of work in the depression of 1921-1922, Air Service vacancies exceeded 3,000 enlisted. There were good reasons for this lethargy

Among them was a natural loathing of all things military following the horrendous American Expeditionary Forces (AEF) losses in the trench warfare of WWI. Of those officers that did enter the Army, less than a quarter were physically qualified for duty involving flight. The fact that the Air Service suffered nearly half of all deaths in the Army from 1921—1924 surely dimmed the enthusiasm for aviation duty.

Establishing a Permanent Infrastructure

Bird's Eye View of Langley Field in 1920

By necessity, many of the original buildings at Langley Field were hastily built temporary structures, and they too needed to be "demobilized". The permanent structures, such as the officers' quarters, two brick hangars, an airship hangar, Bachelor Officer Quarters (BOQ)s, and a seaplane hangar had been joined by an equal number of sheet iron or steel and stucco temporary buildings that included the hospital, hangars, barracks, and mess halls that had to be replaced before they deteriorated. Construction continued through the 1920s to be home to new organizations.

Among the many new structures of the interwar period was the Laboratory Building. Amazingly, the building continues to serve today as the Headquarters of the Air Force Air Combat Command following stints for NACA, the Air Service Tactical School and GHQ of the Air Forces.

Organizational Changes in the New Air Service

The Laboratory Building in 1919

In 1920, the Air Service had two wings; the 1st Wing resided at Kelly Field in San Antonio, TX and the 2nd at Langley Field. Also located at Langley was the 1st Army Observation Group, (AOG) consisting of the 50th and the 88th Aero Squadrons. In the organization convulsions following WWI, the 88th was deactivated and personnel assigned to the 50th. Then the 2nd Wing and the 1st AOG were deactivated in 1921. By August 1923, the 2nd Wing was reactivated as the 2nd Bombardment Group that had been transferred from Kelly to Langley the previous month.

Units On-board

In April 1923, the Langley tenant organizations looked like this:

2nd Wing
    2nd Bombardment Group
    20th Photo Section
    58th Service Squadron
    50th Observation Squadron
    19th Airship Company

The 2nd Bombardment Group consisted of:

    11th Bombardment Squadron
        Martin MB-2/NBS-1
    20th Bombardment Squadron

49th Bombardment Squadron
96th Bombardment Squadron
2nd Photo Section
59th Service Squadron
Group Headquarters

The 2nd Bombardment Group would remain at Langley for twenty years of storied accomplishments.[2]

2nd Bombardment Group

Aircraft Assigned in the 1930s

There were many different aircraft flown at Langley in the 1920s, including the trusty holdovers from WWI, the DeHavilland DH-4 and the Curtis JN-4. Most of the aircraft, however, were assigned to the 2nd Bombardment Group.

11th Bombardment Squadron
 Martin MB-2/NBS-1, and later the LB-1
 20th Bombardment Squadron
 Martin MB-2/NBS-1, Keystone LB-5,—7
49th Bombardment Squadron
 Martin MB-2/NBS-1, Keystone LB-5,—7
96th Bombardment Squadron
 Martin MB-2/NBS-1, Keystone LB-5,—7
2nd Photo Section
59th Service Squadron
 1 Loening amphibian, 2 Loening Air Yachts

Huff-DeLand LB-5 and the Martin MB-2

Army Air Service School of Application and Subsequent Derivations[3]

Maj Henry Claggett, General William Mitchell, Grover Loening at Bolling Field

One of the more interesting and ultimately influential tenants was the Army Air Service School of Application. WWI had proved that the Army needed officers who could fight from and in the air. The Air Service thought it to be very important to train its officers in the disciplines of air combat, standardize tactics, and develop the future air doctrines, and as explained in Chapter Three, the school became the source of most AAC Doctrine for years to come.

Maj Thomas DeWitt Milling reported to Langley in July 1920 to establish the school.[3] Although it was initially named the Air Service Field Officers School, there were not enough field grade officers available, and most students were Captains or lieutenants. In 1922, the name was changed to Air Service Tactical School, and ultimately to the Air Corps Tactical School (ACTS) in 1926 in conjunction with the reorganization of the air arm.

Maj W. N. Hensley was the first commandant of the school, but wore two hats as he was also the base commander, and as a result, the office-in-charge and assistant commandant ran the school. In the years that Langley hosted the school, there were two assistant commandants: Maj Milling (1921-1926) and Maj E. L. Naiden (1926-1931). Due to the rapid expansion of the Air Corps and lack of facilities at Langley, the school moved to Maxwell Field, AL in 1931.

Establishment of the GHQ Air Force

On March 1, 1935, the Army Air Corps underwent a major reorganization as explained in Chapter Two. Langley Field became the center of tactical aviation in the Army with the establishment of the General Headquarters Air Force, or GHQ AF, a first step in the creation of an autonomous air arm within the Army. The purpose of the GHQ was to create the mobile air force ready for deployment to support the conventional ground forces with strategic bombing and close tactical firepower. The GHQ reported directly to the Chief of Staff and supervised all tactical units while the Chief of the Air Corps had responsibility for technical training, acquisition, production and other non-combat functions. There were now two parallel air forces and success would ride the shoulders of the leaders' ability to cooperate.

A Unique View—I Was There

Yogi Berra of the New York Yankees was famous for his "sayings" and one of those attributed to him was: "When you come to the "Y" in the road, take it." Such was the case with co-author LtCol Bill Braxton, USAF (RET):

"I suppose everyone who is old enough must wonder what would have happened to them if at a certain point, they had taken a different path. In my case that certainly is true with a decision that I made in the fall of 1936 when I was barely nineteen years old. In August, 1936, after I had purchased my discharge from the Army (you could do that at that time), I returned to my native Rocky Mount, N. C., where I had grown up. Things had not changed a great deal since I left. The depression was still in full swing with slight chances of a good job, and I soon tired of sitting around doing nothing and putting a strain on my parents who were having their own troubles with unemployment. Anyway, I had always intended to return to the Army, although not in Panama.

"I had been in the Coast Artillery on my last assignment in Panama and had heard a lot about Fort Monroe, VA, the headquarters of the Coast Artillery in the Army, and decided that I would try to enlist again at Fort Monroe. Fort Monroe is located near Newport News and Hampton, VA, along the coast of Chesapeake Bay. Late in October, 1936, I hitch-hiked to Newport News, and spent the night with my brother Gene who was working at the shipyard there. The next morning, October 27th, I climbed aboard the streetcar which ran from Newport News to Phoebus, near the main gate of Fort Monroe. As we were traveling through Hampton, I noticed a large billboard advertising enlistment in the Army Air Corps at Langley Field near Hampton. That sounded much more exciting than the Coast Artillery, so I asked the motorman on the streetcar how to get to Langley Field. He stopped the car and pointed out a streetcar sideline which led to Langley and I immediately got off and mounted in the Langley streetcar, a decision that certainly changed my life.

The Langley Trolley That Changed My Life

"Within a few minutes I was crossing a bridge which led to the main gate at Langley. If I had gone on to Fort Monroe, I am sure that I would have ended up as probably a corporal or sergeant in World War Two somewhere in the Army artillery.

"As soon as I arrived at Langley, I was directed to base headquarters and to the personnel office. I was immediately greeted by a sergeant and then by the personnel officer who administered the oath of office, and told me that I was now an airman in the Army Air Corps.

"In 1936 Langley Field was one of the main bases of the Army Air Corps along with March Field in CA, Selfridge Field, MI, and Barksdale Field, LA, the main bases for the combat forces of the Air Corps. After President Roosevelt was elected in 1932, a public works program was started throughout the United States under the Works Progress Administration (WPA). The Air Corps greatly benefited from this program, and permanent barracks and other buildings were constructed on all the main bases of the Air Corps. All of the new buildings at Langley were made with red bricks, and these buildings remained pretty much the same until after World War Two.

"As you entered the main gate from Hampton the first building on the right was the Officers Club. Nearby were two buildings for bachelor officers. As you moved along from the officers club, there were married officers' quarters on both sides of Dodd Boulevard, the main street running through the base. Dodd Boulevard pretty much paralleled the Back River all the way through the main base and ended up in the non-commissioned officer area on the opposite side of the flying field from the main base. Further along Dodd Boulevard was a chapel on the left, a post school, and a headquarters building for the NACA (now NASA) headquarters. The base headquarters building was located on the left side of Dodd Blvd just before the enlisted barracks area. In the next block after the base headquarters there was one barracks building on the right. Behind these barracks was an enclosed swimming pool and gymnasium and post theater. On the left side of Dodd could be seen a long barracks for the 8th Pursuit Group and a similar long barracks for the 2nd Bombardment Group. Also on the left were the commissary and Post Exchange. Between the two long barracks buildings were several other barracks buildings for various units. The enlisted barracks for

Hq. GHQ was the last building on the left as Dodd Blvd turned around the flying field. On the north side of the barracks buildings were the two rows of hangars, too small for the B-17s. Also, along the Back River parallel to Dodd Blvd were a base hospital, a dental clinic, and a set of nurses' quarters. In addition, the large home for the base commander and several other large homes were scattered along the same area as the hospital. All of the buildings on the main base remain pretty much the same today as they were in 1936 although some new buildings have been added to this area since World War Two.

"Base Headquarters was a long two story brick building on the left side of Dodd Blvd. On the first floor were the office of the base commander and various activities of the base. The commander of GHQ (MajGen Frank Andrews) and the commander of the Second Wing, GHQ (BrigGen Gerald Brant) were located on the second and third floors of the base headquarters. The offices of the 8th Pursuit Group, the Second Bomb Group, and the various squadrons were located in the hangars on the flight line.

"On the far north side of the base was the family housing for noncommissioned officers. The noncommissioned family housing and a balloon hangar were separated from the main base by the flight line and runways, and Dodd Boulevard led from the main base to the noncommissioned officer area. In addition, there was a noncommissioned officers club, and a balloon hangar built after World War One. After the arrival of the B-17s in 1937 the balloon hangar was used for maintenance of the aircraft as the regular hangars were too small for the B-17. There was a joke going around the base that the balloon pilots in order to get their four hours flying time every month would go to the balloon hangar and climb into a basket about three feet from the floor and play cards for four hours while suspended from the balloon above within the hangar. Also, in this area were two large multi-room family homes which were used for warrant officers. I was assigned one of these homes when I was promoted to warrant officer in 1942.

"As you entered the main gate if you turned left and traveled several hundred yards, you came to what was then known as the Shellbank area with a large farm house which still stands today and is used for office space. The Shellbank area was unoccupied in 1936 but shortly after 1940 the base began to extend to this area, and today most of the area is taken up with new buildings of all types including a hospital, exchange, commissary, barracks, and officers' quarters. The main entrance to the base today is in this area although the base still maintains what is known as the Hampton gate near the officers club.

Early Aerial View of Langley
(Note the lack of runways)

"As soon as I enlisted I was directed across the street to the barracks building which housed the men of the air base squadron. I could not believe my reception when I arrived in the first sergeant's office. The sergeant shook hands with me and asked if I had had lunch. He took me into the dining room and told the mess sergeant to give me whatever I wanted for lunch. It was already past lunch time, and I had never heard of such a thing. In the Infantry if you missed a meal, you waited until the next meal. I was seated at a table for four with the first sergeant and mess sergeant for company. Shortly after, an airman dressed in a white jacket brought out a plate filled with meat, potatoes, and several vegetables. In all my time in the Infantry and Coast Artillery I had never had such a meal. I found out later that several of the mess halls maintained a separate table for one of the base generals who might stop in for lunch. Each squadron had its own mess hall, and the food and appearance of the mess hall would depend on the mess sergeant and the mess officer. A food allowance of 21 cents per day per airman was allocated to each mess hall, and the mess sergeant was responsible for procuring the food and its preparation. Later on in 1940 when I was assigned to Hq GHQ Air Force I found that the GHQ mess was considered one of the best in the Air Corps and for good reason: General Andrews stopped by for lunch on a periodic basis. His personal pilot lived in a room on the third floor of our barracks." (Bill provided a menu from the Thanksgiving Meal of 1935 that certainly supports his opinion of the good food found at Langley Field! It is included as Appendix C.)

"My first job after enlistment was as a clerk in the Sub Depot which was something like a parts department in an auto repair shop. The Sub Depot was located beside the hangars and extended for several blocks along the flight line. I quickly learned where most things were located, but the job was extremely boring, and I spent much time trying to find something else to do. There was an air mechanic's school operating on the base at night, and I signed up for that hoping to get a job on the flight line; however, shortly after the New Year in 1937, I was informed that I was to go to the clerical and court-reporter school at Fort Monroe. Langley Field had been allotted two spaces in the spring class, and I was to fill one of these spaces. I reported to Fort Monroe on January 31, 1937, and spent the next five months learning typing and shorthand. In addition, much time was spent on military court-martial procedures and Army regulations. In 1941 this course turned out to be a life saver for me when I took a national test for warrant officer as I easily passed the test and was promoted to warrant officer. I graduated from the Coast Artillery School on June 26, 1937, with academic honors as No. 1 in my class, and returned to Langley Field.

"As soon as I arrived back at Langley, I was assigned to the Base Sergeant Major's office. The Base Sergeant Major was responsible for the various administrative tasks directly under the Base Commander. My immediate job was to record any Court-Martial as well as general typing of special orders, daily bulletins, and rosters of flying personnel. At this type of work I soon became familiar with many of the pilots in the flying units as well as pilots in base headquarters. One of the pilots assigned to our office directly out of flying school was Lt Beirne Lay. Lay had just had published a book "I Wanted Wings" which was later made into a movie. I worked directly with him and heard many stories about his flying training. Later in World War II he became one of the B-17 pilots. Another of my duties was to maintain a roster for Officer of the Day, and here I got to know many of the officers personally as they reported to me before going in to receive instructions from the Base Adjutant.

"My duties as a court-reporter began immediately after my return to Langley. In my very first court, I reported to 1stLt Curtis LeMay who was to be Trial Judge Advocate, a job similar to prosecuting attorney in civil courts. I was pretty scared not only because I wasn't sure I could keep up with the court proceedings, but the fact that I had almost never even spoken to an officer in my time in the Infantry and Coast Artillery. 1stLt LeMay immediately put me at ease by telling me that I could stop proceedings at any time when anyone talked too fast for me to record his words. The court-martial was a fairly simple case of Absent With Out Leave (AWOL), and I soon found out that all procedures followed the court-martial manual to the letter and made it easy to record. I finished recording all procedures, and Lt LeMay praised me for my work and for typing the court record. Later I recall working with Lt James Walsh of the Second Bombardment

Group who was one of the B-17 pilots on a goodwill flight to South America. I might add here that all officers in those days were pilots who were assigned additional duties such as operations officers, mess officers, squadron adjutants, etc., as needed.

"When I first reported back to Langley from the Coast Artillery School, the Second Bombardment Group was well on its way to receiving all of the first twelve B-17s. The first B-17 was delivered to Langley by Maj Barney Giles on March 1, 1937, and the remainder of the aircraft arrived before the end of the summer. These airplanes became famous in a very short time, and single ship and formation flights were very familiar to local residents. In addition, the names of LtCol Bob Olds, and Majs Vincent Meloy, Harold George, and Caleb Haynes were used so often as squadron commanders and flight leaders that everyone knew who they were. Also, the B-17s used a local bombing range known as "Bull Island", and the sound of exploding bombs was heard distinctly on the base. The local newspaper *Daily Press* frequently carried stories about the exploits of the first B-17s and their pilots, and although the 2nd Bomb Group had B-10s and B-18s, the big news was the new four-engine bombers. One thing that caused a great deal of excitement was the filming of the movie "Test Pilot" with Clark Gable, Spencer Tracy, and Myrna Loy in late 1937 and early 1938. One of the scenes in the movie was the loading of sand bags into one B-17 to simulate the weight of bombs as Clark Gable and Spencer took the B-17 for a test flight. The loading of the sand bags was actually filmed at Langley with several enlisted men of the 2nd Bomb Group loading the sand bags. The actual flying scenes were filmed at March Field, Riverside, California, with the twelve B-17s being used in the final scenes of the movie with Gable and Loy, and John Barrymore."

In the 2000s, Bill would journey back to Langley Field where so many of his early memories resided, and he took a number of pictures of the Air Force Base today. It was like coming home, as many of those wonderful between-the-wars structures are still in use today. Several of the snapshots can be found in Appendix E.

McCook/Wright Field versus Langley Field

The Aviation Section, U.S. Signal Corps and its successor the United States Army Air Service operated McCook Field in Dayton, OH as an airfield and aviation experimentation station by from 1917-1927. It was named for Alexander McDowell McCook, a Civil War general and his brothers and cousins, who were collectively known as "The Fighting McCooks". The field was located approximately one mile north of the downtown area between the Greater Miami and Stillwater rivers (now the present-day Dayton park, Kettering Field). Constructed during World War I, it became the location of the Aviation Service's Engineering Division in 1919.

Before the end of WWI, the Army Air Staff realized that McCook Field, where much of aviation research had been conducted, suffered from the lack of physical facilities and sought a permanent home, with Langley Field in Virginia frequently mentioned as a likely site. After the war, there were a number of competing proposals submitted from cities across the country, offering land and facilities to house engineering activities. John H. Patterson, President of The National Cash Register Corporation (NCR), vowed to keep Army aviation in Dayton and began a local campaign to raise money to purchase a tract of land large enough for a new air field and then be donate it to the U.S. Army with the understanding that it would become the permanent home of the Engineering Division.

Patterson's intensive campaign netted $425,000, enough to purchase 4,520 acres of land east of Dayton, including Wilbur Wright Field adjacent to Fairfield (now Fairborn), OH, already leased by the Air Service. This far exceeded all others, and in August 1924 President Calvin Coolidge accepted Dayton's gift. As with any such undertaking, the political and bureaucratic path was strewn with obstacles, but ground was finally broken on April 16, 1926 for Wright Field. Construction proceeded slowly and McCook laboratories began moving to their new quarters as the buildings were completed. During the summer of 1926 the Air Corps Act was enacted,

Construction of Wright Field in 1927

changing the name of the Army Air Service to the Army Air Corps, and dividing the Corps into three divisions. Gen Mason M. Patrick, Chief of the Air Corps, located the largest of the three, the Materiel Division, at Wright Field.

The Materiel Division (combining the former Engineering Division and Field Service Section) was originally headquartered at McCook Field. The Materiel Division moved seven branches to Wright Field in 1927. Although funding for their activities was still inadequate, the new facilities built specifically to house scientific functions were far superior to what had been left behind. The enthusiasm for invention that had made McCook Field famous thrived at Wright Field. Among the divisions were Powerplants, Equipment, Instruments, Propellers, Armament. a Structures Development and Test Laboratory, an Aircraft Radio Laboratory that all created an Army aviation "center of excellence" to use a recent term. Recognition of the human element in increased combat capabilities spawned the Physiological Research Laboratory where pilots were subjected to simulations involving extremes of speed, pressure, and temperature.

Along with their previous responsibilities, the Materiel Division added a new assignment-procurement. It became obvious that the division of responsibilities between McCook and Langley would be contentious and important for the future of the Air Corps. It would eventually shake out to be technical research and development (R&D) versus operational strategic, tactical and procedural development.

As a result of these decisions (or lack of them) at the Washington level, the future of Army aviation, and, in fact, that of aviation in general, was formulated. NACA would be destined to probe fundamental research that would lead to the development and application technologies. The Army Materials Division (and later the Wright Labs) straddled the research, development, application and acquisition arenas and met the military needs for technological superiority. Langley would become the spot where all of the research, development, acquisition, and production would coalesce in an airframe whose capabilities would then be taken beyond specifications and translated into operational procedures[4].

Langley Center Stage for Air Corps Proof of Concept

Arrival of the Y1B-17

It may be difficult today to assess the impact, excitement, and yet the consternation over the arrival of the Y1B-17 at Langley field. The joy of being on the cutting edge of the bomber performance was tempered by the fact that the Army Air Corps was under the glaring spotlight of military, legislative and public scrutiny to determine if the expense of this acquisition was justified. But first, the euphoria of the arrival was universal, and well documented.

Y1B-17s Arrival at Langley Field

As explained in the last chapter, it was through a legal loophole that the Air Corps was able to procure 13 Boeing Y1B-17s, and a 14th for structural testing at Wright Field, that the hopes for the future of strategic bombing would ride on these twelve aircraft and the pioneers that flew them.

The Beat Goes On—The Air Combat Command

The fall of the former Soviet Union caused a re-evaluation of the U.S. military establishment by senior Defense Department planning personnel. The Cold War solution was not well-suited for the new international scene. The likelihood of a large-scale nuclear conflict was becoming more remote and armed forces were being called upon to fight smaller scale regional wars and participate in humanitarian efforts. In face of these changes, the Air Force began to focus on what the terms "strategic" and "tactical" really meant. The differences between the Tactical Air Command (TAC) and Strategic Air Command (SAC) were disappearing, or at best becoming blurred.

In 1991, the Chief of Staff and the Commanders of SAC, MAC and TAC converged on the concept of a streamlined Air Force. As a result, most assets of SAC and TAC were merged into a new Air Combat Command (ACC) and a reorganized MAC became the Air Mobility Command (AMC) by June 1992. Following the inactivation of SAC at Offutt AFB, Nebraska, a new unified command, the US Strategic Command, stood up at Offutt AFB created to manage the combined strategic nuclear forces belonging to the Air Force and the Navy.

Air Combat Command (Clip Art)

The ceremony at Langley signaled the birth of the Air Combat Command which would be responsible for providing combat-ready forces assuming control of all fighter resources based in the continental United States, all bombers, reconnaissance platforms, battle management resources, and intercontinental ballistic missiles (ICBMs). Furthermore, ACC also had tankers and C-130s in its composite, reconnaissance, and certain other combat wings. The legend of Langley Field continues to evolve as Langley AFB and the home of the ACC.

1. Langley Field. The Early Years, R.I Curtis, J. Mitchell, M. Copp, Office of History Langley AFB, VA 19771

2. Ibid

3. Ibid

4. *Remarkable Journey,* Diana Good Comelisse, History Office, Wright Patterson AFB. OH

CHAPTER XI

Selling the Package

MajGen Andrew's efforts to obtain 65 Flying Fortresses despite the crash of the Boeing Model 299 failed. However, he was successful in pleading his case to the War Department and gained approval for the acquisition of 13 Y1B-17s basing his argument on the potential synergism in transferring technology to the commercial aircraft arena. He was indeed right, as was seen in Chapter VII. The 13 aircraft possessed many improvements over the prototype Model 299, including more power in the switch from the Pratt and Whitney R-1690 850 HP engine to the Wright R-1820 930 HP engine which translated to improved performance. Part of the performance improvements could be attributed to a better understanding of the relationship of the relatively new constant speed propellers, automatic mixture settings, and power settings.[1] A 14th aircraft was destined to go to Wright Field for structural testing. While the first Y1B-17s were under construction, negotiations were conducted to make the Wright ship a test bed for turbo-supercharging. The Air Corps wanted to go higher and faster for their strategic bombing offense, and this would help get them there.

Improvements were not limited to the engine upgrade, but in a number of other areas. An annoying tail wheel shimmy that plagued initial Model 299 flights was damped. The perfectly functioning yoke type structure that supported the main landing gear oleos was changed to a simple stub axle to facilitate tire and wheel changes. The complex-to-build, and hence costly, side gun blisters were changed to Plexiglas moulding (later to be eliminated altogether). Other detailed changes included a revised fuel tanking system and rubber de-icer boots on the leading edges of the flight surfaces.

Now that the big birds were on their way, the Air Corps was committed and was going to put its reputation on the line and attempt to show just how capable this advanced aircraft was. Capitalizing on the 1931 Gen MacArthur/Admiral Pratt agreement that the Army Air Corps would be responsible for Coastal Defense beyond the range of the Coast Artillery, Andrews stretched that foundation to the limit, but in so doing, made it abundantly clear that the Air Corps could not afford a single mistake in the introduction of the Flying Fortress. The War Department was on the verge of concluding that no requirement existed in the US Army for a long-range, four-engine bomber and that close air support of the infantry was to be the focus. Andrews pressed on to the goal of a stronger strategic air force. As an illustration of just how precarious a situation the visionaries' leadership was in could readily be seen in the passing over of MajGen Andrews for command of the Air Corps with MajGen Westover's passing in 1938. Andrews was thought to be too aggressive and pushed too hard for the supremacy of air power. It did not deter him, however, in his quest to demonstrate the theories and his aggressiveness continued in his command at the Air Corps GHQ. It set the stage for a similarly inclined officer to arrive on scene and prove Andrew's concepts.

The 2nd Bombardment Group and the First Twelve YB-17s

Coinciding with the first delivery, Maj Robert Olds was assigned to command the 2nd Bomb Group on March 1, 1937 and promoted to the rank of lieutenant colonel. It was his enviable lot yet extremely demanding responsibility to train the group in operating the most advanced aircraft of its day, develop entirely new techniques and demonstrate how the Y1B-17's performance was critical to the Army's, and the War Department's, success. Not only did he have these crushing tasks, they would have to perform under the watchful and critical eyes of General Andrews and his entire Air

Corps GHQ, co-located with him at Langley Field. Fortunately, there was probably no one in the Air Corps better prepared or personally equipped for the job.

Robert Olds had a meteoric career in the Army and was always on the leading edge during its formative years. He had managed to confront and conquer every challenge presented to him in the early days of aviation, and did so with an élan that endeared him to his superiors as well as those supervised. When assigned to Washington DC, he had assisted BrigGen Billy Mitchell before the Morrow Board, and had laid his career on the line in testifying for the General during his court-marshal three months later.

He was no stranger to Langley as he attended the ACTS in 1927 and after graduation, continued on as an instructor. He was recognized for his untiring efforts there and he was assigned to the 2nd Bomb Group as the Operations Officer. He continued to not only organize, but lead high profile events such as the Group's flight at the 1932 National Air Races in Cleveland, awing the crowds with night-time bombing demonstrations. Rewarded with an assignment to Command and General Staff School, he again was able to testify, with obvious potential career-ending impact, for the pro-aviation elements before the Federal Aviation Commission and the Baker Board, before returning to GHQ and General Andrews' staff. The Army Air Corps may have searched for others, but Robert Olds seemed the perfect fit.

First Things First

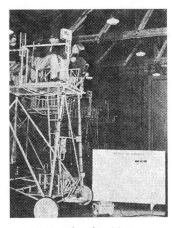

A2 Bombardier Trainer

Admonished by Andrews to "Train your group to go any place in the world, in any kind of weather and hit your objective", Olds would accept this directive, realizing that to satisfy this requirement, he had to accomplish two things. One, every pilot had to be trained to take off and land in instrument weather conditions; and two, crews had to become absolute experts in navigation over both land and water. He would prove to be just the right man for the job, though his aggressiveness and desire to succeed placed him at odds with superiors at times. But succeed he would under the always present threat of; if Olds' Group "cracked up one of these B-17s it would be the end of procurement of that airplane."[2]

Getting the Group in Shape

Train. Train. Train. The crews of the 2nd Bombardment Group were immediately turned to on a rigorous regimen of training. All of the officers assigned were pilots, so all were run through the same routines in bombing, navigation, visual day-time cross country, night cross country and instrument under the hood flying. All of the training was not in the air, as they were subjected to one of the first "simulators" for bombing—a small ten-foot tower on wheels that would roll along the hangar floor. The fledgling bombardier rode a seat atop the tower and aimed his Norden bombsight at a paper target on the floor. At the appropriate time after "bombs away", a plumb bob would drop and mark the paper as to where the bombs would have struck.

Instrument Flying—Flight without Visual References

Perhaps the most demanding skill to be acquired was that of flying "blind". Flying in inclement weather, or even at night in "ink bowl" conditions, was not a skill that many aviators could claim in the 1920s. Commercial flights were conducted during the daylight hours only, landing in the evening and transferring passengers to rail for the night time portion of their travel. Military combat operations were essentially conducted under Visual Flight Rules (VFR). By the late 1920's the need was starting to be felt for the effective training of pilots in the skills of "blind" or instrument flying. In the 1920s, there was slow but steady progress in the development of cockpit instruments for flying during inclement weather. A look at the austere cockpit of the Martin NB-2 bomber and the Curtis P-6E Hawk aptly shows the simplicity of these early combat aircraft instrument panels and why they were restricted to VFR.

Martin NB-2 Bomber (left) and Curtis P-6E Pursuit (right) Instrument Panels

But progress on a number of fronts offered some real hope for using the advances in performance that were being made in the aircraft of the period. Some of the most important emanated from the engineering entrepreneur Lawrence Sperry. His company was founded in 1910 as the Sperry Gyroscope Company by Lawrence's father Elmer Ambrose Sperry, to manufacture navigation equipment such as the marine gyrostabilizer and the gyrocompass. During World War I the company diversified into aircraft components including bomb sights and fire control systems. In 1918 Lawrence split from his father to compete over aero-instruments with the Lawrence Sperry Aircraft Company, including the new automatic pilot. In 1924 following the death of Lawrence on December 13, 1923, the two firms were brought together. The company became Sperry Corporation in 1933. Typical of the innovations from the elder inventor Sperry was the introduction in 1915 of a three-way gyrostabilizer to steer and stabilize bombers to improve the accuracy of bomb runs. That success led to the application of gyros to other aircraft uses, primarily in the compass and attitude indicators, and then to more sophisticated autopilots. The Army Air Corps followed these advances closely, and was intimately involved in developments.

Many times advances in aviation technology happen through the efforts of private citizens. Such was the case when Florence and Daniel Guggenheim established a foundation for the promotion and funding of benevolent causes. Son Harry, who had served as a WWI pilot, teamed with his father to found the Daniel Guggenheim Fund for the Promotion of Aeronautics on June 16, 1926. One of the funded projects was tackling the problem of "blind" flight. Army Lt James Doolittle, on loan from the Air Corps, worked with the Guggenheim Foundation, and with Sperry's Preston Bassett on the problems associated with the effort. Three years later using a Sperry compass and attitude indicator, Doolittle took off from Mitchel Field, Long Island, N.Y., flew a 15-mile course, and landed safely without ever seeing the ground. Lt Benjamin Kelsey served as a safety pilot in the front cockpit should some kind of emergency develop, but during the complete flight he held his hands outside the cockpit where they could be seen at all times.

Lieutenant Doolittle sat completely isolated beneath a specially constructed canvas canopy in the rear cockpit of a Consolidated NY-2 *Husky*. A specially designed short-range radio beacon system was installed on the field for Doolittle to home on to return to Mitchel. With the aid of his bank-and-turn indicator, airspeed indicator, stopwatch and the newly developed directional gyroscope and artificial horizon, Doolittle completed two separate 180° turns and then commenced his descent to the range station on the eastern boundary of the field. He was well prepared, for during the preceding eleven months, his special "blind" flight navigational techniques had been practiced and re-practiced during endless flight tests, but this flight was the official demonstration of a practical, instrument-only blind flying method developed by the Full Flight Laboratory of the Daniel Guggenheim Fund for the Promotion of Aeronautics.

Doolittle, and the modified Consolidated NY-2 Instrument Panel

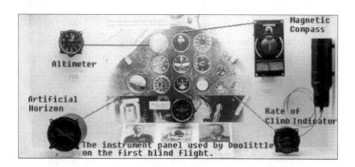

The instrument panel used by Doolittle on the first blind flight.

Doolittle, an expert flier with a deep knowledge of aeronautics, had wanted to make the first official blind flight alone. But he was over ruled because of the chance of a mid-air collision, something his instruments could not warn of. Doolittle's flight marked the end of an aviation era characterized by "seat-of-the-pants" approaches and silk scarves hung from struts. And while it did not represent a complete solution to the problem of flight in bad visibility, it did lay the essential groundwork for the sophisticated instrument techniques used today.

The first solo blind flight was achieved by Maj A. F. Hegenberger on May 9, 1932. Flying a Douglas BT-2 airplane equipped with standard Air Corps instruments, Hegenberger took off, made a five-minute flight, and landed safely without once seeing outside his cockpit. He made his final landing approach by lining up on two radio transmitters through the use of a radio compass in his airplane. The quest to equip the Air Corps' aircraft with adequate instrumentation was a few years away, as the military and commercial officials sought sufficient funds to become available to establish a radio navigational network across the U.S., equip all planes with necessary radios and instruments, provide airfields with proper ground transmitters and receivers, and to train all Air Corps pilots in the proper procedures designed to save their lives. By 1934, instrument flight was no longer an experiment, but becoming a practical reality.

Executing MajGen Andrews' Dictum

Even with this progress, landing and taking off in instrument conditions were not de rigueur in 1937, and there seemed to be no easy way to learn these demanding phases of operations, other than to "stick your nose in it." That was a risky approach. The pilots assigned to the 2nd Bombardment Group for the arrival of the first 13 Y1B-17s were not neophytes in the Army Air Corps and had distinguished themselves in a number of aviation endeavors, some heralded in this book. However, if LtCol Olds was to comply with the primary guidance of MajGen Andrews to "Train your group to go any place in the world, in any kind of weather and hit your objective", the crews were going to have to step up to some rigorous training. The Y1B-17 was equipped like no other bomber they had the opportunity to fly, so they needed to become intimately familiar with it, and hone their instrument skills in the Link Trainer.

Colonel Olds was stymied by the War Department's lack of funding support for the emerging Link instrument trainer he deemed so important to their operations. He scrounged what materials he could, enlisted the support of the airlines, and cobbled trainers together in the base shops. He

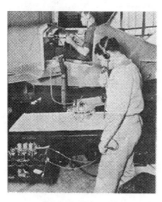

Link Trainer

issued a directive stating that "Nobody would be cleared to fly a B-17 two months from this date unless he holds a certificate over my signature stating that he is qualified in instrument landings and take-offs." Not wanting to be left behind, every pilot in the group, including Olds himself, had completed the qualifications.[3] His Group became proficient, but the importance seemed to fade in the later rush to qualify pilots for WWII, causing drastic increases in the accident rates.

Another Skill Required

Long range navigation was the next requirement to be mastered if the B-17 was to have the ability to fly anywhere in the world. The crews quickly achieved expertise in visual reference and dead reckoning navigation for it was built on their past experience. But no one knew a thing about celestial navigation. Celestial navigation could be used anywhere in the world, over land or sea, and was essential ingredient for long-range deployments of the period. Olds stressed that navigation training flights take place over the ocean to emphasize the need and to preclude shortcuts. Fortunately, Langley Field was located in coastal Virginia and the Atlantic was just a few minute's flight away, so finding a place to practice did not prove difficult. The ability to conduct long-range navigation missions over water and unfamiliar terrain would be critical to the success of Olds' future missions.

Early Demonstrations

A serendipity part of the training was to combine the need for cross-country flights to become familiar with the aircraft and the desire to show-off the new aircraft in as many venues as possible to generate public support. A few days after the arrival of the aircraft at Langley, it was wisely decided to bring the birds to Washington DC LtCol Olds and Maj Giles flew the Y1B-17 to Bolling Field so that the Army ground and aviation hierarchy, and the important people in the War Department and Congress, could see this aeronautical wonder first hand.

**The Y1B-17 at Bolling Field,
Washington DC, March 9, 1937**

The publicity would not be limited to static displays, for the capabilities had to be brought home with a series of flights that would awe and amaze the populace and convince the doubtful military. On May 16, 1937, LtCol Olds led a flight of four ships on a cruise to the north and Augusta, Maine, then west to Cleveland and back to Langley via Pittsburgh and Richmond. They covered 20 cities, 15 states in 11 hours.

Six of the ships took part in an aerial review put on for the American Legion Convention in New York City. A number of speed runs brought home the here-to-fore unheard of distances and times that the B-17 could accomplish with seeming ease. They flew from Miami to Langley in five hours; the same time from Kelly (San Antonio) to Langley; Wright (Dayton) to Langley in 1 hr and 45 min.

Despite having to buck the normal west-to-east prevailing winds, on January 6, 1938, LtCol Olds flew the 2,317 miles from Langley to March Field (Riverside, CA) in 13 hrs. and 27 mins. Three days later, he took advantage of the winds and returned to Langley in 11 hrs. and 1 min. His crew for this record-breaking flight consisted of:

The Y1B-17s on the Ramp at Langley
A Sight the Visionaries Worked so Hard to Achieve!

The Y1B-17s over New York City's Central Park

Maj Edwin R. MacReynolds
1stLt Robert F. Travis
1stLt Edwin L. Tucker

SSgt James J. Boutty
Sgt William H. Dodson
Pvt Joseph H. Walsh,
MajGen Emmons, GHQ commander and LtCol Clifton Russell from the HQ
were aboard as passengers.

Newspaper coverage of the flights appeared in the Newport News *Daily Press* on Monday, January 10, 1938.[4] In a previous edition on Sunday January 2, 1938[5], the paper had considerable coverage of the filming of many of the "atmosphere scenes" for the movie *Test Pilot* starring Clark Gable, Myrna Loy and Spenser Tracy. The timing of the flight to March Field in Riverside CA, shortly after the Langley filming would lead one to believe that LtCol Olds was not only setting speed records, but also insuring that the filming of the movie was proceeding with the Air Corps' best face forward. LtCol Olds would break this speed record a few short months later in April 1938, just before the premiere of the movie *Test Pilot* at the Palace Theater in Los Angeles on April 26th. On April 23-24, he took off one hour flat from his previous East-to-West time, and picking up a more favorable tail wind, he managed to cut 16 minutes off the March Field to Langley Field time.[6]

His crew for this round trip record breaker consisted of:

Maj Caleb V. Haynes
Cpt Benjamin W. Chidlaw
Lt Richard T. King
SSgt James J. Boutty
Pvt1stClass Archie R. Jester
Pvt1stClass Joseph H. Walsh
Pvt Kenneth E. Trout

The flights were made in the same aircraft as that used in Olds' successful Buenos Aries flight in February, and he manned it with the same enlisted crewmembers. Never one to let an opportunity for favorable publicity to pass, when LtCol Olds presented his wings to the Mission in Riverside, CA for inclusion in the shrine to famous flyers, the *Los Angeles Times* was there to document it.

LtCol Olds Adds His Wings to the Wall at Mission Inn

LtCol Olds and Maj Haynes Flank Mrs. Ulysses Grant McQueen, founder of Women's International Aviation Association at the Mission Inn in Riverside CA

Enlisted Personnel Policies Promote Stability

Co-author Bill Braxton had some interesting insights into the enlisted personnel policies in existence at the time of the arrival of Y1B-17s at Langley Field. As a young Private in GHQ, he had a ringside seat to view the between-the-wars scene at the lower enlisted ranks. Some of his observations:

"In 1937 each squadron in the Air Corps was set up to be self-sufficient. When I arrived at Langley Field, I found that each squadron had its own complete community unto itself. It was a far cry from the infantry experience I had in Panama. At Langley, we had three story barracks, with the first floor set aside for a dining room, kitchen, office for the commander and First Sergeant, and supply room. The enlisted men were quartered on the second floor in large rooms (bays) with a couple of rooms set aside for senior noncommissioned officers. Most of the senior NCOs were married but we always had two or three who were single and lived amongst us in the barracks. The primary feature in bringing the unit together was the fact that each squadron had its own mess hall, its own Mess Officer and a Mess Sgt.

"At this time, the ration allowance for enlisted men was 21 cents a day, and the Mess Sgt was in charge of living within the budget and buying the necessary food and making up the daily menu. Naturally, the best food was found with the most talented and skillful Mess Sgt. In my barracks, we had the best I had ever seen anywhere in the military, due in part to the fact that the Commanding General, MajGen Andrews occasionally dropped by unexpectedly for lunch, and we always maintained a separate table set up for him.

"Self-sufficient capabilities even included our own barber chair on the first floor; everyone had to get a weekly haircut. We also had a "day room" or recreation room on the first floor with a pool table. Pay Day occurred once per month, and on Pay Day, the day room orderly ran poker games there. If you had seen the movie *From Here to Eternity* you would have a good idea on how we lived.

"Stability was established through the squadron Table of Organization, which was established by Air Corps GHQ, to show exactly how many officers and enlisted men were assigned to each squadron. Each was allocated a fixed number of sergeants, corporals, privates first class, and privates. These enlisted ranks belonged to the squadron, and if a corporal or sergeant was transferred from the squadron, he lost the rank and reverted to private and the squadron retained the open billet. Therefore, it was not unusual to see an enlisted man remain in one squadron for his entire 30 years until his retirement. In my Base GHQ squadron, I saw only a couple of enlisted vacancies during my whole three-year enlistment. They occurred when a corporal did not enlist and a Tsgt died. That stability enabled LtCol Olds to form an extremely capable air crew roster in the 2nd BG.

"Between-the-wars promotion was exceedingly slow for officers and enlisted alike. In 1940 I was promoted to corporal in the 2nd BG but lost my stripes when I transferred to GHQ HQ. To compensate, my mentor Col Blair saw that I was promoted in a hurry during the next two years. Promotion was crazy with the big build-up in 1939, but it still tended to create stability. Our pilot officers were not separated into specialties and dedicated to "flying only" but were assigned to various administrative squadron duties. I was 1stLt Curtis E. LeMay's court reporter for a Group administrative hearing."

Some Views of Robert Olds

With the perspective of being a charter member of the ACTS "Bomber Mafia", a pilot with Billy Mitchell's Project "B", one of the old hands in the 2nd Bomb Group serving under Robert Olds, and Commander of the Air Transport Command (ATC), LieutGen Harold George, looked back on Olds' tenure.

"Training and preparation for the maximum utilization of these airplanes were carried out under very trying circumstances. Without question, the future of this country's airpower depended upon the quality of leadership possessed by the officer commanding the Second Bombardment Group. Fortunately, that person had the attributes which make him a great leader. He had a brilliant mind, he was an outstanding pilot, anything associated with flying he could do not only as well as the next person but usually a little better. He could grasp instantly, vexing details which usually make up difficult problems and, grasping them, he had the priceless ability to make a decision. He did not mull over what to do—having studied the problem, having arrived at a decision, he made it at once. He was a rare individual indeed!"[7]

Shortly before the arrival of the B-17s, 1stlt Curtis LeMay was assigned to Langley Field arriving with the reputation as an expert navigator, having opened a navigation school while in Hawaii. (At this time, there was no separate navigator rating and pilots were expected to handle that job on their progression up the experience ladder.) He was slated to start up the navigator school for the 2nd Bombardment Group at Langley, but weaseled his way out by "volunteering" fellow pilot John Egan for the job[8]. He was assigned to the 49th squadron as the Assistant Operations Officer, and later as the Operations Officer. By June, there were several Y1B-17 aircraft on Langley's ramp and Curtis LeMay fell in love with the aircraft.

He was equally in awe of his new boss, LtCol Olds, stating that he really did not know what it was all about until he served under him. He learned that the whole purpose of the Air Corps was to fly and fight in a war, and to be ready to fly and fight in that war at any given moment. Olds strived to make that requirement paramount in the minds of his personnel and in the status of their equipment.

Gen LeMay is fond of telling the story of his temporary assignment to be the Group Operations Officer and having LtCol Olds pass his desk every day, loading him down with three days' work every day. On one morning as he passed LeMay's desk, he asked for the weather report. LeMay was so overloaded, he did not even know the local weather and confessed to that fact. Olds unloaded on him and made the point that if they had to lay on a mission to Wright Field, or San Antonio, he'd have to know the weather and not spend time trying to dig it up. LeMay never came to work again without visiting the Weather Room first. He also boned up on the status of all of the aircraft for that was information he was expected to have at his fingertips.[9]

LeMay was not selected to ferry a Y1B-17 from Seattle to Langley, much to his chagrin. As a relatively low-ranking pilot, it was left to the likes of Barney Giles to pick up the first ship, followed by Caleb V. Haynes, Harold George, Vince Meloy, Neil Harding and A.Y. Smith to do the honors.

Joint Exercises—The Army/Navy Feuds

As noted in Chapter Four, Project "B", covering BrigGen Mitchell's 1921 successful bombing of the German dreadnaught *Ostfriesland*, the Navy took a publicity beating and every attempt was made to keep the story under wraps. The Air Service, being placed as an Army auxiliary to support ground troops, could not exert the influence the Navy was able to bring to the fore, and so the results remained relatively obscured. In the ensuing decade following the Navy's embarrassment, the Air Service, and in 1926, the Air Corps continued to seek publicity and generate favorable public opinion for the development of the all-metal monoplane bomber and the use of long distance. The January 1931 MacArthur/Pratt agreement ceding the coastal defense role to the Army's land-based aircraft seemed to be the opening needed to demonstrate Army capabilities as there was a limit to the distance off-shore for that defense.

The "Shasta Disaster"

In August 1931, then LtCol Frank Andrews proposed to bomb another ship during joint maneuvers with the Navy off the North Carolina coast. A WWI cargo ship, the USS *Mount Shasta* was made available and towed to a point 60 miles off the Currituck Beach Light. A dozen B-3A and B-5 bombers from the 2nd Bombardment Group from Langley were to locate and then attack the *Mount Shasta*. Unfortunately for the Army airmen, the weather turned bad and they suffered communications failures and they were unable to locate the ship. On top of the failure, it was witnessed by reporters, newsreel crews and a broadcast team from NBC News. The Navy was quick to publicly mock the Army, and when the aircraft were only able to score a few hits three days later, it became known as the "bombing flop". The Navy had evened up an old score.

By 1933, the Navy repudiated the 1931 Army/Navy roles and missions agreement and a "Joint Action Statement" was issued by the Navy, and in a turn of events, agreed to by MacArthur, Army Chief of Staff. It essentially limited Air Corps roles to support of the "mobile Army". Not to be deterred, the long-range bomber advocates interpreted the statement language to mean that the Air Corps could conduct long-range reconnaissance, attack approaching enemy fleets, and reinforce distant bases. All of this, of course, to prevent an air attack on America!

LeMay mused in his memoirs that in those early days, a pamphlet entitled Joint Action of the Army and Navy contained the following statements concerning co-operation:

1. Neither service will attempt to restrict in any way the means and weapons used by the other service in carrying out its functions.
2. Neither service will attempt to restrict in any way the area of operations of the other service in carrying out its functions

3. Each service will lend the utmost assistance possible to the other service in carrying out its functions.

The Joint Exercises of 1937 were conducted in a manner that one would wonder if the pamphlet had ever been promulgated, and if it was, did anyone read it.

Joint Air Exercise No.4—The Bombing of the Battleship *Utah*

LeMay reported that upon looking into the official records of this exercise in 1965, one would find only extracts of the operations:

> "34 B-10Bs, three B-18s, and seven B-17s from the bombardment group, three OA-4s, one OA-5 and one B-18 from Reconnaissance and four C-33s from Cargo participated. The exercise was completed at 1200 13 August 1937. A supplementary exercise took place on 14 August."

Despite the 1931 and 1933 Army/Navy roles and missions agreement, it appeared that the same relational standoffs that existed in the Billy Mitchell tests continued unabated to 1937.

With the July 10, 1937 authorization of President Roosevelt, and former Secretary of the Navy, the Navy had configured the battleship *Utah* with partial wooden planking so that Navy pilots could practice bombing the ship with water-filled bombs and not inflict any damage. It was to represent a hostile fleet of two battleships, a carrier and nine destroyers. A Navy patrol wing of 30 planes commanded by RADM Ernest J. King was assigned to locate the enemy fleet and a force of 41 Air Corps bombers would attack it. A number of Army B-10 and B-18 aircraft were to participate.

When Olds heard of the Navy exercise, he petitioned to participate with the B-17s. Initially, the Navy was reluctant to add the longer range aircraft to the mix, but MajGen Andrews was successful in interceding and gaining permission for the Langley fliers to join in, and nine of the Y1B-17s were penciled in. The stated purpose was to determine if the Air Corps aircraft could first find the *Utah* and if successful in doing so, bomb it. BrigGen Mitchell's success at sinking the German ships more than a decade previous did not seem to have made a dent in the Navy's poor opinion of airpower versus their warships.

The 1937 Joint Exercise was to be the first deployment of the B-17, a mere four months after their arrival at Langley. The pressure was on to show just how capable the aircraft would be in the defense of the U.S. coast. Olds thought of this exercise as more than inter-service competition or rivalry, but an event that could make or break the future of the B-17 and perhaps the GHQ. Without sounding too altruistic, Olds and his men thought that the exercise was really an issue of national concern[10]. They wanted to not only prove the capability of their new birds, but on a larger scale, they wished to demonstrate just how dangerous an aggressor nation with superior airpower could be.

Not surprisingly, the Navy did all they could to "sandbag" the Langley fliers. They positioned the *Utah* 300 miles at sea off San Francisco, California. They also selected August for the time of the exercise, knowing that at this time of the year, coastal fog nearly blanketed the off-shore areas. They also specified that Navy Mark VII 50 lb water-filled bombs were to be used. Essentially a stove-type metal tube with fins, they were designed to cause minimal damage to a ship, should a direct hit occur. Obviously, this strange and unique ordnance had undocumented ballistic characteristics, and the Air Corps requested samples to study the differences from standard munitions. The Navy said that they had "supply difficulties" and could not honor the request.

The Navy's attempt to drive a final nail in the coffin was the specification that the exercise would be conducted from noon on 12 August until noon on 13 August, and no bombs could be dropped after dark. Thus, the Navy had designed the mission for Air Corps failure, knowing full well that the allotted time would not allow for the Navy reconnaissance aircraft to fly the 300 miles off shore, locate the *Utah*, radio the position back and have the B-17s proceed to the scene before dark. LtCol Olds knew that too, but he had a plan to overcome the disadvantage.[11]

He launched his B-17s in advance of any spotting alert, and placed them in a holding pattern 200 miles offshore orbiting above the fog. When the radio message came in from the Navy aircraft <u>one hour</u> prior to the time for closing of the exercise, Olds led the formation down through the fog, and guided by his lead navigator 1stLt Curtis LeMay, headed for the reported position. When they broke out, there was nothing in sight.

Executing square searches, they did not sight the *Utah*. Olds was irate and immediately accosted LeMay and wondered aloud if he knew where the "boat" was supposed to be. LeMay was sure of his position. Olds asked how he knew, and LeMay took a celestial sight, and stated that they would recover at Oakland at a specified time—they did. Olds wondered then, why had they not found the *Utah*? Could it have been that Navy gave an erroneous position?

The Navy was to maintain surveillance of the *Utah* during the night, but not surprisingly, they reported that contact was lost. During the night, the Navy reported that the position that was previously provided was in fact one degree off the actual position—60 miles! However, to the uninitiated, all that seemed to be known was that the Navy spotted the *Utah*, but the Army could not find it.

The next and final day of the exercise, Navy aircraft were initially reported to be fogged in, and Olds saw the clock running out to the noon deadline for exercise completion. He decided to launch to the midpoint of the area without any definitive position and was determined to find that ship. The Navy continued to load the game to their advantage and delayed the reporting of the sighting of the *Utah* until one hour before the exercise completion deadline of noon. Lead navigator LeMay plotted the position, worked out the intercept solution, and it looked as though they could not make it prior to the end of the exercise. The only solution appeared to be was to drop below the fog and spread the formation out in a fingertip arrangement. They headed south and lo and behold, they found the *Utah*. Once again, the position provided was a degree in error.[12] Could it be that the Navy tried the same trick once again had made such a gross error intentionally?

The Olds-led 2nd Bombardment Group located the *Utah* 285 miles off shore five minutes before noon of the final day! The first bomb splintered the deck and in the ensuing three minutes, they had claimed three direct hits and many near misses.

USS *Utah* (BB31) Now an AG-1 Target Ship in 1935
(Note that the armament has been removed, decks covered with timbers)

Back at March Field, the Army celebrated their achievement but was unable to release the information to the public because of Navy objections, The Navy opined that they never had a chance because the planes had snuck in under the cover of fog and they did not have the opportunity to use evasive maneuvers. Never mind that historically opponents in thousands of years of wars had taken advantage of the weather. Olds was infuriated and challenged the Navy to come out from under the fog, get underway at any speed and he would bomb from altitude. The Navy was backed into a corner and could not logically refuse.

The next day, the Navy was underway, executing evasive maneuvers and the Army's B-18s made their runs from 8,000 while Olds' aircraft bombed from 18,000 ft. The results were devastating—23 % (37) of the water-filled bombs were direct hits. Obviously, the many hours spent with their new Norden bomb sights traversing the hangar floor atop a tower and out on the bombing range against battleship cutouts paid big dividends! Not surprisingly, the Navy once again wished to keep this news under wraps. But somehow(?) the news did reach a well-known newscaster who broke the information to the public. Famed radio newscaster Boake Carter had been leaked the information and to refute any denials stated that he had the photo proof in his hands. LeMay reported that he would never forget the cat-who-ate-the-canary smile on Olds' face.[13]

Rendezvous with the *Rex*

Spurred on by world events, military joint exercises became increasingly important and in May 1938 the Air Corps conducted the largest maneuvers in its history under the direction of the GHQ Commander, MajGen Frank Andrews. 450 officers, 2,300 enlisted men, and 300 aircraft were drawn from all three wings of the GHQ Air Force and based at 19 airports in the northeast United States, from Schenectady, NY, and Aberdeen, MD, westward to Harrisburg, PA. Among the deployed aircraft were B-18 bombers, P-36 pursuits and A-17 attack aircraft, however, LtCol Olds brought the stars of the show, nine of the 13 new B-17s, and parked them on the ramp at Harrisburg, PA. Andrews established his headquarters at New York's Mitchel Field.

The scenario was to face and thwart the deployed elements of an aggressor bent on capturing the industrial northeast with a combination of airplanes, warships and troops. This scenario called for the Navy to be busy in the Pacific, so the GHQ Air Force had to defend the eastern seaboard. Air Corps aircraft would launch well in advance of the enemy forces getting airborne from their carriers and reaching any point near the U.S. The plan was for the U.S. Air Forces to attack their fleet, turning back the invasion force. The Navy was deeply involved in its own Pacific exercises and could/would not provide any ships to be located and neutralized by the Air Corps, so it seemed that the GHQ Air Forces would be relegated to simulating the situation. But, an alternative arose.

LtCol Ira Eater had been borrowed from the Air Staff to serve as G-2 for the maneuvers. Eaker had just completed a degree in journalism and a course in news photography at the University of Oklahoma. He was the ideal man to use the maneuvers as a platform for publicizing both the capabilities and materiel deficiencies of the Air Corps. His assistant was 2ndLt Harris Hull, a reservist on temporary duty for the exercise and was a reporter for the Washington Post in civilian life. When newspapers, including the *Los Angeles Times*, criticized the maneuvers for using a "mythical fleet" as a target, Hull suggested that an ocean liner be substituted for naval vessels. He had learned that the Italian Line's SS Rex was bound for New York and would pass the 1,000-mile mark on 11 May. Eaker recommended the interception of the liner to Gen. Andrews, who concurred and received approval from the office of the Army's Chief of Staff while Hull arranged to receive position reports from officials of the line. Italian officials readily agreed to participate, thinking of the publicity that would accrue to the vessel, and the War Department came aboard as well. The stage was set for the *Rex* intercept to play a pivotal role in the exercise and in the ongoing struggle over roles and missions. It was also another make or break opportunity for the 2nd Bombardment Group to find itself in the center of.

Olds moved three of the B-17s, numbers 80, 81, and 82 from Harrisburg to Mitchel Field in Long Island, crewed by his first team. Maj Vincent Meloy would command the three-ship formation from number 80, piloted by Maj Caleb Haynes, and Cpt Cornelius Cousland had 81, while Cpt Archibald Y. Smith piloted 82. The proven best navigator in the Air Corps, 1stLt Curtis Lemay, would again play the pivotal role of lead navigator in the command ship. It is well to remember that at this time, there were only a handful of officers, all pilots, who were skilled in long range navigation beyond the availability of landmarks and lighted beacons. LeMay had taught navigation, had the ability to use celestial and drift calculations over water, and had proved himself in the bombing of the *Utah*. The Navy was about to be upstaged once again.

Disagreement had continued over the MacArthur/Pratt agreement over roles and missions that gave the Air Corps a coastal defense mission, but the Air Corps noted and took full advantage of the fact that there was no limit as to how far off shore that mission could be executed. The Navy was also upset over the success of the 1921 and 1923 Mitchell bombings of dreadnaughts and the Y1B-17 success over the battleship *Utah* in 1937. They made every attempt to quash dissemination of this information over the ensuing years. However, since this scenario called for the Navy to be "occupied" with a Pacific threat, they had little to say about the conduct of the 1938 Blue and Black Air Corps exercise. The Air Corps was to have full sway, and arranged for civilian members of the press and radio to be aboard to observe their intercept. In addition to Olds, Meloy, Haynes and LeMay, number 80 carried an NBC announcer, two NBC engineers and their radio transmitter. Aboard 81 with Cousland was C.B. Allen of the New York *Herald Tribune*, and 82 had the *New York Times'* Hanson W. Baldwin aboard. Additionally, Maj George Goddard, the Air Corps top photographer, flew in 81 with his large format Graflex camera. They had the coverage, now all they had to do was find the "needle in the haystack".

When the aircraft arrived at Mitchel on May 11, a radiogram from the *Rex* reporting their noon position awaited them. LeMay calculated that on the following noon, should the *Rex* proceed at her normal speed, she should be 600 miles off Sandy Hook, the entrance to New York Harbor.

Although they waited for an evening update, one never was received. The next morning, May 12th, the weather at Mitchel had deteriorated in squalls with blowing rain, and was predicted to be virtually WOXOF (ceiling and visibility zero) at the predicted *Rex* position. The whole mission seemed to be on the verge of cancellation. Determined to succeed, Olds asked LeMay to predict an intercept time based on the information he had. LeMay worked the solution accounting for known routes, *Rex* speed-of-advance, and its last noon position report and stated that it would be 12:25 pm, and unbeknown to him, that time was provided to NBC and they scheduled a short-wave broadcast from the bomber for that time.

Not to be deterred by the elements, Olds had the three aircraft taxi out during a rain squall at 8:30 am on May 12th, ready to take the risk of missing the *Rex* because of weather or error in position report. As they were taxiing out, there was a pounding on the door of the lead ship, and when it was opened, there was a man holding the 0800 *Rex* position report! The ship was 725 miles from New York and somewhat to the east of LeMay's original navigation solution, but it was as recent as it could be. The risk was just mitigated somewhat, but they still had the weather to contend with. Takeoff from Mitchel was at 8:45 a.m. and continued in rain, hail, downdrafts and clouds that precluded LeMay from taking drift readings until 10:00 am and again at 11:15 a.m. He again calculated the intercept time to be 12:25 pm accounting for unexpected headwinds.

The B-17s encountered more low clouds, and they flew on instruments through them, spreading the three planes out on a line abreast with 15 miles between each aircraft. At 12:23 pm, they broke out of a squall line, and Cousland in 81 shouted over the radio "There it is! There it is!" As if by magic, the three planes flew over the *Rex* at 1225 some 610 miles from Sandy Hook! Number 80 with 82 on the wing passed down the *Rex*'s port side and Maj Goddard used his Graflex to take a series of photographs. Passengers were lining the decks waving at the planes as they passed by. Stationed in the waist position of 80, Meloy made contact with the *Rex*'s captain and was invited to dinner but respectfully declined. NBC reported the intercept live on a coast-to-coast radio broadcast.

Number 82 on the wing of Number 80 on a Port-Side Pass of the *Rex*

The weather on the return was even worse than on the outbound leg, and upon safely landing at Mitchel, Cpt Cousland summoned LeMay over to his aircraft to look at the nose and leading edges of the wings. They were pebbled and pitted as if someone had used a ball peen hammer on the surfaces, mute testimony to the severity of the weather that they had penetrated.

Maj Goddard's photographs appeared in many newspapers the next day, and Hansen Baldwin described the mission in the *New York Times*. Baldwin thought that valuable lessons concerning the defense of the United States would be learned from the mission. The Navy was fit to be tied, and tried to diminish the accomplishments of the 2nd Bombardment Group's aircraft and personnel. They claimed that the *Rex* transmitted a homing signal for the B-17s to home in on, but it fell on deaf ears, as the War Games continued to capture the attention of the general populace. But the Navy's organizational superior position in the War Department enabled them to push through flight restrictions on the Air Corps. Army Chief of Staff Gen Malin Craig telephoned MajGen Andrews and instead of congratulating him as might be expected, issued an order to restrict Air Corps aircraft to operate within 100 miles of the coast.[14] Despite requests for providing the order in writing, such a document could never be found.

There were many other activities taking place in the "Blue—Black" war games, but the B-17s were certainly the stars with their intercept of the *Rex*, even in the Navy-oriented Hampton Roads across from Langley Field. Some Air Corps historians did not think that the Navy was behind the restriction, while others claimed it to be sourced to them. Exceptions to the restriction soon became the norm as the written restriction never surfaced. One month after the intercept of the *Rex*, the B-17s intercepted the SS *Queen of Bermuda* 300 miles at sea, and Army aircraft in Hawaii twice located an Army transport at similar distances in the summer of 1938. In March of 1939, General Arnold, as Chief of the Air Corps, was given specific authority by the Chief of Staff to grant exceptions as he saw fit, provided that the Army would not publicize them and he notified the War Department in advance. In any event, the restriction did nothing but increase the interservice enmity which never abated until the hands were joined for WWII.

One would think that requests for more B-17s would engender more support following success, but in fact the opposite was true. In July, Secretary of War Harry Wooding cancelled an authorization for 144 more B-17s. The coming of WWII however was looming on the horizon, and President Roosevelt felt the need to increase the defenses of the Western Hemisphere. He reversed the Army policy and ordered an expansion of the Air Corps. If the names of some of the leaders who participated in these events, and those that will be recounted in subsequent chapters, seem familiar, there is good reason for it. These visionaries were on the cutting edge of advancing the preeminence of airpower and rode their convictions into WWII where they were proven to be correct, and recognized for it.

- As a Maj, Henry "Hap" Arnold faced down a potential court martial for supporting BrigGen Billy Mitchell in 1921, but was rescued from exile by Army Chief of Staff Summerall, made chief of the Air Corps by Summerall's successor, Gen Craig and then Chief of the newly formed Army Air Forces in 1941. A storied WWII career led to his retirement as the only five-star USAF General.
- MajGen Frank M. Andrews—Commander GHQ—demoted to Colonel and exiled until Gen George C. Marshall promoted him. Eventually achieved the rank of LieutGen and appeared to be

groomed for command of the Normandy invasion, but was killed in a Greenland air crash in 1943.

- Reservist 1stLt Harris Hull called to active duty in WWII, then remained in the Air Force as a career, retiring as a BrigGen in 1964.
- Meloy served as a BrigGen in the Air Transport Command (ATC) retiring in 1946.
- Maj George W. Goddard became the recognized aerial photography expert in the USAF, retiring as a BrigGen in 1953.
- Maj Caleb V. Haynes retired as a MajGen in 1953 after a series of distinguished bomber and ferry commands throughout the war.
- Maj Robert Olds was eventually promoted to MajGen and commanded the Second Air Force, dying unexpectedly of a heart ailment in 1943.
- LtCol Ira Eaker went on to important commands in strategic bombing commands in WWII, taking command of the Eighth Air Force in 1942 and the Mediterranean Allied Air Forces in 1944. Retiring in 1947 as a LieutGen, he was promoted to Gen on the retired list in recognition of his accomplishments.
- 1stLt Curtis LeMay advanced through one of the pioneer B-17 Groups in the Eighth Air Force in 1942, and on to B-29 commands in the Pacific in 1944-45. He was the first commander of the Strategic Air Command (SAC) and the fifth Chief of Staff of the USAF.

They were indeed visionaries whose convictions were so strong that they not only caused friction within the Army, but dissention between the services. But they would not back down, learning from mistakes, capitalizing on the burgeoning technologies and eventually basking in their successes. The *Rex* did not enjoy an analogous post-intercept future. She was laid up in Bari, Italy and seized by Nazi Germany when Italy surrendered in 1943. She was destroyed by the RAF near Trieste in September 1944 so as to prevent her use to block the harbor entrance.

1. *The B-17 Story* Roger A. Freeman and David Osborne
2. *The Most Outstanding Leader, Lieutenant General Harold L. George*, Aerospace Historian 1968
3. *Ambassador of American Airpower: Maj General Robert Olds*, Scottie Zamzow, Air University Maxwell Air Force Base, Alabama June 2008

4. Newport News, VA *Daily Press* Monday, January 10, 1938.
5. Newport News, VA *Daily Press*, Sunday, January 2, 1938
6. New York, NY *New York Times*, Sunday, April 24, 1938
7. *The Most Outstanding Leader*, Lieutenant General Harold George, 1968 Aerospace Historian
8. *Mission with LeMay*, Curtis E. LeMay, Doubleday & Company
9. ibid
10. *Ambassador of American Airpower: Maj General Robert Olds*, Scottie Zamzow, Air University Maxwell Air Force Base, Alabama June 2008
11. ibid
12. *Mission with LeMay*, Curtis E. LeMay, Doubleday & Company
13. ibid
14. *Redezvous with the Rex* John T. Correll, Air Force magazine December 2008

CHAPTER XII

Expanding the Envelope

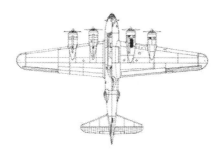

The year 1937 was an exciting and demanding one for the 2nd Bombardment Group at Langley Field. From the showing of the Y1B-17s to the "Brass" at Bolling Field in Washington, DC a few days after the arrival at Langley, to the intense crew training, the 20-city tour of the eastern United States, and the successful west coast deployment for the exercise of locating and "bombing" of the USS *Utah* in August 1937 aptly demonstrated the potential for the Y1B-17. Following the January 1938 speed runs detailed in Chapter Nine, the Group was ready for bigger things, all with the intent to create favorable opinions for Air Corps strategic bombing tenets.

General Andrews Anniversary Comments

MajGen Frank M. Andrews, Commander of the Air Corps' GHQ, reviewed the events of the preceding year in a January 9, 1938 interview. He noted that the B-17 had been thought to be too much of an airplane for air corps personnel and was too large, complex and costly. In 1937, the GHQ personnel had proved beyond any doubt that the four-engined high-performance bombardment plane was not only a valuable asset, but absolutely necessary for the GHQ to execute its war time mission. The 2nd Bombardment Group had flown thousands of hours in all types of weather, dropped thousands of bombs on stationary and moving targets, and if anything, set a trend line for even larger bombardment planes. "Within a short period of time I am certain the B-17 will be considered a small airplane", he opined. He indicated that 1937 showcased two outstanding achievements. One was perfection of the Air Base System, and the other the successful service test and universal acceptance of the B-17 as the prototype of the future basic element of the air corps[1]. 1938's accomplishments would overshadow even the past year's achievements.

Goodwill Flight to Buenos Aires, Argentina

The State Department dropped an opportunity in the Air Corps' lap by requesting the War Department provide a Goodwill Flight to Buenos Aires, Argentina for the inauguration of Roberto M. Ortiz as President of Argentina on February 20, 1938. Conditions were inching their way toward another World War, despite the hope that WWI would be the "War to end all wars". Hitler was menacing Europe, Japan had already occupied Manchuria, Korea and sections of China. Argentina had developed a rather warm relationship with Germany, and it would be beneficial to show our flag at the inaugural of the president of this nominally neutral country, and especially so if the attendance was accompanied by a display of our armed forces superior weaponry. The capabilities of the Y1B-17 seemed to be tailor made for such a show.

MajGen Andrews selected LtCol Olds to command a six-plane flight of the B-17s and the 2nd Bombardment Group eagerly accepted the challenge on February 10th, allowing only ten days for planning and execution of the mission. Andrews and Olds thought that if they could arrive in Buenos Aires the day following departure from the U.S., it would make an

LtCol Robert Olds

indelible impression not only in Argentina, but to every country in the world. It would establish and cement the U.S. position as a leader in strategic airpower. The concept was great, but as always, the devil is in the details. Properly planned, there could be 48 hours to accomplish the mission. To say that there was a need for attention to detail would be an extreme understatement, for flying vast distances over the oceans and uncharted territory presented tremendous problems. A measure of LtCol Olds' grasp of the situation and the drive he instilled in his staff was illustrated in the fact that one day later, a detailed plan was published, and can be reviewed in Appendix C.

The Selected Crews and Aircraft

Olds selected the best of his Group to crew the six aircraft. He would command the flagship, Number **10**, with:
Maj Edwin R. McReynolds
Cpt Robert B. Williams
1stLt John W. Egan
1stLt Edwin L. Tucker
SSgt James J. Boutty
Pvt1stCl Archie R. Jester
Pvt Joseph H. Walsh
Pvt Kenneth E. Trout
Number **51**, would be commanded by Maj Vincent J. Meloy, with:
Cpt Alva Harvey (Former enlisted crew survivor Alaskan crash of the World Cruisers)
1stLt Frederick E. Glantzberg
1stLt Torgils G. Wold
SSgt Jack A. Franske
Corp Clarance D. Lake
Pvt1stCl John W. Yankowsky

Number **52**, would be commanded by Cpt Neil B. Harding with:
    1stLt David R. Gibbs
    1stLt Ralph E. Koon
    1stLt Gerald E. Williams
    TSgt Besola Cobb
    Sgt Lewis Hayduke
    Pvt1stCl Harold J. Nycum
    Pvt Frederick W. Woitineck
Number **80**, would be commanded by Maj Caleb V. Haynes with:
    1stLt Thomas L. Mosley
    1stLt Curtis E. LeMay
    2ndLt Joseph B. Stanley
    TSgt Adolph Cattarius
    SSgt William J. Heldt
    Corp James E. Sands
    Pvt1stCl Donald F. Lowney
Number **82**, would be commanded by Cpt Archibald Y. Smith with:
    Cpt Cornelius W. Cousland
    1stLt Richard S. Freeman
    1stLt John A. Samford
    Sgt George R. Charton
    SSgt Troy V. Martin
    SSgt Henry P. Hansen
    Pvt1stCl Russell E. Junior
Number **61**, Would be commanded by Maj Harold L. George with:
    Cpt Darr H. Alkire
    1stLt William A. Matheny
    1stLt Paul G. Miller
    TSgt Gilbert W. Olson
    SSgt Everett Kirkpatrick
    Corp William A. Withers
    Pvt1stCl Norbert D. Flinn

The Navigational Problem

    1stLt John W. Egan, navigator for LtCol Olds in the flagship, related the frantic preparations that took place to make the historic flight[2]. If the aircraft were to make the flight in the two days desired, it was going to be necessary to deploy them to Miami, FL, and use it for the initial departure point. The leg from Miami to Lima, Peru was 2,343 nautical miles and the leg from Lima to Buenos Aires was 1,984 nautical miles. Fuel would have to be conserved as these distances were near the range of the B-17 with reserves, and best ranges would be achieved at 12,000—15,000 ft.

Weather was predicted to be cloudy over the greater part of the route, scattered or broken overcast at altitudes below 10,000 ft. Equatorial storms could reach up to 20,000 ft. Low clouds and fog were predicted along the Ecuadorian and Chilean coasts. Charts, or more accurately, the lack of them, were another problem that had to be surmounted. The Hydrographic Office had published charts for the coast line of Central and South America, but the only interior maps were being published by the National Geographic Society in Washington. They were not of the right projection and hence good only for Visual Flight Rules (VFR) pilotage.

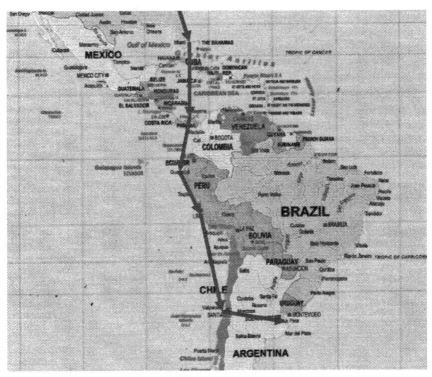

Goodwill Flight to Bueno Aries
Return Flight retraced with stops at Santiago, Lima and Canal Zone

To make the "two-day trip" a reality, the Miami-Panama portion of the leg to Lima would require an "o-dark-thirty" departure, and so it would be conducted in darkness. Celestial navigation using observations of the stars would be the only method available to determine position. Panama-Lima would be in daylight, so dead reckoning, and drift readings, if breaks in the clouds would permit, would have to suffice, with an occasional observation of the sun to augment the navigational solution. The Lima-Buenos Aires leg was to once again include a night departure from Lima so as to arrive at the Andes Mountain pass between Valparaiso and Mendoza after dawn. The crews would have less than six hours on the ground to rest and refuel, as well as repair any discovered mechanical problems.

Three of the B-17s had two navigators each while each of the remaining three had one. Since the entire flight would be conducted above 10,000 ft, continuous use of oxygen would be required. The Air Corps had no oxygen masks available at the time; the method to obtain the life-giving gas for each crew member was to stick a tube in the crew member's mouth. This was a clumsy and less than desirable situation, and clenching down on the tube with the teeth closed down the flow. Some crew members devised a method of taping the tube in the nose so as to free up the hands, or to use a smoking pipe stem clamped between the teeth[3], but this too was less than acceptable.

The stop in Lima was slated to last only as long as it took to refuel the aircraft, hence the navigators would be working for two straight days with no assistance. Crew Rest was not a consideration, and navigators seemed to be particularly affected. No attempt was made to try and divide duties in a watch-stander type of environment, and all sensed that the mission depended solely on them.

Despite the almost impossible short dwell time to get ready for the flight, a Navigation Plan evolved. A list of maps and charts went to the Chief of the Air Corps. The Navigation Branch at Wright Field pulled out all of the stops and provided Maxton Computers and training on how to use them; gathered every map of the area they had, expedited two driftmeters for the B-17s that were not so equipped, and calibrated spare octants.

Armed with the data and information the navigators worked in excess of fifteen hours a day to pre-compute star lines using the Ageton Method, alternate courses plotted to accommodate unpredicted weather, magnetic variations calculated. Some time was spent studying the Southern

Hemisphere constellations for none of the navigators had flown below the equator. The new radio compasses were installed in five of the six aircraft, completion occurring just a day before departure. The navigators had never used the radio compass and how to operate the loop antenna and thus did not rely heavily on them. A hasty check made on the ground revealed that they too needed to be calibrated so as to provide accurate bearings, so in essence they became a homing device, not a bad thing in and of itself.

Navigation Techniques to be Used

1. Dead Reckoning was to be the standard procedure used, with particular attention paid to time/distance/heading documentation in a standard format.
2. Pilot's compass was found to be more reliable than the D-4 Aperiodic compass because of unpredictable deviation, and satisfactory solutions could be derived from the pilot's compass.
3. B-3 and B-4 driftmeters would be used whenever the surface was visible. Double drift technique would be used to determine groundspeed. (One of the navigators was knowledgeable of pressure pattern navigation and was able to obtain accurate groundspeeds using a stop watch, zero prism angle on the driftmeter, and using pressure altitude variation from normal and corrected for temperature.)
4. Celestial navigation would be used constantly, as most of the legs would be above the clouds. Night fixes would generally provide better accuracy, with the daytime sun lines subject to the inaccuracies of the running fix.
5. The A-5 and A-6 Octants were used with two being available in each aircraft.

Another View of the Navigation Problems

1stLt Curtis LeMay was the navigator aboard Maj Caleb V. Haynes' Y1B-17 number 80 and although not in the flagship, he was the lead navigator. Because of this, he had the only gyro stabilized driftmeter, and their plane was placed in the middle of the formation. He would relay by radio his observation of drift with this superior device. As Lt Egan had discovered, maps and charts of the area were generally not available and LeMay used the good auspices of the National Geographic Society. Additionally, he borrowed more detailed maps from Pan American Airways, who had pioneered many air routes to South America. Seeking every available source, he even brought along a standard wind chart used by sailors, providing monthly averages in various areas. Although it could not be relied on for specific information, it did provide an inkling as to what to expect. All in all, there was nothing more than rudimentary information for the navigators to undertake the longest flight the Air Corps had ever attempted.

Indeed, the navigators had to be resourceful. For example, after landing at Lima, Peru, refueling the six aircraft seemed to take an eternity with only one slow rate-of-refueling truck on the field. LeMay used the time to the maximum extent. Although he did not relate how he decided on the methodology, he stated that they would call selected Andes Mountain mines possessing telephones located at various levels up and down the sides of the mountains. He would ask the operator to go outside and look at the stars, if he could. His calls were made to a series of mine operators up to 16,000 ft and all reported clear skies. It was time to depart. These men were a collection of rather ambitious young aeronauts.[4]

Flight Progress

At 9:00 am on February 15, 1938, a bitingly cold Tuesday morning, the last of the six Y1B-17s departed Langley, winging their way to Miami carrying the greetings of President Franklin D. Roosevelt to the President-elect of Argentina, Roberto Ortiz. LtCol Olds maximized the training aspects of the flight by having the aircraft depart at two minute intervals, and instead of joining up on the lead navigator's plane, each conducted his own track monitoring, maintaining radio contact. Five hours and 45 minutes later, the birds landed at Miami.

There was precious little time to enjoy the southern climes, as the mechanics went over the ships with fine-toothed combs and the pilots and navigators pored over the maps and available weather reports. Shortly before 1:00 am on the 16th, they were airborne once again, this time setting out on the long leg to Lima. LtCol Olds had hoped for the flight to Lima to be non-stop, but he recognized the vagaries they were facing and briefed that a go-no-go decision would be made over Panama. Once again the planes flew on alone, but were to assemble over Colon.

Six hours and 14 minutes after takeoff from Miami, Olds assembled the ships over Colon at 7:07 am. Bad weather continued to be reported over the Equator and unknown beyond that. Weighing the skimpy information and all of the factors as best he could, Olds directed "Continue to Lima". He decided to himself that they would continue for another four hours as they swung down the west coast of South America. Things became a bit dicier as the headwind component increased and ground speed slowed to 125 kts, and the radio report of this slowing caused the Langley staff to scramble for their computers. However, with the next report came the news that the groundspeed had increased to 150 kts.

The expected equatorial storm appeared off Guayaquil, Ecuador, and the ships gradually found it necessary to climb ultimately to 23,000 ft and remain there for the next 300 miles to top the storms. The awkward oxygen hose arrangement was again employed periodically, and LeMay noted that his performance was severely degraded by hypoxia. Descending once again to the appointed rendezvous at Point Salinas, just north of Lima, Peru, the aircraft landed at Limatambo airport at 4:25 pm, having flown the 2,695 miles in 15 hrs. and 32 minutes for an average speed of 173 mph.[5]

1stLt LeMay reported that in-flight communications with Lima were not very good, and there turned out to be good reason for it. The personnel in Lima had been advised that each airplane would transmit on 6230 Kcs, and it was only after a lapse of many hours was it determined that they were on 5692 Kcs. Additionally, they had been told that the call sign would be GBB 10 when the aircraft actually were using RT 8. The final straw was the fact that the Lima personnel had been told that the flight commander would notify the American Embassy of their Estimated Time of Arrival (ETA) 24 hours in advance. Unfortunately, Olds was never informed of the requirement. In fact, Olds did not know with whom to communicate with and eventually contacted Pan American Grace Airways (Panagra) with the information[6].

Despite the confusion, there were a good many people at the aerodrome when the aircraft arrived, some having been there three or four hours. The crowd included the aide-de-camp of the president, the president of the Cabinet, and the Ministers of War, Navy, Aviation, Public Health and Justice. The mayor of Lima and ranking members of the military rounded out the official crowd along with businessmen, editors, cameramen and hordes of children. They had set up a wonderful buffet, right on the ramp, for the visiting crews. But with all of the activities necessary for the immediate launch for Buenos Aires, they had to be satisfied with a quick grab of chicken, meat or seafood, and no vino!

LtCol Olds fulfilled his role as a goodwill ambassador, spokesman and leader of the flight and spoke to the assembled crowd at 5:00 pm. The speech was carried in the U.S over a nationwide radio hook-up, and the joy at the GHQ, 2nd Bomb Group staff, and individual crewmembers' homes was without bounds.

Employees of Panagra turned to and assisted the Air Corps crews in any way they could in the refueling and readying the ships for departure. Maj Meloy's aircraft needed a propeller adjustment and it looked as though they would be unable to make the takeoff time. The remaining five aircraft departed seven hours after landing and turned to the south to hug the coast south to the vicinity of Santiago, Chile, where they would turn east and climb enroute to 21,000 ft to ensure clearance over the Andes bound for Buenos Aires.

Contact with Lima was lost after the planes crossed the Andes and dropped down to the coastal plains, so there was no word concerning the status of Maj Meloy's B-17. Colonel Olds and his five-ship formation landed at Buenos Aires' El Paloma airport just under 12 hours after departure from Lima and they were met by U.S. ambassador Alexander W. Weddell and a large contingent of Argentine dignitaries.

As it turned out, Maj Meloy, with a huge hand from Panagra, was able to depart Lima at 6:20 am, some seven plus hours after his five companions. For two, three, and four hours he reported back to Lima, but then contact was lost and no word was received for some time. Finally, the relay station at Buenos Aires picked up his position report at 2:00 pm, and the growing anxiety disappeared. Meloy was not out of the woods, however, as he ran into a"pontero", or tornado, and he had to skirt around it and delay his landing by an hour. Despite the delay, he shattered the record with an elapsed time of 11 hrs. and five minutes.

The crews found that their money was useless in Buenos Aires, and other cities, and they were wined and dined as visiting dignitaries. The enlisted crewmembers were quartered and fed at the Argentine noncommissioned officers barracks without any charge. The officers were dined by the ambassador and his wife. The highlight of the trip, however, occurred on Sunday, February 20, when the six B-17s flew overhead during the inaugural ceremonies; an awesome appearance and tribute to U.S. technology, not lost on audiences everywhere.. The detailed planning, strenuous flying over unexplored territories and demanding post-flight appearances took its toll, and the crews were mentally and physically exhausted. LtCol Olds wisely had the crews take a day's rest and "recharge" their batteries.

The Flight Home

They had performed flawlessly conforming to a tight schedule, so the flight home offered the opportunity for a more leisurely journey. Five of the B-17s took off from El Palomar at 7:10 am on Tuesday, February 22nd, bound for Santiago, Chile. The sixth aircraft, commanded by Archibald Y. Smith, was delayed by a minor incident when a main wheel broke through thin cement when being pushed away from the refueling pit. He was finally able to depart by 12:45 pm The first five ships landed at Santiago's Los Cerrillos Airport at 12:05 pm, followed by Smith at 4:45 pm. Smith was to experience engine trouble on the next leg and remained overnight at Arica, Chile, but joined the rest of the flight at Lima.

While the five ships were in Santiago, LtCol Olds once again made a broadcast to recount the progress of the return flight. They left Santiago on Wednesday, February 23rd at 8:00 am and arrived in Lima at 5:05 pm. Prevented from providing traditional Peruvian hospitality on the trip south, the residents of Lima took advantage of the return opportunity to royally fete the crews. On Friday, February 25th, reluctantly, LtCol Olds launched his flight from Limatampo for Albrook Field in the Panama Canal Zone arriving there after a flight of nine hours. The ships had by now accumulated more than 40 hrs. of flight time away from any substantial maintenance resources, and it was decided to bring them to the France Field Panama Air Depot for in-depth inspection and servicing. The "Look-See" revealed no problems, a testimony to the reliability of the B-17, and plans were made for their non-stop flight home to Langley. LtCol Olds seldom missed an opportunity to use every flight hour to its maximum use, and once again dictated departures for Langley would be at two minute intervals, and each ship would navigate independently. He briefed that they would assemble over Norfolk for the triumphant return to Langley. It was quite a welcome!

The Welcome and Deserved Accolades

When the crews crawled from their ships, they were met first by a cold, raw day, certainly bringing home to them the extent of their globe circling mission. They then were astounded by the more than five thousand military and civilians that were there on the ramp to welcome them. Reporters, cameramen, and at the forefront was MajGen Andrews holding a handful of telegrams and radio messages of congratulations, and justifiably so—the flight of six large bombers returning from a 12,000-mile, 10-day mission with a success that had world-wide implications resounded with the country. One member of the welcoming party was co-author LtCol Bill Braxton, then an enlisted man attached to the GHQ on the adjutant's staff.

"Back in those days, newspapers were the primary source of information for us. The local Newport *Daily Press* ran a daily account of the progress of the goodwill flight of the B-17s to Buenos Aires. Reporters followed the planes from take-off at Langley Field to return on Sunday, Feb. 27, 1938. Of course, we eagerly read about the flight every day, and heard a lot of scuttlebutt around Base HQ from the officers and noncoms alike. It was the prime subject of our days.

"On Friday, Feb 25th, we were alerted in the barracks that there would be a big inspection and parade on Saturday, so we spent all of Friday night in the barracks polishing and shining everything and getting our Class A uniforms ready for the inspection. Of course, we knew from the newspapers that the B-17s were returning from South America, but we did not know that we would be involved. Saturday morning we not only had an inspection in the barracks but we lined up outside and drilled most of the morning. Two years before, I had been an infantryman in Panama on my first between-the-wars tour, and drill had become second nature to me. In the infantry, we spent two or three hours every day practicing close-order drill which was quite complicated. Despite the Army's attempts to make the drill less complicated, it was something else to see

Air Corps troops marching. It was not very sharp, to say the least.

"Still, this was the Air Corps, and we didn't spend much time in marching; only when it was necessary to move a large group from one place to the other, and that was just not a normal activity for us. We had airplanes and balloons to get in the air! On Saturday afternoon we were told that most of us would be restricted to the base on Sunday, so we knew we were in for something big. This didn't bother us too much since it was close to the end of the month, and no one had enough money to go out, anyway. On Sunday morning we were told at breakfast that we would be in parade formation on the flight line that afternoon when our B-17s returned from Argentina. We formed up in front of the barracks at about one o'clock, and it was quite cold although we were dressed in standard winter uniforms without overcoats. Much to our surprise, in addition to the Base HQ Squadron, we were joined by troops from the 8th Pursuit Group and the 2nd Bombardment Group.

"They marched us down to the flight line, which was only a block from the enlisted barracks. We stood "at ease" for more than an hour, and there naturally was a lot of grumbling because of the cold and having to march around on Sunday. Suddenly, at about 1500, the B-17s roared overhead and soon landed one by one and lined up with the other six B-17s in a row facing the hangars and the assembled troops.

"As the crews dismounted from the planes, they lined up in front of their individual planes with LtCol Olds and his crew in the center. They were greeted by several general officers and VIP civilians. We recognized General Andrews, and General George Marshall, who had recently been appointed Chief of War Plans. Of course, we were called to attention while everyone waited until the official greeting was made to Col Olds. In addition to the military welcome, there was a large crowd of several thousand civilians present, since this affair had received so much publicity. When the official greeting was over with Gen. Andrews making a short speech, we were dismissed and allowed to mill around the airplanes and talk to the enlisted crews who had been on the flight. Of course there were numerous reporters and photographers present, and on Monday the local papers were full of the story with high praise for the crews."

General Andrews read greetings from Secretary of War the Honorable Harry H, Woodring, and Army Chief of Staff, Malin Craig[7], and then he congratulated the men himself.

Woodring's message was:

"Please convey to all the members of your command my personal and official congratulations on the completion of your remarkably successful flight to and from Buenos Aires. Your splendid achievement has greatly strengthened the bonds of friendship which so closely unite us with our great neighbors In South America. The President and the people of the United States are highly appreciative of the demonstrated efficiency of you and your companions which alone made such an amazing flight possible."

Craig said:

"My hearty congratulations to you and your men on the brilliant success of your great flight. Such an undertaking could only succeed through fine organization, splendid leadership, and remarkable efficiency. The entire Army has followed the details of your flight from day to day and is proud of your achievement. You may expect to hear further from the War Department."

BrigGen Oscar Westover, Chief of the Air Corps, dispatched the following to Andrews:

"I have just learned of the landing of the B-17 flight from Panama after a record performance. My congratulations to the GHQ Air Force. With this successful demonstration of the efficiency of the organization and the high state of training and skill of the personnel. The whole Air Corps holds a debt of gratitude to your men for the striking demonstration of the speed and mobility of air power. It will have a wholesome effect throughout the corps. Please convey the following message to Colonel Olds, commander of the flight: "The whole air corps has watched the progress of your flight from beginning to end with keen interest. I now congratulate you and your personnel for a truly magnificent performance. You and your men have executed a difficult tiring and trying task in an efficient and modest way. You deserve fully what you now have, the admiration and gratitude of the whole corps."

Senators Robert McReynolds of North Carolina and Millard Tydings of Maryland lauded these men and their leader, LtCol Olds, and recommended that all 49 men be awarded The Distinguished Flying Cross (DFC). Olds was awarded the DFC and the 2nd Bombardment Group was awarded the MacKay Trophy for 1938.

LtCol Olds Receiving MacKay Trophy from Secretary of War H.H. Woodring

Things Go Sour for MajGen Andrews

By the summer of 1938, however, the B-17 was in trouble, with the War Department threatening to shut down production in a cost-cutting effort. Senior Army officers believed that larger numbers of short—and medium-range, twin-engine bombers could do a better job than smaller numbers of large, expensive, long-range bombers with four engines.

Andrews, still a temporary Major General, invited BrigGen George C. Marshall, new chief of war plans on the General Staff, for an all-day briefing at his Langley Field headquarters. Marshall accepted and was favorably impressed. Andrews followed that up with an extended inspection trip for Marshall, visiting GHQ combat units across the country. Among visits to support units and aircraft manufacturers was a crucial stop at Boeing's plant in Seattle, and Marshall saw firsthand the actual B-17 production line. He was favorably impressed and became convinced of the Army's need for this aircraft. Marshall's trip with Andrews marked the beginning of a professional relationship between the two that would be of great importance to the future of the Army air arm.

Andrews spent four crucial years as head of GHQ Air Force at Langley. Although eminently successful in the eyes of most, his actions did not sit well with Malin Craig, the Chief of Staff of the Army. On March 1, 1939, Andrews completed his command tour at GHQ Air Force and Craig declined to offer Andrews a new assignment in a general officer's post. Andrews was forced to revert to his permanent grade of colonel and was sent to San Antonio, as VIII Corps air officer, finding himself in exactly the same job that Billy Mitchell had been relegated in 1925. Craig's decision, however, could not change the fact that the consolidation of air combat units under Andrews in GHQ Air Force represented an important milestone in the strategic development of American airpower. Andrews was "rescued" and returned to General rank when President Roosevelt passed over many and appointed Marshall Chief of Staff, and Marshall in turn recalled Andrews to be the first air officer to serve on the General Staff.

1. *Daily Press*, Newport News, VA, January 9, 1938
2. *The Navigator*, 1stLt (Col) John W. Eagan, Summer Edition 1963
3. *Mission with LeMay*, Curtis E. LeMay . Doubleday and Company, New York, NY 1965
4. ibid
5. Letter dtd February 19, from American Ambassador to Peru to War Department vis State Department
6. *The Argentina Flight, As Seen by Langley Field Correspondent*.7. Newport News, VA *Daily Press* February 28, 1938
7. *Daily Press*, Newport News, VA February 28, 1938

CHAPTER
XIII

Expanding the Envelope II

The world sat up and took note of the fantastic accomplishment of the 2nd Bombardment Group's six B-17s in their February 1938 round trip to Buenos Aries, Argentina. (They had shed the Y1B-17 designation and were now just B-17s and not B-17As. The next model delivered to Langley in 1938 was the B-17B. It would be first used on a flight to Brazil.) The mission had demonstrated that a flight of heavy bombers could proceed over essentially uncharted land and sea and arrive at destinations at distances up to 2,800 miles away. Of course, then they had to land and refuel, but that also meant that they were capable of traveling on a seven and one-half hour mission to a target and return without refueling. If the "Brass" did not notice, air forces the world over did, especially our own.

It was one thing to be able to fly these unheard of distances with such accuracy, but the airplanes had to be capable of more than navigation precision. It must be a strategic weapon of war. The Air Corps was now putting together an impressive record. Shortly after the arrival of the first aircraft at Langley, the group had demonstrated its bombing skill off the coast of California in August 1937, scoring many water bomb direct hits on the USS *Utah*. A 20-city flight over Midwest and eastern industrial areas showed off the ease of moving multi-plane formations over populated areas. Then came LtCol Olds' record speed runs from Langley to March Field in California and return in January and April of 1938. Flush with the long distance Argentina success, two months later, three of the ships flew 700 miles to sea, and located the Italian liner *Rex* in almost impossible weather conditions.

Goodwill Flight to Bogota Columbia

The success of the *Rex* intercept and the Goodwill Flight to Argentina led to the laying on of another Goodwill Flight to South America, this time to Columbia. The State Department was sensitive to conditions in South America and sought War Department support for another Goodwill Flight to a presidential inaugural, this time for President-elect Eduardo Santos of Columbia. The requirements were sent down to Air Corps GHQ and then the 2nd Bombardment Group and quickly accepted as another chance to show-case the B-17. This flight, however, was not to be commanded by LtCol Olds, but by Maj Vincent J. Meloy. Maj Harold L. George would command another of the ships, and Maj Caleb V. Haynes would command the third aircraft.

Personalities Intrude on Years of Success

Always known as somewhat of a maverick ever since his testimony in support of BrigGen Mitchell during the general's court martial, LtCol Olds had gradually repaired his image and was recognized as a born leader. His special leadership capabilities had been demonstrated many times since his elevation to commander of the 2nd Bombardment Group where he demanded much of his crews, and of himself. However, there were rough periods where he had rankled Army seniors, Navy leadership and War Department civilians. Another event was to trip him up.

Sometime after the return of the goodwill flight to Argentina, an unwelcome official cablegram was sent to the U.S. State Department by the Argentina government. It alleged that while in Argentina, LtCol Olds had told a newspaper reporter that the Argentina Government was purchasing obsolete Martin B-10 bombers from the U.S. and they had not been used in years. An official congressional investigation was initiated and it appeared that the Argentine Secretary of War might lose his job. Needless to say, the State Department was embarrassed, and complained bitterly to Secretary of War H. H. Woodring and in turn to Army Chief of Staff, Gen Malin Craig. The onus for responding eventually landed in Olds' lap.[1]

Deputy Army Chief of Staff Stanley D. Embrick told Air Corps Deputy Chief H.H. Arnold, acting in MajGen Westover's absence, to have Olds report to Woodring and Craig in person and explain himself. Apparently Arnold tried to shelter Olds and pointed out that Olds was not under his command, but that of the GHQ, and he and Westover had no say in the matter. The excuse did not work, and Olds was ordered to Washington, where he strongly denied having ever made such a statement.[2]

Louis B. Johnson, Assistant Secretary of War and staunch protector of the image of air power was not convinced and fumed that Olds abilities were not worth the trouble he caused. He ordered that Olds not be permitted to lead the upcoming goodwill flight to Columbia. MajGen Andrews argued, without success, that the authority for assigning flight commanders was his, and that Olds was the only man who had the experience to conduct such a mission. Andrews recognized the futility of further argument and juggled the assignment of crews.

The Selected Aircraft and Crews

The crews selected for the run to Bogota were made up from the three 2nd Bombardment Group squadrons, many of them veterans of the previous record-shattering mission to Argentina.

Number **51** from the 20th Squadron:
Maj Vincent J. Meloy (One of the ship commanders to Argentina)
Cpt Alva L. Harvey (of World Cruiser Fame)
Cpt Ford J. Lauer
1stLt Frederick E. Glantzberg
1stLt Edwin L. Tucker
SSgt Henry L. West
Corp John F. Gray

Corp Clarence D. Lake
Pvt Joseph H. Walsh

Number **62** from the 96th Squadron:
Maj Harold L. George
Maj Charles Y. Banfill (General Staff Passenger)
Cpt Carl B. McDaniel
1stLt William C. Bentley
1stLt William A. Matheny
MSgt Floyd B. Haney
SSgt Ralph W. Spencer

Sgt Frank B. Conner
Pvt1stCl Norbett D. Flinn

Number **80** from the 49th Squadron:
Maj Caleb V. Haynes
1stLt Curtis E. LeMay
1stLt Richard S. Freeman
1stLt Torgils G. Wold ((Langley Weather Officer)
2ndLt James H. Rothrock
TSgt Adolph Cattarius
Corp James E. Sands

Pvt1stCl Russell E. Junior

LeMay noted that the extra crew members were "human mechanical insurance"[3].

Number 80 was tapped to be the lead ship, and LeMay as the lead navigator once again, based on his growing reputation as the Air Corps' best navigator. This in turn provided him with access to the latest evolving navigation equipment. The gyro stabilized driftmeter was aboard each aircraft, as was the new radio compass, which allowed radio bearings to be taken on any type of ground radio station. Each of the navigators was trained in celestial navigation, at times the only available method when above the clouds and/or over water. As with the Argentina flight, all of the ships were equipped with the Sperry Autopilot.

They also carried a significant outfit of emergency equipment in recognition of the route of flight over water and uncharted jungles. Pneumatic individual life vests and jungle kits with mosquito nets, medicine, emergency rations, drinking water, fishing gear, guns and ammunition were available for each of the crew. In addition, each aircraft had two rubber inflatable boats (rafts). The aircraft also was equipped with an emergency flotation system which would expel gasoline and enable the evacuated tanks to become flotation devices to keep the aircraft afloat if ditched on water.

This turned out to be different from the flight to Argentina, yet there were a number of similarities that the crews would eventually recognize as basic to all of the communities visited. But this one almost was a non-event.

Lead Ship Officers. LeMay on the left alongside Maj Haynes

Tragedy in Bogota

On Sunday, July 24th, a new military airfield, the Campa de Marte, was being dedicated at Santa Ana, near Bogota, and more than 50,000 people were amassed for the occasion. They were celebrating the 150th anniversary of Simon Bolivar's birth, and one of the events was the aerobatic display of a Columbian Air Force aircraft. The pilot was stunting wildly a mere 90 ft above the crowds who were justifiably awed and amazed. President-elect Santos looked at the display disapprovingly and remarked to his War Department Minister that he did not like such foolishness, and received no argument from him. Within a few moments, the stunting acrobatic pilot, Lieutenant Abadia, slammed into the crowd going at full speed, spreading himself, his airplane, and more than 60 members of the crowd over a wide area. The carnage was terrible. The Army Air Corps assumed their goodwill flight would be cancelled, but it was still on.

The Flight to Bogota

The August time frame for the flight made a close examination and evaluation of the weather necessary, as it was the rainy season in Columbia, and an 8:00 am to 12:00 pm arrival time would avoid the afternoon showers and thunderstorm build-ups. Additionally, it was the hurricane season, and although lacking the forecast tools of today, reports from the greater and lesser Antilles provided enough information to delineate the formation of storms along the route. To arrive in Bogota in the morning hours, it would require an early morning (approximately 2:00 am) departure from Miami, once again selected for the jumping off point. With the inauguration scheduled for Sunday, the three planes departed Langley Field on Wednesday, August 3rd, with ship 80 off at 8:55 am, 62 at 9:04 am, and 51 at 9:06 am, arriving in Miami 2:35 pm.[4] The planes were given a routine inspection, groomed and refueled and made ready for the flight to Bogota, which was planned for 2:30 am August 5th.

The airplanes were airborne again from Miami at 3:05 am in the darkness and headed for Barranquilla where they would join up for the remaining leg to Bogota maintaining visual contact and landed within 30 minutes of the ETA that had been provided to legation the day prior.

LeMay said that the welcome was somehow becoming routine, what with the immaculate uniforms of the senior officers, so different than ours, formal greetings, flowers, and handshakes all around. Mr. Jefferson Caffery, a well know diplomat and Special Ambassador was present, but the Military Attaché was not there. The US Navy, however, had Marine Cpt John C. Munn fill in, and despite inter-service, rivalry, LeMay stated that he could not have done a better job. So much so, that on return, Maj Meloy recommended that a Letter of Commendation be issued up through War Department channels.

One of the many details so well-handled by Cpt Munn was crew participation in a memorial service for those killed in the July 24th airshow disaster. Among all of the many dignitaries, the crew proffered a wreath which was deposited at the entrance to the cemetery vault. Maj Meloy spoke, followed by the President. All was not somber for the crews, however, as they attended a corrida, where the Matador, taking a cue from the crowd attitude, dedicated a bull to the visitors, an unheard of recognition of foreigners. LeMay had another take on the spectacle, relating that they were sea-level bulls, and at the 9,000 ft altitude, they would take a turn around the arena and collapse[5]. Oh well, the gesture was appreciated.

The Return to Langley

Prior to the departure from the high field elevation field at Bogota, a considerable amount of time was spent in two mechanical situation discussions. One over which they had no control, but could be vociferously complained about, was the lack of a full-feathering propeller. The unwelcomed event of an engine failure was somewhat mitigated by the fact that the B-17 had four engines, but having the unwanted drag of a windmilling propeller driving a dead engine could be devastating to performance until the engine froze up and stopped. A full-feathering propeller with associated engine system shutoffs was considered essential.

The other discussion considered a more immediate concern and that was how to use the two-stage supercharger installed on the B-17 R-1820 engines. Lacking the turbo-chargers that would show up on later models, the crew spent a lot of time pondering whether to take off with the engines in high or low blower (two-stage supercharger). High blower would push more of the less dense air into the intake system, and recover some of the sea-level power, but require more horsepower from the engine to drive it. Low blower would provide less manifold pressure, but require less power to drive it. A definitive solution was never arrived at and the ships were loaded with a diminished fuel load of 1,000 gal and departure was uneventful.[5]

The flight gave President Santos another farewell flyby salute at 9:22 am on August 9th and headed for France Field in Panama, a relatively short flight of three hours and 17 minutes for the long-legged ships, averaging 207 mph. The times might have been even swifter had they not been required to deviate to avoid thunderstorms. Circling the field for a few minutes, they landed in drizzling rain at 12:39 pm. Departure for Miami Municipal was slated for the 11th.

It was another opportunity for a triumphant return of the strategic bombers, and LtCol Olds was not about to let it pass, despite his prohibition from leading the mission. He had picked up the mammoth Boeing XB-15 at Seattle, and was putting it through its paces, and it just seemed natural for him to fly on down south to Miami and meet the returning B-17s over Chapman Field outside Miami. They would then join up for a turnabout Miami while the press was given the chance to fawn over this display of massive airpower. All that was necessary was for lead navigator Cutis LeMay to provide an ETA over Chapman for all of this to take place. Unfortunately, LeMay blew the calculation, and although it was corrected in sufficient time to "make the scene", he received more than a little chastisement[6]. It would seem that once again, the lack of, or the poor quality oxygen, caused mental lapses and it was to be the focus of concentrated efforts to correct.

On the 12th, all of the ships returned to Langley, again showing the "legs" of the strategic bombers such as the B-17 and the "super flying fortress" XB-15.

The One and Only "Super Flying Fortress"

As noted in Chapter Nine, new Boeing President Claire Egtvedt shared a belief with the Air Corps "Bomber Mafia" that there was a great future for larger bombers, although as an astute businessman, he knew there would be synergies. What flew well in the military would have application in the transport arena and vice versa. At the same time that his engineers started the legendary B-17 design, he responded to an Army query and request for a large bomber with a 5,000 mile range. Originally, the Boeing Model 294 was designated the XBLR-1 (Experimental Bomber Long Range), it but it eventually became the XB-15.

It first flew on October 15, 1937, and LtCol Olds received it in the 2nd Bombardment Group in 1938 when it had finished testing and proving capable of lifting unheard of payloads. It was a great aerodynamic design, as shown with the payload capability, but it lacked power. Originally designed to be powered by 1,000 HP liquid cooled engines, the 850 HP Pratt and Whitney R-1830 engines were unable to propel the aircraft beyond the meager 145 kts with a full load, and it became a one-off orphan. The 2nd Bombardment Group made good use of it, however, and the accompaniment of the returning Columbian B-17s was a classic example of its use as a symbol of Air Corps air power. It eventually received a cargo door and became the XC-105.

The XC-105 in Panama

True to the Boeing large aircraft thrust and the translation of "what works" to other applications, the wing design of the XB-15 was used on the Boeing Model 314 Clipper for Pan American Airways. The R-1830 engines were replaced with Wright Double Cyclone R-2600 engines of 1,600 HP, and another Boeing legend was born with a first flight in June 1938. Similarly, the unpressurized B-17 fuselage was replaced by a circular pressurized passenger configuration, and the Boeing 307 Stratoliner first flew on December 31, 1938. It was a busy, and successful, time for Boeing.

1. *Ambassador of American Airpower: Maj General Robert Olds*, Scottie Zamzow, Air University Maxwell Air Force Base, Alabama June 2008
2. ibid
3. *Mission with LeMay*, Curtis E. LeMay, Doubleday and Company, NY, NY
4. Newport News, VA *Daily Press*, August 4, 1938
5. *Mission with LeMay*, Curtis E. LeMay, Doubleday and Company, NY, NY
6. ibid

CHAPTER XIV

Expanding the Envelope III

Personalities Continue to Dictate Events

The 1938 American Legion Convention in Los Angeles offered another stage for the Army and Navy to again vie for public support. MajGen Arnold opined that it appeared that the Army and Navy would be constantly involved in a running series of shows to gain people's support.

The Navy Shows its Power at the 1938 Los Angeles Legionnaires' Convention

The Navy sent three battleships of the Colorado class to strut their stuff for assembled Long Beach/San Pedro harbor crowds. The Air Corps intended to show the B-15 and B-17 to crowds at the Los Angeles Air Show, held in consort with the convention, particularly in light of the acclaim received at the Cleveland Air Show the week before. At the time, it was common for the services to take every advantage of trotting out their latest weaponry for public review to encourage recruiting and seek support for funding of what they considered necessary expansion.

LtCol Olds found himself at crossed swords again when he bruised Assistant Secretary of War Johnson's ego by inviting aviation authorities to accompany him to Los Angeles in the B-15 without obtaining War Department approval. Both Secretary Woodring and Assistant Secretary Johnson were Legionnaires of note, and had plans for their own invitations. Johnson was angry, stating that the planes belonged to him, and not to Olds. He banned both the B-15 and Olds from the show[1].

Bigger Fish to Fry

Despite the sometimes intense internal personal differences, the rapidly evolving world events demanded the full attention of the United States Government, from the President down through his Cabinet and all of the military Chiefs. Though rivalries would continue, there would be a focusing of efforts for the better good. The World events of 1939 ominously foretold of a conflict on a scale not previously envisioned. Nazi Germany took Czechoslovakia in March, annexed Austria, and the Spanish Civil War wound down after providing Germany with a "lab" for weapons testing. Germany invaded Poland in September, France and England declared War on Germany, Germany and Russia signed a non-aggression pact. Wise leaders in the U.S. feared the conflagration might spread to the Americas.

Many years before, the Monroe Doctrine of 1823 stated that further efforts by European countries to colonize land or interfere with states in the Americas would be viewed by the United States of America as acts of aggression requiring US intervention[2]. It asserted that the Western Hemisphere was not to be further colonized by European countries and that the United States would neither interfere with existing European colonies nor meddle in the internal concerns of European countries.

The Monroe Doctrine generally met with a favorable response in South America, as the former colonies emerged from under the boot of European colonization. But as time went on, the United States influence in South America took a more sovereign role and Teddy Roosevelt added the Roosevelt Corollary in 1904 which in essence asserted the right of the United States to intervene in Latin America in cases of "flagrant and chronic wrongdoing by a Latin American Nation". [3] Critics, however, argued that the Corollary simply asserted U.S. domination in that area, essentially making them a "hemispheric policeman". In 1928, J. Reuben Clark, President Calvin Coolidge's Secretary of State responded with the Clark Memorandum. It was not released until 1930 under the presidency of Herbert Hoover, and it answered critics by concluding that the United States need not invoke the Monroe Doctrine as a defense of its interventions in Latin America. The Memorandum argued that the United States had a self-evident right of self-defense, and that this was all that was needed to justify certain actions.

The Importance of Brazil

But times had changed, and by 1939, the major countries of South America were well established entities and cooperation rather than dictation was needed. Franklin Roosevelt's Secretary of State Cordell Hull had met with leaders in Lima, Peru, and the change to "Good Neighbor Policy" was in vogue. A series of high level meetings between Brazilian and American officials followed the Lima cooperation. Under Secretary of State Sumner Welles telephoned Brazilian Minister of External Relations, Osvaldo Aranha, and said that he would like to ask President Getulio Vargas to have Aranha visit Washington in February 1939 for a five-week stay, to discuss items of mutual interest. They did not have to ask twice, as Brazil's debt was considerable and the opportunity to seek financial aid seemed to be ripe. While Aranha was enroute to the U.S. via ship, President Roosevelt held a secret meeting of the Military Affairs Commission. He laid out his views in a post-Munich World. Peace had failed, an aggressive alliance of Germany, Italy and Japan was on the move, and America's first line of defense was in the Pacific. Therefore, the United States must rely on the continued independence of a large group of nations on the Atlantic and Brazil had to be one of them. New Army Chief of Staff, General

George C. Marshall secretly asked the Army War College to examine what steps would be necessary to protect Brazil.

With Roosevelt's framework well understood in the highest levels of Government, Aranha had a full schedule on arrival and was shepherded from one Department to another and had several meetings with Roosevelt, Hull, and Welles. Mid-trip, Aranha reported to Vargas that the U.S. was "favorable to our intensions." Vargas and company, however, saw the threat to Brazil from the south and not the northeast, and in addition, had a large and varied plan of spending U.S.-provided aid. Economic accords did emerge from the visit, including a promise from the Export-Import Bank to arrange credits to finance purchases in the United States and to lend Brazil $19,200,000 to pay off its debts. The U.S. promised to send an expert to Brazil to assist in the development of methods for the export of commodities from Brazil and to request congressional approval for a $50,000,000 gold loan to capitalize a proposed Brazilian central bank[4].

Both Welles and Aranha were optimistic that the accords reached during the visit would bring the two countries into closer economic ties. But Aranha's return in March, 1939 was met with disappointment due to the lack of promises for "things" such as planes, tanks and ships, or "something for nothing" as the ambassador said. Significantly, the navy and war ministers were not at pier side on arrival, and General Góes Montiero, who was to make the welcoming speech, was out of town. It was clear to the military that tying the Brazilian currency to the U.S. dollar via the loan to a central bank would adversely affect their ability to buy German weaponry. The implementation of the accords was slow[5].

In February 1938 the German High Command had invited Brazil's General Góes Montiero to visit Germany and to command a division in maneuvers. A hastily arranged tour of England, France and Italy followed, and some Brazilian leaders thought that a visit to the U.S. might offset any adverse reaction to the European swing. Aranha recommended that General Marshall visit Brazil, and return with General Montiero, which met with favorable response on both sides. The mission was to be political in nature, but if military aspects needed discussion, they should be raised by Brazil. General Marshall went to Brazil aboard the USS *Nashville* in May 1939 and had a successful 12-day visit, and there was a mutual cordiality among all of the participants. Not one to be overwhelmed by the effusive welcomes, on the trip down, he instructed his staff to obtain definitive information on Brazil's military structure, resources and problems. Experienced Brazil hand Col Lehman W. Miller and War Department's Chief Latin American Planner, Maj Matthew B. Ridgway would have more than cocktail parties and visits to orphanages on their minds.

Meanwhile, the Army War College study had concluded that Brazil would be unable to defend the vital coastal city of Natal and the northeast portion of Brazil, and that was of prime interest to the U.S. because of the short Natal, Brazil—Dakar, Senegal flight route to the anticipated European War Zones. There were basically only two air routes to the European battlespace—one through the treacherous icy north and the Natal-Dakar route.

Hence, there was a strategic need to protect Brazil and it was the geographic position of Natal, a "bulge" extending into the Atlantic and only 1,400 miles from Dakar, French West Africa (Senegal) that begged for protection. But the Brazilians did not see the strategic situations as the Americans did, thinking more in terms of intra-South American conflicts with Argentina. The northeast area of the country had excellent harbors but was not connected by any means of transportation. The Brazilian Air Force was primarily involved with air mail and had no combat aircraft.

Marshall emphasized the need for an American presence in Natal, and the discussions continued on the return trip with General Montiero and then during his visit. The jousting continued with the General claiming to weary of the "mental gymnastics". Summarizing the situation, Maj Ridgway correctly thought that a critical factor for the approval of U.S. presence in the northeast would be the supply of arms to Brazil. Accordingly, General Montiero submitted a list of essential military equipment and argued for an advantageous price and payment schedule, hoping that exchange of raw materials would form the payment. President Vargas was pleased but worried that the neutrality Law may create an insurmountable obstacle. The Army could not legally provide arms from its arsenals nor match the German pricing.

Montiero returned to Brazil in August and had in hand a basic agreement for military cooperation, but it was years in the signing because of U.S. slowness in providing the requested arms. The general was impressed with America's industrial capabilities and other resources but was sensitive to isolationist elements in Congress. The events of the day impacted thinking in Brazil as in almost every country, and they were determined to establish strict neutrality, but anxious to obtain U.S. arms. The Pittman Resolution, which would authorize the army and navy to assist Latin American countries, did not move in Congress, so Marshall caused surplus coastal artillery pieces and anti-aircraft cannons to be sold to Brazil. President Roosevelt himself became more concerned over the Brazilian situation and turned his personal attention to it. The stage was set for another goodwill flight of the Langley B-17s, this time to celebrate the fiftieth anniversary of the Brazilian Republic on November 15, 1939.

The Brazil Goodwill Flight

Although the Air Corps had demonstrated the Y1B-17's capability in a series of impressive missions, a goodwill flight to Rio de Janeiro, Brazil obviously would be more than just another exercise for them. This mission carried the prestige of the United States to a country that was of strategic importance to the Western Hemisphere's defense, and the reputation of the War Department, the Army, and the United States was on the line. MajGen Delos C. Emmons, GHQ commander since March of 1939, would be the flight commander. LtCol Robert Olds, commander of the 2nd Bombardment Group would be his deputy, Maj Harold George was assigned as Executive Officer. The navigator par excellence, 1stLt Curtis LeMay, would be recognized for his skills and be assigned as Operations Officer. He was still going to be de facto Lead Navigator, for his ability was above reproach, and trusted by all. Seven ships with the best crews of the 2nd Group would make the trip. In addition to Meloy and Olds in the flagship, the remaining ships were commanded by Maj Harold L. George, Cpt Robert B. Williams, Cpt Alva L. Harvey, Cpt Carl B. McDaniel, Cpt Thomas L. Mosley and Cpt William D. Old. Along to lend his Latin expertise and to act as interpreter was Maj Matthew B. Ridgway.

Capt Robert B. Williams   1stLt James H. Rothrock
2ndLt Bela A Harcos   2ndLt H.S. Williams
TSGT W.W. Fry   SSGT J. A. Piper
SSGT R.R. Illick   PVT G.F. Lowney
Maj   Pax   Maj   Pax

MajGen Delos C. Emmons CG
LtCol Robert Olds   1stLt Curtis E. LeMay
2ndLt G.C. Nye   1stLt Torgils G. Wold
Col A.S. Pedicrine   SSGT J.E. McDonald
PVT A. R. Jester   Corp J.H. Walsh
PVT T.M. Domzal

Maj Harold L. George   Capt William A. Matheny
Capt D.R. Lyon   Capt Charles H. Caldwell
TSGT John A Mauro   SSGT D.F. Hamilton
SSGT E.W. Latham   SGT W.A. Withers
Capt J.A. Baird ~ MC   Capt V.C. Bartcellos Pax

Capt Alva L. Harvey   Capt I.R. Selby
2ndLt C.M. Longacre   2ndLt A.D. Clark
SSGT A.W. Meuhl   SSGT C.D. Green
SGT C.C. Knar   OVT P.F. Rochetti
Capt P.B. Martins Pax   Capt P.C. Lucas   Pax

Capt William D. Old   1stLT C.J. Corchoran
2ndLT H.C. Corhlan   2ndLT C.R. Bond, Jr
TSGT T.W. Martin   SSGT H.P. Hansen
SGT A.C. Moore   PVT R.E. Jungar
Capt A.P. Bello Pax

Capt Carl B. McDaniel   2ndLT T.R. Spring
1stLT J. H. Walsh   2ndLT W.M. Banks
SSGT W.J. Duffy   SSGT L.A. Baker
SSGT L.L. Henry   PVT Norbert D. Flynn
Capt A.B. Catalance Pax Capt O.A. Landini Pax

Capt Thomas L. Mosely   2ndLT W. P. Ragsdale
2ndLT J.R. Ambrose   2ndLT K.K. Compton
TSGT D.M. Capps   TSGT L.H. Burger
SSGT D. Bradley   PVT G.C. Snydder
Capt R.L. Guerreariro Pax   Capt M.J. Venhals Pax

The Brazil Goodwill Fight Crewmembers

(The careful Reader will note that the crew member names indicated here, drawn from the 2nd Bombardment Commemorative Chart Prepared in 1939 do not agree with those in the OpOrder contained in Appendix D. We have been unable to reconcile the two.)

Maj Harold L. George and Three of the Brazil Crews November 1939

The typical detailed pre-planning of required navigational information on a flight of this magnitude is an immense undertaking, as the crews try to anticipate every eventuality. Weather phenomena, seasonal trends, geographic peculiarities and selection of suitable alternative fields are just a few of the additional considerations that become so important to the execution of a mission of this undertaking in an era of fledgling long-range flying.. Gathering of the Hydrographic Office (H.O.) tables, calibration of equipment such as sextants, drift meters, pelorises, radio and magnetic compasses and selection of charts are just a few of the tasks. The route of flight was intentionally designed to provide an opportunity to secure the maximum available information from a standpoint of air operations from the all-important Natal area.

LeMay again found a dearth of needed charts and recommended "that the information section of the Chief of the Air Corps procure and maintain sufficient quantities of the best maps available——" and since the Government was not a source for them, they should be sourced "from Pan American, Air France, Pan-Grace and the various South American Air Forces, and even oil and mining companies conducting air operations in the areas."[6]

Three of the seven aircraft were from the batch of 39 B-17Bs authorized in 1939 with deliveries that summer. In addition to the major reconfiguration of the nose section and the incorporation of a larger dorsal fin, the B-17B incorporated a number of other small refinements. Most importantly from the long range flight point of view was the shifting of the navigator's position from behind the pilots to the nose, where he would have better visibility and would not have to run about the ship trying to find a view for celestial navigation. The fabric flaps reverted to aluminum, and the brakes were changed from pneumatic to hydraulic operation. The B-17B was also fitted with the top-secret Norden bombsight, which was installed under wraps before the beginning of a mission and then taken away in the same way after landing, always under the supervision of an armed guard.

Route of Flight to Rio de Janeiro

The seven B-17s would depart Langley on an 822-mile leg to Miami and remain overnight (RON), then depart on the 1180 mile leg to Albrook Field in the Panama Canal Zone for a second RON. Following the west coast of South America, stops would be made at Lima, Peru, Asunción, Paraguay, and on in to Rio de Janeiro. Lending weight to the importance that the War Department and the Army placed on the mission to Brazil was the high ranking assemblage that wished them well and witnessed the takeoff of the seven ships. MajGen H.H. Arnold, Chief of the Air Corps spoke briefly before departure. His text:

> "The Army Air Corps is honored and gratified that its members have been selected for this important mission, to bear this message from our President to the president and people of Brazil. I shall take no effort to conceal the intense pride which fills me and every member of the corps on this occasion. Your selection for this undertaking is a triumph for aviation and an expression of confidence in you.

> "Last week, I witnessed here a ceremony wherein the Secretary of War, the Honorable Harry H. Woodring conferred upon the Second Bombardment Group of which you are the present flight members, the highly prized Mackay trophy, emblematic

of the outstanding annual achievement in Army aviation, for your flight last year to South America. So this undertaking in which you are about to engage in is not new to many of you. You know that your planes and equipment are fully capable of these overwater and transcontinental flights because they and you have executed these missions before. At the beginning, however, of aerial expeditions of such as these, there must always be the thrill which comes from the anticipation of unusual achievement and high venture.

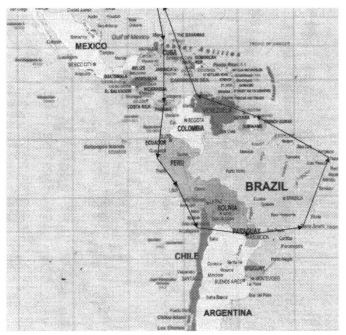

Proposed Route of Flight

"Long transoceanic and transcontinental flights always present varying experiences—the weather, the winds, the visibility, all flying conditions change from day-to-day and from time-to-time. I am fully convinced, however, that no matter what conditions prevail for you on your flight to the south, these planes you man and you, their crews, are fully competent and capable of meeting them. This mission you will perform according to high standard and tradition which have established here in the General Headquarters Air Force."

He went on to discuss the routes to be covered and assured the crews that those left behind would be following their progress with the keenest of interest. He concluded:

> "Your return journey will complete a flight of more than 10,000 miles and the record of your achievements will add to that long list which army Air Corps fliers have written in the chapter (that) history will label 'the great expeditions of the first generation of human flight."[7]

This was high praise and a rousing confidence builder for the crews about to take on this mission of national importance. Not only was General Arnold there, but General George C. Marshall, Chief of Staff was present to see them off, as was BrigGen Arnold N. Krogstad, 2nd Wing Commander, BrigGen Fred W. Martin, Commander of the 3rd Wing, at Langley temporarily to fill in for Emmons.[8]

Army Chief of Staff, General George C. Marshall Sees LtCol Olds Off on the Brazil Mission

The aircraft lifted off from Langley Field at four minute intervals commencing at 9:00 am Friday November 10, 1938 for the relatively benign and shortest leg to Miami carrying the message from President Roosevelt to President Vargas of Brazil. Festivities had already begun in Brazil on the 10th, as it was two years previously on that date that Brazilians had awakened to troops in the streets following a bloodless coup that brought Dr. Getulio Vargas to the Presidency. Congress had been dissolved, a new regime installed, a new constitution declared and Francisco Campos installed as Minister of Justice and Interior. The 15th would be the 50th anniversary of the founding of the Republic.

It was up early the next morning for the 1180 mile flight to Cristobal and Albrook Field in Panama. Along the way, at 11:00 am and 10,000 ft, MajGen Emmons reminded the airborne crews over the radio that November 11th was an important anniversary as well. General Emmons transmitted that 21 years ago, Armistice was declared, and he suggested that they all say a prayer that the United States had as yet been untouched by the war in Europe. The flight was uneventful, save for a few squalls and showers and upon landing at Albrook, Emmons was greeted by General David L. Stone, Commanding Officer of the Canal Zone, William Dawson, U.S. Ambassador to Panama, and BrigGen Herbert A. Dargue, and a joint review of the honor guard took place. A review of a formation of 18 attack and 36 pursuit aircraft was followed by lunch at the Officer's Club. After lunch, General Emmons flew some 70 miles to view a new field constructed in Rio Hato in the Republic of Panama.[9]

The ships were airborne early in the morning and arrived at Lima at 1:40 pm, having traversed 1,530 miles, all at an altitude of 8,000ft to 10,000 ft. The Peruvians had not forgotten the mighty Fortresses' visit the previous year, nor had they become blasé, and the field swarmed with a welcoming crowd. The next leg over the Andes to Asunción, Paraguay would present more a challenge in the way of terrain, weather and the uncharted South American interior.

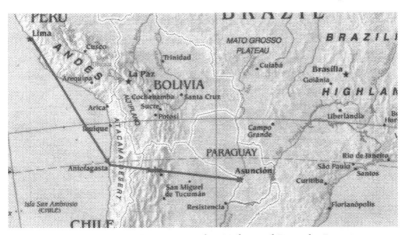

Lima to Asuncion Route over the Andes and Into the Interior

LeMay remembered that it was clear on the west side of the Andes, but that there were clouds up against the highlands on the east side. There were no passes cutting through the mountains, so it was on up to 25,000 ft and on oxygen for all of the crews of the unpressurized planes. LeMay had only one large scale map of all of South America and nothing at all of the details of Paraguay. Lacking any details of the mountainous terrain, the planes remained at 25,000 ft longer than they probably needed to, and instances of props running away, hunting and failure to maintain synchronization placed pressure on LeMay to let them know immediately when they could start to descend. He factored in a generous amount of extra time on his dead reckoning estimates before giving his "Okay".

Sliding on down the eastern slopes into the interior presented more navigational problems. With only that large scale map of South America to consult, LeMay used a plotting sheet with latitude and longitude plotted on it, and calculating that they could raise Asunción by knowing its location in relation to the Rios Parana, Paraguay and Verde, he set out a heading for a point 25 miles upriver, from whence they would turn down to Asunción. They all hit the city on the nose save for Don Old, who had come down the wrong side but eventually found the city. The six landed at 1:02 pm , followed by Don Olds at 3:01 pm.[10] They were welcomed by Paraquay's Ministers of War, Foreign Relations, Interior and Justice as well as the Commander in Chief of the Armed Forces and the United States Legation staff. They were slated to depart at 5:00 am on the13th for Rio.

At Asunción, the "perfectness" of the trip was spoiled somewhat. The field at Asuncion was soft, and number 81 slipped into the mud and damaged three propellers, delaying her arrival in Rio for four days. Number 90 lost its navigational aids on the way to Asunción and as the weather in Rio appeared to be IFR, the lack of a radio compass would be a concern. Low clouds and rain caused MajGen Emmons to delay the departure for a day.

Rio Arrival a Challenge

Although Rio de Janeiro is situated on the Atlantic, the geography can be unforgiving for "scud runners", or those who would attempt to sneak beneath the clouds at low altitudes in the vicinity rising terrain. In the immediate vicinity of Rio are peaks that rise several hundred, even one thousand meters in height. The famous Sugar Loaf is 395 meters (or close to 1,300 ft) and it sits immediately adjacent to the bay. The aircraft had successfully made the trip, but the weather at Rio was poor, so the flight proceeded out over the ocean and let down over the water—they broke out at 400 ft, and this in the days prior to radio altimeters! They proceeded carefully into Rio, avoiding terrain, cable cars and associated obstacles. With 81 awaiting repairs at Asunción and 90 being forced to land in Porto Alegra due to its inability to proceed in the adverse weather, the mission was now down to five ships.

The arriving Fortresses were warmly welcomed by the American Ambassador, Brazilian authorities, and chief of the Brazilian Air Force, General Pedro Goés Montiero. The public was also enthusiastic, having missed out on the previous year's visit of the aircraft to Argentina. The 57 crewmen were regarded as persons who bring a special message of good will from the United States and joined in the festivities, mingling with visitors from Chile and Columbia. After President Vargas' address to the throngs, he reviewed a military parade and received the American aviators at Cattete Palace. The Americans had carried the message from President Roosevelt in which he recalled his visit to Brazil in 1936 and he declared that the mutual friendship of the two countries was based on the mutual respect and the right of the New World nations to realize their destiny without extraneous interference.

Minister of War General Enrico Gaspar Dutra asked the American Ambassador, Jefferson Caffery, that the departure of the aircrew be delayed so that the Brazilian military could pay tribute to the men. On the 18th, the five ships flew over the city for a 50-minute orientation flight for passengers President Vargas, Chief of Staff General Montiero, MajGen F.J. Dutra, Maj Gen F.J. Pinto, Secretary to the President, and Jefferson Caffrey, the Ambassador, cementing friendships and further thrilling the Brazilians, and significantly, Brazilian leadership.

Time to Return Home

Natal, the all-important potential jumping off point for Europe-bound aircraft, was the first stop for the flight of homeward bound B-17s, now back to full strength of seven. The Natal of 1939 was not a thriving metropolis, and the crews were hard-pressed to find quarters. Compounding the problem was the inclusion of ten Brazilian officers as passengers, headed by Col Sergio Veloso Pedeneiras and Maj Jose Sampaio De Macedo of their Air Force, bound for some orientation in the U.S. The single hotel was inadequate to house all, and the overflow was accommodated in the hospital, courtesy of the local catholic nuns. They not only provided quarters, but hustled to feed the entourage.

Natal was not without aeronautical aids, as Air France flew a bi-weekly flight from Paris to Dakar, and on to Natal, homing on a radio beacon that they had erected there. The Army had made arrangements to have the beacon turned on during a specified period of time to assist in their arrival, and six of the seven aircraft successfully used it and landed on November 22nd. Thinking that all of the ships had landed, the Frenchman in charge turned the beacon off, and no amount of persuasion would move him to turn it back on. LtCol Olds, and then 1stLt LeMay, he of the French name, but not speaking French, yelled, gestured, had the maintainer make calls, but to no avail. Despite their failure to get the beacon turned back on, Cpt Al Harvey eventually arrived safely.[11]

The next stop was Paramaribo in Dutch Guiana, followed by Maricaibo, Venzuela. The 2,100 mile non-stop flight from Maricaibo to Bolling Field in Washington DC was the longest leg of the mission. No 90 once again suffered from problems, this time apparently from bad gas obtained in Maricaibo, and had to land at Jacksonville, FL. Their complement of Brazilians was picked up by No 70 for the remaining portion of the flight to Bolling Field. General Emmons was greeted by Louis Johnson, Assistant Secretary of War, General George C. Marshall, Army Chief of Staff, and MajGen H. H. Arnold, Chief of the Air Corps and many other high-ranking officials. The Brazilian officers were greeted by members of their embassy staff, Walter M. Walmsley, Chief of the State Department's Division of American republics, and Thomas Burke, Chief of the Division of International Communications[12].

On November 27, 1939, at 1825, five of the seven planes returned to Langley Field, having traversed 10,939 miles. The sixth aircraft, delayed in Jacksonville, having to retrieve the stranded Brazilian officers, landed at 1900. The seventh aircraft remained in Jacksonville to cleanse its tanks. All things considered, especially including the primitive enroute facilities, the B-17s had demonstrated performance capabilities and reliability standards that had never been achieved before.

LtCol Robert Olds stated that "It was the most wonderful and interesting trip that I have ever taken. We were given a marvelous reception by the people and were quartered in the finest hotels in the city. We were the guests of the Brazilian Government and each officer was decorated while the enlisted men were each awarded an honorary insignia of air mechanic and radio operator of the Brazilian Government. Over 600 troops attended the ceremony with a full military band and cheering crowds. A special police escort was given us on sight-seeing tours all over the city."[13]

The *New York Times* opined that once again the Army had demonstrated the potentialities of their resources for hemispheric defense.[14] They lauded the well-executed mission and the contribution to the enhancement of inter-American commercial flights

The mission would pay eventual dividends. With the signature of the Land Lease Act in March 1941, the Air Corps was tasked with expediting delivery of bombers to Great Britain. Olds was selected by MajGen H.H. Arnold to head the newly-formed Air Corps Ferrying Command, reporting directly to Arnold, to accomplish this mission. He staffed up with those he trusted, such as Col Caleb V. Haynes, and quickly developed a plan for the expansion for the transfer of 1,000 planes per month. Anticipating the future needs for the transport of personnel and cargo between the United States and the war zones, he drew up ferry routes for a courier-passenger service. One was the northern route, the other to the south from Natal to Dakar. Promoted to BrigGen on January 16, 1942, he personally handled the successful negotiations with neutral Brazil for the activation and use of Natal. His success was easily measured as 7,100 airplanes were delivered to their pick-up points in the first nine months of operations.

1939 Through the Eyes of a Private First Class

Bill Braxton's second enlistment was up in 1939 about the time of the Brazil mission, and despite urgings from the base sergeant major to re-enlist, Bill opted to get out, but with a plan in mind. He wrote the CO at Chapman Field in Miami and found that he had an opening. If Bill could get there on his own, he could re-enlist there. He'd have to revert to private, but there were monetary compensations in that the men there were paid subsistence. So it was off to sunny south Florida and a small operation, not realizing that the upheaval in Europe was to cause the Air Corps to explode in size.

President Roosevelt had just announced expansion of the Air Corps to 25 groups, and the men at Chapman all thought it was ridiculous. He soon found out that the President was serious, and after hardly unpacking his bag in Miami, he received orders transferring him back to Langley.

Needless to say he wasn't too happy when he found most of his private peers had been promoted. He eked out a step up to corporal, but realized had he stayed put, he would have jumped to staff sergeant. Hundreds of new recruits and men were being transferred in from all over the country.

Breaking up that Old Gang of Mine

The 2nd Bomb Group was also impacted. Having been staffed with an elite cadre with the arrival of the Y1B-17, the Group was gutted of officers and men to form the 25th Bomb Group headed for Puerto Rico, and the 29th Bomb Group headed for MacDill in Tampa. Braxton was sent to the 25th as a corporal working for men who had been under him in the Sergeant Major's office. Stopping by the GHQ one day after work, he told them of his qualifications as a stenographer. A Col Blair welcomed him with open arms, and he worked for him for the next two years, and through this relationship, eventually made his way to Warrant Officer rank, then to OCS, pilot training and a satisfying career ending up as a LtCol in the USAF.

1. *Ambassador of American Airpower: Maj General Robert Olds*, Scottie Zamzow, Air University Maxwell Air Force Base, Alabama June 2008
2. *The New American Empire* (pp. 133-134Rodrigue Tremblay (2004) ISBN 9780741418876,
3. Theodore Roosevelt (1904-12-06). "State of the Union Address"
4. *The Brazian-American Alliance 1937-1945* Frank D. McCann Jr, Princeton University Press
5. ibid
6. *Mission With Lemay*, Curtis E. LeMay
7. *Daily Press*, Newport News, VA, November 11, 1939
8. ibid
9. ibid
10. *Mission With Lemay*, Curtis E. LeMay
11. ibid
12. *Daily Press*, Newport News, VA, November 27, 1939
13. ibid
14. *New York Times*, New York, NY, November 28, 1939

CHAPTER XV

The Movie *Test Pilot*

The Golden Age of Aviation

The twenties and thirties were a veritable heyday for aviation in the United States and around the world, especially during the mid-to-late thirties, and the period was aptly called the "Golden Age of Aviation". Hardly a day went by that there wasn't a headline story about an aviation exploit. Technology was introducing improvements in structures, avionics, propulsion, and weaponry at a dizzying pace. The exploits were not limited to any one organization or country as it seemed that the advances were being announced virtually everywhere and a competitive environment was endemic. The times found the Army Air Corps blazing new trails by flying the U. S. air mail, and introducing new aircraft into the inventory. Daring entrepreneurs were tackling transoceanic flights that rapidly became relatively routine commercial flights with passengers. New record flights in speed, altitude and range were made by both civil and military aviation entities seemingly every day. Names such as Jimmy Doolittle, Amelia Earhart, Paul Mantz, Wiley Post, Howard Hughes, Al Williams and Admiral Richard Byrd became household names, and the exploits of Lindbergh and his wife Anne were detailed in newspapers and newsreels. Many of the pilots trained in WWI bought surplus Army planes and barnstormed around the country carrying passengers for cheap thrills and performing at air shows.

Publisher Ralph Pulitzer sponsored the Pulitzer Trophy Race for military airplanes at Roosevelt Field, Long Island, New York, in 1920 in an effort to publicize aviation and naturally for him, his newspaper. The races eventually moved to Cleveland in 1929 and were known as the Cleveland National Air Races. They drew the best flyers of the time, including Doolittle, Post, Frank Hawks, Jimmie Wedell, and the flamboyant Roscoe Turner. The races included a variety of events, including the Bendix Trophy cross-country races that ended in Cleveland, the Thompson Trophy Race, a closed-course event around pylons, landing contests, glider demonstrations, airship flights, and parachute-jumping contests. In 1929 Cleveland was the venue for the first Women's Air Derby, which developed into the Powder Puff Derby, that featured well-known female pilots such as Amelia Earhart, Pancho Barnes, Bobbi Trout, and Louise Thaden.

Unfortunately, not all the aviation exploit news was good; Wiley Post and Will Rogers were killed in a crash in Alaska, Knute Rockne, famed football coach of Notre Dame, was killed in a commercial plane crash, and deadly crashes occurred at the Cleveland Air Races and other aviation spectaculars. Because of the inherent perils and concomitant publicity, test pilots stood atop the idolization pyramid and the public heaped adoration on them.

In the middle thirties, the new profession of test pilot was a very dangerous one, and one that some considered almost suicidal. There were only about 100 test pilots in the United States at the time, and most of them were in their twenties and thirties and became famous through their escapades. Some of them participated in movie-making, performing dangerous stunts such as flying through buildings, mid-air crashes, and flaming ground crashes. These daring contributions to the salability of a film only added to the aura of test pilot invincibility.

The Motion Picture Industry Captures the Thrills

The movie industry has always been keen to recognize fads, trends, and what the current American public focus is, and it was quick to

attempt to film stories that captured the thrill of flying exploits wrapped in the ubiquitous love story. The 1927 *Wings* won the first ever Best Picture Oscar in 1929, and must have had the full support of the Air Corps, for a virtual armada of 220 of their aircraft participated. Shot at Kelly and Brooks Fields, and Camp Stanley, Texas in 1926, the types used include two Spad VIIs, two Fokker D.VIIs and two 2 MB-3s deliberately crashed. USAAC units included the DH.4s of 90th BS, SE.5s and Thomas Morse MB.3 Scouts of 43rd PS, DH.4s and MB.2s of 11th BS, Curtiss P-1 Hawks of 17th PS, 27th PS, 94th PS, 95th PS, of the 1st PG, and Vought VE-7s from Langley Field. Thomas-Morse

1927 Motion Picture *Wings* Poster

MB.3 and DH.4 camera planes were allocated from San Francisco's Crissy Field, and one Curtiss NBS-1 camera plane and even USAAC balloons. *Wings* was the 1927 equivalent of *Top Gun*, with marvelous air combat scenes and just enough plot to keep the film moving at other times and contains some of the best flying sequences ever captured on celluloid. It was directed by William Wellman, a respected aviation expert, who was credited with recommending the Merlin engine for the North American Aviation (NAA) P-51.

1930 saw two movies of note about the thrills of the aviation times. The *Dawn Patrol* was issued that year, and again in 1938 with Errol Flynn, Basil Rathbone and David Niven. Probably one of the best orchestrated early aeronautical films was Howard Hughes' *Hells Angels*.

Starring Jean Harlow, the story line was not as memorable as the WWI airborne sequences, which were exceptionally well done. 1933 found the MGM movie *Night Flight* with the Barrymore brothers, John and Lionel, Myrna Loy and Clark Gable. This was based on a story by Antoine de Saint-Exupery, who went on to be a WWII pilot and was lost in a P-38 on a mission off Italy.

The Y1B-17 Captures the Public's Imagination

When the radically new Y1B-17 Flying Fortress burst on the scene, it became an instant headline grabber. The escapades of these new behemoths assigned to the 2nd Bombardment Group at Langley Field in the latter thirties created sensational aviation news, as they broke records, cemented diplomatic relations, demonstrated strategic capabilities, and competed with the Navy at every opportunity. The names of Col Robert Olds and his chief pilots became household words as they were highlighted in many of those stories. It was inevitable that the movie studios would want to find a way to get the new B-17s into a movie. They were capturing the imagination of the country with every well-publicized mission and the Air Corps' March Field at Riverside, CA, was near Hollywood. The abundant publicity surrounding their exploits appeared in the *Los Angeles Times* and other local newspapers. In the fall of 1937, Metro-Goldwyn-Mayer (MGM) approached officials of the War Department and Air Corps about using the new bomber in one of their movies. Former commander of the GHQ's 1st Wing stationed at March Field, General "Hap" Arnold, was in an Air Corps command position to respond positively to the request, and undoubtedly he, General Andrews, and Colonel Olds enthusiastically approved the idea. Anything that would bring favorable attention and accolades to the Air Corps was sure to get top priority.[1]

At this time, MGM possessed the rights to a book *Test Pilot* by Jimmy Collins, who had been

**Tracey, Gable, and Barrymore
(Photo Credit www. doctormacro.com)**

a test pilot himself. The movie was scheduled for filming in December, 1937. In the film Clark Gable is seen as Jim Lane, ace test pilot for the Drake Company, Myrna Loy as Ann Barton, his love interest, Spencer Tracy as Gunner, the dependable sidekick, and Lionel Barrymore as Mr. Drake, owner of the Drake Corporation.

There was a supporting cast of Marjorie Main, Samuel S. Hinds as General Ross, Gloria Holden, Virginia Grey, Priscilla Lawson, Arthur Aylesworth, and many other minor characters. Victor Fleming, one of the leading directors at MGM, was the director and later directed memorable films such as *The Wizard of Oz* and *Gone With the Wind*. Location shooting was scheduled for 35 days, with a 70-day shooting schedule.

The *Test Pilot* Story Line

The plot line is about two simple love stories and how they interact. One is the love of a woman and the second is the love of flying. California-based Drake Aviation, headed up by Mr. Drake, has a new pursuit aircraft named the "Drake Bullet", well-played by the Seversky P-35.

Seversky P-35 and Clark Gable, the "Stars" of *Test Pilot*

His ace test pilot Jim Lane is forced to land on a Kansas farm while trying to break a cross country speed record. The farm is owned by the Barton family, and Ann Barton, the daughter, comes out to meet Jim. Ann and Jim are immediately attracted to each other.

They spend the day together while waiting for Jim's friend and mechanic, Gunner Morse, to arrive and repair the plane. Although Jim

and Ann have a good time together, Ann announces her engagement that evening to a local sweetheart.

The next day Jim leaves but soon comes back, and he and Ann fly off together to get married. Mr. Drake and Gunner are surprised and annoyed at the marriage and Drake considers that marriage and aircraft testing are not compatible. However, Jim's love of flying keeps him in the business of flight testing and he continues his fun-loving highjinks on the ground. He narrowly escapes death in one plane he is testing while Ann watches. They attend the Cleveland Air Races, and a friend of Jim's is killed, leaving behind a wife and child. Ann is horrified, but Jim goes out during the evening and gets gloriously drunk. Ann tells Gunner that she will stick with him, no matter what and so Jim keeps flying, blissfully ignorant of the devastating effect that his recklessness has on both Ann and his best friend Gunner.

Myrna Loy, Clark Gable and the P-35 (Photo Credit: www.doctormacro.com)

On a flight to test the new B-17 Flying Fortress bomber, Gunner rides along to help. The plane reaches 30,000 feet, but suddenly goes into a spin. The sand bags used to simulate bombs break loose and pin Gunner down. Jim finally straightens the plane out, but it is too late to avoid a crash. Gunner is killed in the crash, and Jim is devastated.

When Jim arrives home, he is confronted by an almost hysterical Ann, saying that she wishes that Jim had died. They are separated, and Jim decides to quit flying. He goes to Drake's office, and Drake convinces him that he loves Ann, and calls Ann to tell her Jim will come to see her. The two are reconciled. In the last scene of the movie, Jim is seen on the tarmac addressing the actual 2nd Bombardment Group pilots in front of a line of nine B-17s. The B-17s then take off and the final scene of the movie shows Jim watching as they pass in formation with Ann proudly present with their young son.

Film Facts

According to Dr. Macro's High Quality Movie Scans on *Test Pilot*, the title *Test Pilot* was first announced by MGM in 1933. Jean Harlow, Wallace Beery, and Jimmy Durante were to star in the film with Clark Gable. The film was to be filmed partially on location at Wright Field in Dayton, OH, by special permission from the U. S. War Department. On February 1, 1936, a Hollywood Review news item noted that MGM was buying the story *Test Pilot* by Frank "Spig" Wead to be adapted for a film for Clark Gable. Wead had been a naval aviator and ace pilot until injured in a fall and was a paraplegic, but he nevertheless was given the task of writing the screenplay for which he received an Academy Award nomination.

On January 2, 1938, the following story appeared in the *Daily Press* newspaper, Newport News, VA, which routinely covered news from Langley Field:

"SCENES FOR HOLLYWOOD FILM RECORDED AT LANGLEY FIELD

Atmosphere scenes to be used in Metro-Goldwyn-Mayer's screen production Test Pilot, starring Clark Gable, Myrna Loy and Spencer Tracy were "shot" last week at the Peninsula airdrome. A group of ten photographers and technicians from the Hollywood company have been active at the local base several days, making scenes both on land and in air. In the scene at top the cameras record one of the scenes to be used in the film. The persons in white are enlisted men at Langley, dressed in uniforms of the "Drake Aircraft Corp, loading sandbags on one of the giant four-engined flying fortress bombers, preparing it for Clark Gable who is supposed to pilot it on a "test flight" in the picture. Larry Williams, first cameraman, is silhouetted near the picture machine in the foreground. His assistant is George Welstead. Included in the group on the platform in the background where another camera is located are Cullen Tate, director of the unit; Jack Smith, born near Norfolk, director of photography; Don Brigham, Smith's assistant, and Jack Doran, Tate's assistant.

The "men in white" (below) await their turn at loading the sandbags into the bomber while Director Tate (with dark glasses) looks the situation over. The hangar of the National Advisory Committee for Aeronautics is in the background. Much time was consumed in the shooting of the above scenes Friday, the troupe bring forced to stall for correct lighting effect. Other members of the party were Cooper Smith, operating cameraman, Eddie Bagley, still photographer, and Pop Arnold, known as the "grip" or handyman. Clark Gable (left) who plays an important part in the picture, was not with the unit at Langley. His "double" in the person of Sid Troy, who bears a striking resemblance to the "Hollywood heartbreaker," was on location here. The scenes at Langley were made in conjunction with army officials during routine training." [2]

The remainder of the film was shot at different locations in southern California, including Chino, Van Nuys Municipal Airport, Mines Field Metro Airport (now Los Angeles International), and Union Air Terminal, Lindbergh Field in San Diego, and March Field where the final scenes were shot.

Paul Mantz, a famous dare devil and movie stunt pilot of the time, acted as a technical advisor on airplane scenes in the film. He was sent to Cleveland with a film crew to research and film scenes from the famous Cleveland Air Races and several scenes from actual Races were included in the film. At least eighteen cameras including ground and air cameras were used in the filming bringing realism to a new level.

Some reviews of the film say the story was based on the life of James (Jimmy) Collins who died in an airplane crash in 1935 similar to the Benson Cleveland Air Race crash in the film. Collins wrote a book *Test Pilot* before his death, and his widow sued MGM over rights to the story, but the suit was eventually dismissed[3]. *Life* Magazine noted that parts of the film were made at March Field, and the B-17 crash in the film was based on the crash of Boeing's Model 299 at Wright Field.

The film was previewed simultaneously at Westwood and New York City in April, 1938, and opened to the public the next day. MGM did not expect much praise of the film, but Clark Gable and Myrna Loy had just been voted "King" and "Queen" of Hollywood, and Spencer Tracy had just received an Oscar for his work in *Captains Courageous*. The film received very good reviews and was nominated for three Academy awards. Robert Taylor and Rita Hayworth did a stage adaptation of the film on May 25, 1942. The movie was one of the fifteen top grossing films of 1938 and was voted the best picture at the Venice Film Festival in 1938.[4]

Gable and the Army Air Corps in WWII

Clark Gable was not finished with his relationship with the Army Air Corps or with the B-17 after completion of the filming of *Test Pilot*. His most successful picture, *Gone With the Wind*, was released in 1939, and in that same year, he married his third wife, the successful American actress Carole Lombard. On January 16, 1942, Lombard was a passenger on Trans-World Airlines Flight 3 and was on her way home from a successful war bond selling tour when the DC-3 crashed into a mountain near Las Vegas, NV, killing all aboard, including Lombard's mother, and her MGM staff publicist Otto Winkler (who had been the best man at Gable's wedding to Lombard). Lombard was declared to be the first war-related American female casualty of World War II, and Gable received a personal condolence note from President Roosevelt. The Civil Aeronautics Board investigation into the crash concluded that "pilot error" was its cause.[5]

Gable made a public statement after Lombard's death that prompted Commanding General of the Army Air Forces Henry H. Arnold to offer Gable a "special assignment" in aerial gunnery. Gable had earlier expressed an interest in Officer Candidate School (OCS), but he enlisted on August 12, 1942, with the intention of becoming an enlisted air crew gunner. MGM arranged for his studio friend, cinematographer Andrew McIntyre, to enlist with and accompany him through training. However, shortly after his enlistment, he and McIntyre were sent to Miami Beach, FL, where they entered USAAF OCS Class 42-E on August 17, 1942. Both completed training on October 28, 1942, and were commissioned as second lieutenants. His class of 2,600 fellow students (of which he ranked 700th in class standing) selected Gable as their graduation speaker, at which General Arnold presented them their commissions. Co-author Bill Braxton was also a member of that OCS class and remembers Gable's time there:

"I enlisted in the Army in 1935, and served as an infantryman at Forts Clayton and Sherman in the Canal Zone. It did not take me long to determine that even in a depression, I could do better—and I did. Returning to the Army as private in the Air Corps, I managed to work my way up to Warrant Officer Status, and eventually was selected for Officer Candidate School (OCS) and was ordered to Miami Beach in 1942, a nice place to undergo training to say the least.

"The relatively tough and intense training was made more interesting when it was reported that movie star Clark Gable was also going to be undergoing OCS training following the death of his wife movie star Carol Lombard. Naturally, there was a lot of publicity surrounding his enlistment in the Air Corps and subsequent selection to OCS. It must be said that a lot of special conditions were put in place to accommodate the star, but he did not cut corners because of his stardom.

"All of us wanted to see this national celebrity and movie star Gable at Miami Beach, but there were more than 2000 men undergoing OCS training at Miami Beach, and if you were lucky, you only saw him when his squadron passed in review every Saturday morning when we had a parade for the public.

"About a month after I reported in at Miami Beach, I had to go to sick call for an earache, a fairly common ailment in the tropical Miami Beach. While I was sitting in the waiting room in the typical military processing for Sick Call, who was there but Clark Gable. As a testimony to his wholehearted efforts to prove his mettle, he was suffering from foot blisters. Here I was sitting next to one of the most famous movie stars of the time, and had a half hour conversation with him, sharing stories of our trials and tribulations in OCS. It was easy to be comfortable, because he really did not look like that famous movie star—His hair and trademark mustache had been shaved off on entrance to training.

"On graduation day, we had a typical large military parade, with Army Air Corps General Hap Arnold and Queen Wilhelmina of Holland, along with a number of Washington VIPs wishing to share the spotlight. In what I am sure was break from tradition, graduate Clark Gable gave the graduation address.

"After graduation, the administrative process ground along, and each day we graduates would report to see if we had received our orders. On the third day, my orders came through, and as I was picking them up, I once again ran into Gable, and I asked him where he was going. He responded that he was headed to gunnery school. I thought that was strange as it was for enlisted personnel. He said he had received special permission from General Arnold to attend the school, and that he wanted to get into combat as soon as possible. Next thing I heard after I reported to Langley Field was that he was flying missions with the 8th AF over Europe".[6]

Lt Clark Gable at Gunnery School (Photo Credit www. doctormacro.com)

Arnold then informed Gable of his special assignment, to make a recruiting film in combat with the Eighth Air Force to recruit gunners and Gable and McIntyre were immediately sent to Flexible Gunnery School at Tyndall Field, FL, followed by a photography course at Fort George Wright, WA, and promoted to first lieutenants upon completion.

Gable reported to Biggs Army Air Base on January 27, 1943, to train with and accompany the 351st Bomb Group to England as head of a six-man motion picture unit. Gable spent most of the war in the United Kingdom at RAF Polebrook with the 351st and flew five combat missions, including one to Germany, as an observer-gunner in the B-17 between May 4th and September 23, 1943, earning the Air Medal and the Distinguished Flying Cross for his efforts.

Records of the 351st Bomb Group Crew Member Search Page[6] show the following Gable missions:

MSN NUMBER	DATE	AIRCRAFT	TARGET	COMMENTS
13	26 JUNE 1943	B-17 42-29948	VILLACOUBAY	CLOUD COVER
26	12 AUG 1943	B17 42-29863	BOCHUM, DE	STEEL MILL
38	9 SEPT 1943	B-17 42-29825	LILLE-NORDE	AERODROME
41	23 SEPT 1943	B-17 42-29925	NANTES, FR	PORT FAC

Clark gable's Actual Combat Missions

Not your typical WWII Hollywood star participation in the war effort.

Clark Gable in England with B-17 Crews

During one of the missions, Gable's aircraft was damaged by flak and attacked by fighters, which knocked out one of the engines and shot up the stabilizer. In the raid on Germany, one crewman was killed and two others were wounded, and flak went through Gable's boot and narrowly missed his head. When word of this reached MGM, studio executives began to badger the U.S. Army Air Corps to reassign their valuable screen property to non-combat duty. In November 1943, he returned to the United States to edit the film, only to find that the personnel shortage of aerial gunners had already been rectified.

In May 1944, Gable was promoted to Maj. He hoped for another combat assignment but, when D-Day came and passed in June without further orders, he requested and was granted a discharge. His discharge papers were signed by a captain and president-to-be named Ronald Reagan.

He completed editing of the film, *Combat America*, in September 1944, providing the narration himself and making use of numerous interviews with enlisted gunners as focus of the film.

1. Newport News, VA *Daily Press*, January 28, 1938
2. www.drmacro.com// Test Pilot
3. ibid
4. *Clark Gable: A Biography*. Harris, Warren G New York: (2002). Harmony. ISBN 0609604953
5. *From the Cockpit to the Classroom*, LtCol Bill Braxton
6. 351st.org/loadlist/search

EPILOGUE

Was the "Bomber Mafia" right in their assessment of the supremacy of strategic bombing being a deciding factor in the outcome of wars of the future? Was the promise of the early Y1B-17 performance translated to proven ability to bring the war to the enemy in the sustained force envisioned? The answer can be found in the final compilations of WWII statistics.

Prior to the attack on Pearl Harbor, there were fewer than 200 B-17s in service with the Army, with a total 155 B-17s of all variants delivered between 11 January 1937 and 30 November 1941. Although other WWII aircraft were produced in greater numbers, the production of B-17s accelerated and eventually set the record for achieving the highest production rate for large aircraft. The aircraft went on to serve in every World War II combat zone, and when production ended in May 1945, 12,731 aircraft had been built by Boeing, Douglas, and Vega (a subsidiary of Lockheed). Ask almost anyone today to name an aircraft that epitomized WWII airpower and they will say "Mustang" or the "The Flying Fortress".

During WWII, 148,934 planes were delivered to the Army Air Forces in four years, and they flew in more than 2,360,000 combat sorties and dropped 2,000,000 tons of bombs. 40,000 enemy planes were destroyed. There was a cost of some $37 billion, 23,000 lost planes and 122,819 airman wounded, missing, or dead. 38 flyers of WWII were awarded the Medal of Honor.

Sheer numbers do not measure effectiveness, but the industrial might of the United States did produce an unheard of numbers of aircraft, and air power would never again be questioned. The visionaries of the "Bomber Mafia" did not just focus on the build of aircraft, its weaponry and how to employ it; they knew that support was essential. The creation of the Ferry Command, the Materials Command, and the Training Command fell on the shoulders of many of these men, and few were found wanting.

Those who led in the winning of WWII had the strategic vision that was honed in difficult economic and internationally chaotic times, unbowed by pressures from within and without, and developed the operational doctrines upon which we rely heavily today. The B-17 formed an unforgettable and legendary foundation for the future of airpower to build upon.

APPENDICES

APPENDIX A

ARMY DOUGLAS CRUISER WORLD FLIGHT ITINERARY

	DATE	PLACE	MILES	TIME	
				HOURS	MINUTES
April	6	Seattle to Prince Rupert, B.C.	650	8	10
	10	Sitka, Alaska	282	4	26
	13	Seward, Alaska	625	7	44
	15	Chignik, Alaska	425	6	38
	19	Dutch Harbor, Alaska	390	7	26
May	3	Nazan, Atka	365	4	19
	9	Chicagof, Attu	555	7	52
	15	Komandorski Islands	350	5	25
		Day Lost—180th Meridian			
	17	Paramushiru, Japan	585	6	55
	19	Hitokappu, Yetorofu, Japan	595	7	20
	22	Minato, Japan	485	5	5
		Kasumigaura, Japan	350	4	55
June	1	Kushimoto, Japan	305	4	35
	2	Kagoshima, Japan	360	6	11
	4	Shanghai, China	550	9	10

	7	Tchinkoen Bay, China	350	4	30
		Amoy, China	250	2	47
	8	Hong Kong	310	3	24
	10	Haiphong, French Indo-China	495	7	26
	11	Tourane, French Indo-China	410	6	5
	16	Saigon, French Indo-China	540	7	58
	18	Kampongsong Bay, Fr. Indo-China	295	4	28
		Bangkok, Siam	290	4	2
	20	Tavoy, Burma	200	3	55
		Rangoon, Burma	295	3	8
	25	Akyab, Burma	480	5	38
	26	Chittagong, Burma	180	2	10
		Calcutta, India	265	3	17
July	1	Allahbad, India	450	6	30
	2	Ambala, India	480	6	25
	3	Multan, India	360	5	45
	4	Karachi, India	455	7	8
	7	Chahbar, Persia	410	4	50
		Bandar Abbas, Persia	365	4	5
	8	Bushire, Persia	390	4	5
		Baghdad, Mesopotamia	530	6	30
	9	Aleppo, Syria	450	6	10
	10	Constantinople, Turkey	560	7	38
	12	Bucharest, Rumania	350	4	40
	13	Budapest, Hungary	465	6	50
	14	Strasbourg, France	500	6	30
		Paris, France	250	3	55
	16	London, England	215	3	7
	17	Brough, England	165	1	55
	30	Kirkwall, Orkney Islands	450	5	30
August	2	Hornafjord, Iceland	555		
		New Orleans		9	3
		Chicago		6	13

	5	Reykjavik, Iceland	290	5	3
	21	Fredericksdal, Greenland	830		
		Chicago		10	40
		New Orleans		11	17
	24	Ivigtut, Greenland	165	2	12
	31	Icy Tickle, Labrador	560	6	55
September	2	Hawkes Bay, Newfoundland	315	4	56
	3	Pictou Harbor, Nova Scotia	430	6	34
	5	Mere Point, Maine	450	6	5
	6	Boston, Massachusetts	100	2	8
	8	New York, N.Y.	220	3	40
	9	Aberdeen, Maryland	160	3	38
		Washington, DC	70	1	5
	13	Dayton, Ohio	400	6	43
	15	Chicago, Illinois	245	2	58
	16	Omaha, Nebraska	430	4	48
	18	St. Joseph, Missouri	110	1	48
		Muskogee, Oklahoma	270	3	53
	19	Dallas, Texas	254	3	45
	20	Sweetwater, Texas	210	3	6
		El Paso, Texas	390	6	18
	22	San Diego, California	390	4	3
	23	Los Angeles, California	115	1	25
	25	San Francisco, California	365	5	5
	27	Eugene, Oregon	420	5	20
	28	Vancouver Barracks, Washington	90	1	8
		Seattle, Washington	150	1	43

APPENDIX B

CELESTIAL NAVIGATION USING THE BUBBLE SEXTANT

So what is so hard about taking that "celestial observation" we have discussed frequently during the proving of the Y1B-17's capabilities? Recall first that pilots were expected to attain proficiency in celestial navigation as part of their "tool kit", as it is called today. No rated navigators existed at the time and most pilots had no experience in instrument "blind flying" or in long range navigation. Then imagine aircraft with no dedicated station for the navigator to ply his trade. Even the first Y1B-17s had him located behind the bomb bay with no viable way to take a "sight" with his sextant, forcing him to clamber around the ship until the celestial body could be observed from some "window". Combine that with the lack of sophisticated methods to take a "sight" while advancing at 200 mph and the problem can be seen to become a bit more difficult by today's standards. Aeronautical charts were scarce for most parts of the world, and pilot/navigators created their own from standard plotting sheets.

"Reducing" a Sight—Obtaining a Line of Position

Some Definitions

To understand the basics of a celestial sight reduction, a short dissertation on the terminology is necessary. First, the Earth is considered a perfect sphere with the stars spread about on a fictitious celestial sphere surrounding the Earth. The stars are fixed upon the sphere in relation to each other and thus are called fixed stars and 57 of them are considered bright enough for use in celestial navigation. In actuality, the fixed stars do move, but so slowly that only study of an almanac would reveal it. Planets move among the fixed stars and include Mercury, Venus, Mars, Jupiter, Saturn, the Moon, and the Sun. They confine themselves to a band that extends 8° on either side of the ecliptic, the apparent path that the sun follows through the sky. The ecliptic is tilted relative to the Earth's equator due to the tilt of the Earth's axis.

Positions on Earth are measured in latitude, from 0° at the equator to 90° north and south at the poles, and longitude, running from pole to pole and measured from 0° at the Greenwich meridian (another term for line of longitude) to 180° east and west. Positions on the celestial sphere have corresponding latitiude and longitude: The celestial equator is projected out from the Earth's equator, and its latitude is called <u>declination</u> measured north and south from it to the celestial poles at 90°; Longitude on the celestial sphere is called <u>hour angle</u>, and is measured west through 360° from the starting point. The starting point marks where the Sun crosses the celestial equator in the spring, the vernal equinox, and the angle from it to a celestial body is called the sidereal hour angle, or SHA.

The Basic Concept

If you assume you are standing on the Earth, and looking at one of the navigational stars directly above you, with the known time, you can use the Nautical Almanac (Hydrographic Office publication, or HO 249) to find the position of the star on the celestial sphere, and then the position of the spot directly beneath it on the Earth. That's your location. In this situation, if you measured the angle between the horizon and the star using a sextant, it would be 90°. The line of position (LOP) for a star at an angular altitude of 90° is in fact a dot, called the geographic position, or GP.

Keeping this picture in mind, step back until the angle of the star above the horizon is 89°. The LOP in this case is a small circle around the GP; someone standing anywhere on this circle would get the same measurement of 89°. This circular LOP is also called a circle of equal altitude. Now back up quite a bit to get a good-sized circle and the measured angle is 60°. The LOP now is a much larger circle on the Earth. If we now observe another star at the same time as the first, and its angle measure is

40° above the horizon. There's another large LOP around its GP and the two circles intersect at two points. Anyone standing at either of the two intersections would get the same altitude readings of the two stars. One of the intersections might be on land and the other in mid-ocean thousands of miles away, so it's pretty easy to decide which intersection shows your position. In practice, a third star is measured to resolve the ambiguity; where all three circles intersect is your fix. How do we obtain these circles, or LOPs?

The Bubble Sextant

Since the relatively ancient seagoing sextant was unusable aboard an aircraft, primarily because of the lack of a visible horizon, it was necessary to create one which would provide an artificial horizon (the bubble) and average altitude over a two minute period to accommodate inherent variations, thus complicating the fixing of the position. At a groundspeed of 200 mph, the plane will travel 3.3 statute miles in two minutes. Assuming a two minute period between each observation, it may take as long as 10 minutes between the first and last sight, or more that 30 miles. Little room for error.

So with our trusty bubble sextant, we've managed to take our "sight" and we've plotted celestial LOP which is a line upon which the aircraft must have been at the time the observation was made. Two LOPs are needed for fix, of course, and three to five are more accurate. So we choose more "bodies" and repeat the procedure. We must decide upon an Assumed Position (it will be different for each star observed), perform the calculations from the HO Pub and plot the LOP. Where they intersect would be the fix, although since the aircraft can be moving at hundreds of miles per hour, each LOP will need to be <u>advanced or retarded</u> with the DR before the final fix is determined.

The Proof is in the Pudding

Curtis LeMay and his acolytes were put to the test on their many goodwill flights and joint exercises, and through extensive efforts, made celestial navigation a routine accomplishment and an adjunct to the successful demonstration of the Y1B-17's superior capabilities. Their destiny was literally in the stars.

Appendix C

Langley Field Thanksgiving Menu 1935

Thanksgiving
1936

Base Headquarters
and
First Air Base Squadron
Langley Field, Virginia

Dinner

FRIUT PUNCH

STUFFED OLIVES   SWEET MIXED PICKLES

HEARTS OF CELERY

ROAST MARYLAND TURKEY

COLD ROAST PORK

GIBLET GRAVY   CRANBERRY SAUCE

OYSTER DRESSING

CANDIED YAMS   SNOW WHITE POTATOES

BUTTERED GREEN PEAS   ASSORTED BREADS

LETTUCE SALAD

PUMPKIN PIE   MINCE PIE

ASSORTED LAYER CAKE

ASSORTED ICE CREAM

APPLES   ORANGES   BANANAS

CALIFORNIA GRAPES

MIXED NUTS

CIGARS   CIGARETTES

COFFEE

Roster

COLONEL
Weaver, Walter R.

LIEUTENANT COLONELS
Bender, Walter Guidera, Albert M

MAJORS
Mathis, Paul J. Hutchison, James T.
Temple, John P. Salisbury, Glenn C.
Carey, Edwin F. Moon, Odas
Melansen, Arthur J. Stoner, Rex K.

CAPTAINS
Greer, Jack Hillery, Edward A.
Drumm, John A. Fisher, Ralph E.
Ramsay, David M.

FIRST LIEUTENANTS
Lacey, Julius K. Hockenberry, Earle W. Zimmerman, Joseph B

SECOND LIEUTENANTS
Coursey, Harry Totten, James W

MASTER SERGEANTS
Arnold, William Hixson, William A. Rose, Harry

TECHNICAL SERGEANTS
Ballon, John G. Courtwright, Thos. W. Hutcrens, Peyton E.
Berend, Victor Downing, Harrvey J. McKinstry, Robert F.
Bergman, Henry A. Hopper, Walter S. Rooney, Logan J.
Camire, Henry Hughes, Raymond J.

STAFF SERGEANTS
Ash, Ashby M. Jernigan, William H. Shortridge, M. R.
Bernatchez, A. P. Jutras, Bruno Skidmore, F. J.
Chalk, Sigmund B. Killian, Wiley Smith, Lawrence
Cheatham, Roy D. Lash, Paul Speece, Elmer
Cross, Charles M. McCarthy, John I. Tyler, Fred O.
Ducheane, Joseph O. Michael, Edward Weeks, Alvin C.
Griffis, Isaac Selvey, Eston E. White, Roy.
Hallowell, Rodney G.

SERGEANTS
Adams, Elwood Hargis, Charlie T. Morano, Frank
Bearly, Floyd A. Harris, Gordon A. Oppelt, Joseph L.
Benson, Joseph Harvey, J. Addison Potvin, Alphonse
Byrd, Baus C. Johns, Charles A. Schady, Andrew R.
Cale, Allen E. Johnson, Dayton R. Schode, Martin
Clark, Gibson H. Lasky, William Shemph, Alexander

Roster-Continued

CORPORALS

Boynton, Bernice L.
Burton, Jesse K.
Gerehart, Gilbert C.
Grubb, Edward
Haxson, Harvey D.
Ketcham, Leonard W.
Klopp, Ira
Knaub, Luther R.
Kump, Mathew
McAdams, Samuel A.

McGraw, Jerome R.
Matheson, Samuel J.
Moyer, Clarence M.
Nelson, James F.
Nestor, Leslie M.
Payton, Luther
Petroski, Frank
Purcell, Edward J.
Ramsey, William H.
Ray, Harry
Schov, Ernest C.

Sinclair, Arthur W.
Spraker, Grover K.
Steel, Edward D.
Stinnette, Aubrey L.
Straneva, Mike
Sutton, Joe H.
Tyndall, Thurman
Vetrano, John
Walker, Ransom D.
Zayac, Jacob
Todd, Mahlon

PRIVATES FIRST CLASS

Adkins, Asa O.
Anderson, Benj. H.
Anderson, Charles F.
Anderson, Dennis J.
Barnes, Jessie C.
Barnhart, Clarenre L.
Batts, Charlie C.
Bell, Harry F.
Berger, Adolph A.
Bolvin, Anthony E.
Bradley, Clyde W.
Brewster, John R.
Brumfield, Henry A.
Butts, Thomas K.
Caine, Ezra J.
Camper, William T.
Carlson, Ned H.
Carpenter, Warren W.
Carter, Raymond D.
Church, Cecil G.
Clark, Harold W.
Covert, Harry M.
Cummings, Menelaus
Davis, John G.
Dolan, Thomas J.
Edwards, Preston A.
Frank, Joseph J.
Frazier, James A.
Gable, Richard H.
Garrison, Robert E.
Gibbs, Sidney A.
Gilliland, Gilbert L.
Goldsmith, Roy T.
Goodwin, Walter J.

Griffin, Benj. F.
Grimm, Walter L.
Handforth, Chas. W.
Heape, Wm. C. D.
Heaton, Norris M.
Henderson, Lewis N.
Hill, Wilbur D.
Hite, Glenn W.
Holloran, Chesley H.
Holloway, John J.
Howe, Morgan M.
Huffman, Vernon W.
Hutchko, Joseph
Jeffries, Raymond B.
Jones, Joseph H.
Kaczor, John F.
Kasper, John F.
Kazmiersky, W. P.
Kennedy, Walter A.
King, Frank P.
Klobutscheck, H. C.
Lange, William V.
Lester, Kella E.
Loughery, Geo. W.
MacVicar, Girard E.
McLaughlin, Paul E.
Marion, John A.
Marlett, William T.
Marsh, Edwin F., Jr.
Mason, Herbert W.
Matthews, Calvin M.
Mann, Clyde E.
Meltz, Frank K.
Mort, Clyde O.

Peters, Charles E.
Peterson, Earl M.
Petty, Thomas N.
Phelps, Norvell D.
Polan, Arthur
Price, Gilroy
Proffitt, Wm. J., Jr.
Puzenski, Aloysius B.
Raymond, Harry A.
Rill, Kenneth E.
Roberts, Edgar E.
Robertson, Julius D.
Rountree, Harvey W.
Russell, Peter G.
Schilling, Stephen F.
Schubert, Earl
Shank, Anthony J.
Simmons, James P.
Smith, Eugene G.
Smith, I. A.
Stallings, Peter M., Jr.
Stephenson, Louis J.
Thorpe, Elmer E.
Tomlin, Leslie W.
Vanderwall, Jay J.
Villard, Simon
Ward, Howard W.
Ware, James T., Jr.
Warren, William H.
Welty, Marion E.
Westbrook, Alex
Whitaker, John R., Jr.
Youells, Lyle L.
Zilotti, William G.

PRIVATES

Adams, David W.	Cooley, Marvin G.	Gezzi, Joseph
Allstock, A. G., Jr.	Corbett, Larry	George, Thomas B
Allen, Francis P.	Corinchock, Michael	Gillie, Carl
Andrews, Ralph F.	Cours, Joseph R. A.	Goodhart, Donald W
Anskie, Charles	Cox, Norman L.	Gordon, James M.
Atkins, William T.	Crane, John B.	Gordon, Julian E.
Barksdale, James M.	Cressman, Harry R.	Gorski, Walter V.
Baughan, Clarence R.	Crisham, Thomas D.	Grannell, Charles A.
Baum, Carl W.	Crittenden, W. W.	Green, Joseph
Beattie, John S.	Croak, Lee M.	Griffith, Herbert M.
Beckage, Elmer	Croushore, John L.	Halas, Elmer J.
Beeman, Wayne H.	Crowl, William N.	Hall, Edward L.
Biltheiser, Joseph W.	Crumley, Eugene A.	Hamre, Helge O.
Birk, Fritz	Dalman, Thomas J.	Hankey, Victor H.
Bitner, John D., Jr.	Davis, James T.	Hardtke, Kenneth W.
Black, Miran R.	Dunleavy, Donald W.	Harris, Milton W.
Blasco, Albert	Dayton, Clarence B.	Harrison, George W.
Blumenthal, Thos. H.	Dell'Orto, Frank	Hartsock, Robert L.
Boblett, Willard L.	DeLong, Harold J.	Hicks, John E.
Bolyard, Alden L.	Dickty, Walter L.	Hill, Oscar C.
Bones, Robert	Diehl, Lester W.	Hinebaugh, Joseph G.
Bonner, William P.	Dill, Clarence D.	Hinnant, Archie L.
Borden, George	Dillon, Walter W.	Hirth, Peter J.
Bowers, Crawford L.	DiMaio, Rito M.	Hoffmayer, Joseph G.
Boyles, Clarence W.	Doan, Raybert H.	Holby, Earl H.
Braxton, Leon E.	Dolan, Douglas W.	Huddleston, V. M.
Brennan, C. W., Jr.	Dotson, Otis E.	Hudik, Paul
Brewer, Allen L.	Drakeley, Horace J.	Humphries, J. L., Jr.
Brown, James W., Jr.	Dreher, Earl	Hunsicker, E. L., J-
Brubaker, Vincil	Duble, Carl E.	Hurd, Clarence A
Bunnel, William C.	Dvorshak, Sheldon F.	Hurlbut, Wayne D
Burkett, C. E., Jr.	Earley, Joseph E.	Hyde, Lawrence G.
Bunn, Elmer L.	Edgar, Herbert T.	Irvin, William P.
Butler, Fenton H.	Elliott, Dave W., Jr.	Johnson, John H.
Callahan, Edward M.	Engelman, Daniel W.	Jones, Richard B.
Callahan, John D.	Erickson, Robert L.	Jurkus, Anthony W.
Carpenter, John	Ester, Otis O.	Kahanick, Michael
Carter, Robt. B., Jr.	Faircloth, Carl E.	Keene, James W.
Casper, Joseph F.	Favere, Jess P.	Keene, Worth L.
Casterline, Wm. H.	Ferraro, Alfred W.	Kelley, Jacob P.
Chaney, Herbert L.	Finch, Grant A.	Kerley, Kenneth E.
Cheatham, Charlie	Fitch, Edward R.	Kimmel, E. R.
Chester, John A.	Foxx, Edward W.	Kimmel, Thompson J
Chieffo, Frank R.	Freeman, Euris H.	King, Jesse P.
Cicerone, Angelo J.	Fulcher, John B.	Kline, John D.
Clark, Robert E.	Galloway, Bernon L.	Kline, John M.
Clarke, David D.	Gans, Mike	Knight, Harry B.
	Gasinski, Adam	Koering, Ambrose L

APPENDIX D

2ND Bombardment Group Operations Plan for Buenos Aires Trip

(Obtained from the AF HRA Facilities at Maxwell AFB, AL)

HEADQUARTERS
2ND BOMBARDMENT GROUP, GHQ AIR FORCE
OFFICE OF THE OPERATIONS OFFICER
LANGLEY FIELD, VIRGINIA

February 11, 1938.

PLAN FOR 2ND BOMBARDMENT GROUP FLIGHT

TO

BUENOS AIRES, ARGENTINA AND RETURN

1. ADMINISTRATION:

Command and Staff

Commanding Officer: Lieut. Col. Robert Olds, Air Corps,
S-1 and Finance: Captain Cornelius W. Cousland, Air Corps,
S-2: 1st Lieut. David R. Gibbs, Air Corps,
S-3: Captain Robert B. Williams, Air Corps,
Asst S-3: 1st Lieut. Curtis E. LeMay, Air Corps,
S-4 and Engineering: Major Edwin R. McReynolds, Air Corps,
Asst S-4 and Engineering: 1st Lieut. Thomas L. Mosley, Air Corps,
Communications: 1st Lieut. Edwin L. Tucker, Air Corps,
Mess and Billeting: 1st Lieut. Richard S. Freeman, Air Corps,
Metro Service: 1st Lieut. Torgils G. Wold, Air Corps.

Combat Crews

HQ & HQ SQ, 2D BOMB GP, GHQ-AF

Y1B-17 Airplane, AC No. 36-155 (#10)
Lieut. Colonel ROBERT OLDS, Air Corps,
Major EDWIN R. McREYNOLDS, Air Corps,
Captain ROBERT B. WILLIAMS, Air Corps,
1st Lieut. EDWIN L. TUCKER, Air Corps,
1st Lieut. JOHN W. EGAN, Air Corps,
Staff Sgt. JAMES J. DOUTTY, 6127954, Hq & Hq Sq, 2d Bomb Gp,
GHQ Air Force,
Pfc. ARCHIE R. JESTER, 6814390, Hq & Hq Sq, 2d Bomb Gp, GHQ
Air Force,
Pfc. JOSEPH H. WALSH, 6836218, Hq & Hq Sq, 2d Bomb Gp, GHQ
Air Force,
Pvt. KENNETH E. TROUT, 6846396, Hq & Hq Sq, 2d Bomb Gp, GHQ
Air Force.

20TH BOMBARDMENT SQUADRON, GHQ-AF

Y1B-17 Airplane, AC No. 36-156, (#1)
Major VINCENT J. MELOY, Air Corps,
Captain ALV. L. HARVEY, Air Corps,

RT8

UF4

11

- 1 -

1st Lieut. FREDERIC S. GLANTZBERG, Air Corps,
1st Lieut. TORGILS G. WOLD, Air Corps,
Sgt. JACK A. FRANSKE, 6606254, 20th Bombardment Squadron, GHQ
Air Force,
Staff Sgt. HENRY L. WEST, 6036814, 20th Bombardment Squadron,
GHQ Air Force,
Pfc. JOHN T. YANKOWSKY, 6641086, 20th Bombardment Squadron,
GHQ Air Force,
Corp. CLARENCE D. LACE, 6728329, 20th Bombardment Squadron,
GHQ Air Force.

YIB-17 Airplane, AC No. 36-159 (#52)
Captain NEIL B. HARDING, Air Corps,
1st Lieut. DAVID R. GIBBS, Air Corps,
1st Lieut. GERALD E. WILLIAMS, Air Corps,
1st Lieut. RALPH E. KOON, Air Corps,
Tech Sgt. BESOLA COBB, R-52484, 20th Bombardment Squadron,
GHQ Air Force,
Sgt. LEWIS HAYDUKE, 6788912, 20th Bombardment Squadron, GHQ
Air Force,
Pfc. HAROLD J. NYCUM, 6854183, 20th Bombardment Squadron, GHQ
Air Force,
Pvt. FREDERICK W. WOITHECK, 6389590, 20th Bombardment Squadron, GHQ Air Force.

49TH BOMBARDMENT SQUADRON, GHQ-AF

YIB-17 Airplane, AC No. 36-151 (#50)
Major CALEB V. HAYNES, Air Corps,
1st Lieut. THOMAS L. MOSLEY, Air Corps,
1st Lieut. CURTIS E. LE MAY, Air Corps,
2nd Lieut. JOSEPH B. STANLEY, Air Corps,
Tech Sgt. ADOLPH CATTARIUS, R-1230233, 49th Bombardment Squadron, GHQ Air Force,
Staff Sgt. WILLIAM J. HELDT, 6440692, 49th Bombardment Squadron, GHQ Air Force,
Corp. JAMES E. SANDS, 6839814, 49th Bombardment Squadron, GHQ
Air Force,
Pfc. DONALD F. LOONEY, 6830627, 49th Bombardment Squadron,
GHQ Air Force.

YIB-17 Airplane, AC No. 36-158 (#82)
Captain ARCHIBALD Y. SMITH, Air Corps,
Captain CORNELIUS W. COUSLAND, Air Corps,
1st Lieut. RICHARD S. FREEMAN, Air Corps,
1st Lieut. JOHN A. SAMFORD, Air Corps,
Sgt. GEORGE R. CHARLTON, 6648734, 49th Bombardment Squadron,
GHQ Air Force,
Pfc. RUSSELL E. JUNIOR, 6644912, 49th Bombardment Squadron,
GHQ Air Force,
Staff Sgt. TROY V. MARTIN, 6207265, 49th Bombardment Squadron,
GHQ Air Force,
Staff Sgt. HENRY P. HANSEN, R-1038111, 49th Bombardment Squadron, GHQ Air Force.

- 2 -

Uniform Cont'd.

    (2) Ground wear:

       (a) Officers:

          Daytime:
              Barracks caps.
              Wool O.D. blouse and slacks.
              Cotton O.D. shirts.

          Evening:
              FORMAL:
              White mess jackets.
              Black trousers.
              White caps.
              Dress shirt with collar attached.
              (Note: Insignia on mess jacket will consist of
              following: Group insignia on each lapel; min-
              iature gold wing on left just below Group insig-
              nia.)

              INFORMAL:
              Garrison cap.
              Woolen O.D. blouse and slacks.
              White shirts.
              One cotton O.D. blouse and slacks.

f. Intelligence:

    Press relations will be strictly in accord with directive furnish-
ed by G-2, Headquarters, GHQ Air Force.

    No member of the flight will release any information to the press,
except through the Commanding Officer or the S-2.

2. **OPERATIONS:**

   a. **Flight Plan:**

February 15, A.M. - Depart Langley Field, Va. for assembly at Miami, Fla.

    Flight from United States to Buenos Aires

February 17, A.M. - Depart Miami, Fla., for Lima, Peru, direct.
February 17, P.M. - Arrive Lima, Peru (Stop for service).
February 17, P.M. - Depart Lima, Peru for Buenos Aires, Argentina, direct.
February 18, A.M. - Arrive Buenos Aires, Argentina.

      Return Flight

    Plan I (Based on availability of gasoline at Santiago, Chile
        and Lima, Peru.)

- 4 -

96TH BOMBARDMENT SQUADRON, GHQ-AF

YIB-17 Airplane, AC No. 36-153 (#61)

Major HAROLD L. GEORGE, Air Corps,
Captain DARR H. ALKIRE, Air Corps,
1st Lieut. WILLIAM A. MATHENY, Air Corps,
1st Lieut. WARREN H. HIGGINS, Air Corps,
Tech Sgt. GILBERT 7. OLSON, 6491823, 96th Bombardment Squadron, GHQ Air Force,
Staff Sgt. EVERETT KIRKPATRICK, R-2291273, 96th Bombardment Squadron, GHQ Air Force,
Corp. WILLIAM A. WITHERS, 6809650, 96th Bombardment Squadron, GHQ Air Force,
Pfc. NORBERT D. FLINN, 6830755, 96th Bombardment Squadron, GHQ Air Force.

a. **S-1 and Finance:**

    Duties: (1) Personnel matters.
           (2) Provide necessary vouchers for payment of per diem or other authorized expenditure of funds.

b. **Mess and Billeting:**

    Duties: (1) Arrange for rations to be carried in planes at each stop.
           (2) Arrange for billets for officers and men.
           (3) Keep S-1 informed as to where officers and men are billeted.

c. **Guard:**

    The 2d Wing has been requested to make advance arrangements for necessary guards at all stops.

d. **Landing Facilities:**

    The 2d Wing has been requested to make advance arrangements re parking at all stops.

e. **Uniform:**

    (1) Flying:

        (a) Officers:

            Leather jackets.
            W.O.D. shirts and slacks.
            Normal flying equipment.

        (b) Enlisted men:

            Flight jackets with squadron insignia.
            One spare set of clean coveralls.
            Flight caps (no mechanics caps).

- 3 -

Plan (cont'd.

February 22, A.M.   - Depart Buenos Aires, Argentina, for Santiago, Chile,
                    direct.
February 22, P.M.   - Arrive Santiago, Chile.
February 23, A.M.   - Depart Santiago, Chile, for Lima, Peru, direct.
February 23, P.M.   - Arrive Lima, Peru.
February 24, A.M.   - Depart Lima, Peru, for Franco Field, C.Z., direct.
February 24, F.M.   - Arrive France Field, C.Z.
February 25,   - Necessary 40-hour checks and maintenance at Franco Field,
                    C.Z.
February 26, A.M.   - Depart France Field, C.Z., for Washington, D.C., direct.
February 26, P.M.   - Arrive Washington, D.C.

      Plan II   (Based on the unavailability of gasoline and oil at Santiago,
                  Chile, and Lima, Peru.)

February 22, A.M.   - Depart Buenos Aires, Argentina, for Santiago, Chile, direct.
February 22, P.M.   - Arrive Santiago, Chile.
February 23, A.M.   - Depart Santiago, Chile, for Antofagasta, Chile,
                    direct.
February 23, A.M.   - Arrive Antofagasta, Chile, (Stop for service).
February 23, P.M.   - Depart Antofagasta, Chile, for Lima, Peru, direct.
February 23, P.M.   - Arrive Lima, Peru.
February 24, A.M.   - Depart Lima, Peru, for France Field, C.Z., direct.
February 24, F.M.   - Arrive France Field, C.Z.
February 25,   - Necessary 40-hour checks and maintenance at France Field,
                    C.Z.
February 26, A.M.   - Depart France Field, C.Z., for Washington, D.C., direct.
February 26, P.M.   - Arrive Washington, D.C.

    b. Meteorological Plan:

      See Inclosure No. 1, (Lt. Told will proceed to Miami, Fla., on
February 13 for the purpose of contacting Pan American Airways with reference
to weather reporting service.).

    3. COMMUNICATIONS:

      See Communications Plan as inclosure No. 2, (Lt. Tucker, Group Com-
munications Officer, will proceed to Miami, Fla., on February 13, for the purpose of coordinating communications with Pan American Systems.)

    4. SUPPLY AND ENGINEERING:

      See Supply Plan as inclosure No. 3.

Inclosure No. 1 - Meteorological Plan.
   "   "   " 2 - Communications Plan.
   "   "   " 3 - Supply Plan.

               - 5 -

INCLOSURE NO. 2

Communications Plan

1. The Plan of Communications in General calls for two Radio nets, namely:

   a. Liaison Net: - To be composed of ground stations and air stations. Ground stations to be Langley Field, Va., Chapman Field, Fla., and Quarry Heights, Canal Zone. These to be augmented by Pan Air and Pan Grace facilities.

   b. Air-Command Net: - To be composed of six (6) airplanes of the 2d Bomb Gp.

2. General Plan of Communications:

   a. Langley Field, Va, to Miami, Fla. Contact to be maintained with Langley Field until taken over by Chapman Field.

   b. Miami-Panama-Lima-Valpariso-Buenos Aires. Contact with Chapman Field until taken over by Quarry Heights. When flight has reached proximity of Panama, the Group Commander's airplane will establish contact with existing Pan Grace facilities, two (2) airplanes will guard and intercept all traffic with Pan Grace. The Deputy Group Commander will establish contact with Quarry Heights, one airplane will guard and intercept all traffic on this net. One airplane will be available for Press transmissions.

3. One airplane transmitter will be available for Press duty. Frequency assignments to be made by 2d Wing Hq.

4. The return flight plan will be the same except for reversed schedules.

5. Liaison Officer at Miami and the Canal Zone will be available for co-operation between Army and Pan Air - Pan Grace systems.

6. For details regarding Frequencies, Call Letters, Broadcast Stations, Time Signals, Position Reports, Schematic Diagrams, Radio Procedure and Radio Beacon Stations, see Communications Annex, (Annex to be issued before departure Miami, Fla.).

INCLOSURE NO. 2

Communications Plan

1. The Plan of Communications in General calls for two Radio nets, namely:

   <u>a</u>. Liaison Net: - To be composed of ground stations and air
        stations. Ground stations to be Langley
        Field, Va., Chapman Field, Fla., and Quarry
        Heights, Canal Zone. These to be augmented
        by Pan Air and Pan Grace facilities.

   <u>b</u>. Air-Command Net: - To be composed of six (6) airplanes of
        the 2d Bomb Gp.

2. General Plan of Communications:

   <u>a</u>. Langley Field, Va., to Miami, Fla. Contact to be maintained with
       Langley Field until taken over by Chapman Field.

   <u>b</u>. Miami-Panama-Lima-Valpariso-Buenos Aires. Contact with Chapman
       Field until taken over by Quarry Heights. When flight has reached
       proximity of Panama, the Group Commander's airplane will establish
       contact with existing Pan Grace facilities, two (2) airplanes will
       guard and intercept all traffic with Pan Grace. The Deputy Group
       Commander will establish contact with Quarry Heights, one airplane
       will guard and intercept all traffic on this net. One airplane
       will be available for Press transmissions.

3. One airplane transmitter will be available for Press duty. Frequency
   assignments to be made by 2d Wing Hq.

4. The return flight plan will be the same except for reversed schedules.

5. Liaison Officer at Miami and the Canal Zone will be available for co-
   operation between Army and Pan Air - Pan Grace systems.

6. For details regarding Frequencies, Call Letters, Broadcast Stations,
   Time Signals, Position Reports, Schematic Diagrams, Radio Procedure
   and Radio Beacon Stations, see Communications Annex, (Annex to be issued
   before departure Miami, Fla.).

GENERAL COMMUNICATIONS INSTRUCTIONS

1. RT-8 will establish contact with DF-4 enroute to Miami and change to VL-2 (Chapman Field) before arrival Miami.

2. Upon take-off at Miami, RT-8 will establish and maintain contact with VL-2 (Chapman Field), until contact can be made with WYP (France Field, C.Z.). In the vicinity of the Canal Zone, RT-8 will shift from Army Control and contact Panagra station, frequencies shown in Communication Annex. VL-2 at this time will contact WYP (France Field) and remain under their control until landing at destination. VL-2 will be at liberty to change transmitting frequency when so instructed by WYP.

3. Airplane No. 62 will keep liaison transmitter tuned on 1638 Kcs, and, under air-control orders, will turn same on for Radio bearings by Panagra D.F. stations.

4. Airplane No. 51, continuously, will guard same frequency as RT-8. All weather will come in over this frequency and will be turned over to Lieut. T. G. Wold, weather officer.

COMMUNICATIONS ANNEX

INDEX

Section 2. Frequencies and Call Letters.

Paragraph B., Panair and Panagra (Cont'd).

Tacna, Peru	OOI	Same as Lima	5692.5
Arequipa, Peru	OOH	Same as Lima	5692.5
Arica, Chile	CBZ	3076 - 5610 - 8885	5692.5
Iquique, Chile	CBY	5700	5692.5
Antofagasta, Chile	CBX	3276 - 6552 - 5950 - 8220	5692.5
Ovalle, Chile	CBU	3076 - 5610 - 8865	5692.5
Vallenar, Chile	CBD	" " "	5692.5
Santiago, Chile	CBV	3076 - 5610 - 8885 -12304 13383	5692.5
Lo Ombro, Chile	CBS	3076 - 5610 - 8885	5692.5
Mendoza, Arg.	LYZ	3076 - 5610 - 8885 -11538	5692.5
Villa Mercedes, Arg.	LYH	3076 - 5610 - 8895	5692.5
Moron, Arg.	LVL	3070 - 5585 - 8870 -11538	5692.5

(Note: This station is at airport Buenos Aires.)

Stations thus marked are equipped to give a bearing when a signal of
1638 Kcs., is broadcast from one of the airplanes. In event this is
desired, an air-corand order will be issued to the ship designated
to make the transmission.

(Note: In the transmitting frequencies assigned Panagra and Panair,
the station will always use the station in or near the 5000 series;
for example, when first calling Moron, Arg., expect them to answer
on 5585 Kcs., and then have you shift to the frequency they can use
best. All Panair and Panagra stations will guard 5692.5 Kcs.)

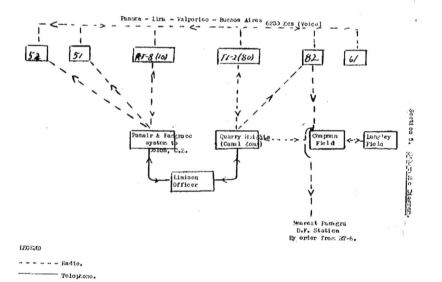

Section 5. Schematic Diagram

LEGEND

- - - - - - Radio.

——————— Telephone.

Section 5   Schematic Diagram

Miami To Panama

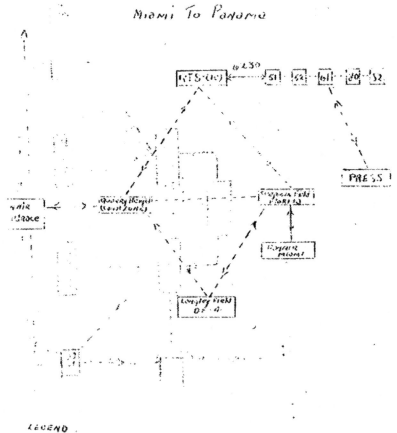

RTS (w)   W230   51   52   61   70   52

PRESS

AIR FORCE

Quincy (Royal Good Zone)

Riffian Field Port SI

Panama Miami

Langley Field OY - 4

LEGEND
- - - - - - Radio
————— Telephone

1. Joint Army-Navy procedure will be used in all radio Telegraph messages.
    A possible exception will be when working with Panair or PanGrace sta-
    tions, in event procedure signals become confusing, straight test will
    be resorted to.

2. Each air station will keep a complete log of all traffic copied   in
    same in to Group Communications when mission is completed.

3. Types of Emission:

    a. Liaison: c.w. (Continuous Wave).
    b. Air-Ground: VOICE.

    (NOTE: In event the distress signal is used, it is permissable to use
    Tone Telegraph to insure attracting attention.)

4. The speed with which an operator can get out an intelligible message de-
    pends on his accuracy and clarity of sending. Experience has taught
    that the 15-word-a-minute man will get through quicker and more accurate
    in a net of the sort that will operate during this mission. For this
    reason, all traffic from airplanes will be of the 15-word-a-minute var-
    iety.

5. Operators will refrain from unnecessary service messages.

Section 7. Radio Beacon and Airdrome Control.

A. Radio Beacons:

    France Field, C.Z.:

                     Call Letter: FF.
                     Frequency: 287.
                     Location: One half (1/2) mile from France Field, course
                                to field 235° magnetic.
                     Bearings: 55 - 134 - 238 - 314.
                     Weather: Irregular.
                     Will operate during this flight.

                     (NOTE: No beacon facilities exist in South American
                     countries. Airdrome control also is non-existant.
                     Arrangements will be made with ground station prior
                     to landing for guard or 6230 Kcs.)

                     By order of Lt. Colonel OLDS:

OFFICIAL: ROBERT B. WILLIAMS,
EDWIN L. TUCKER,   Captain, Air Corps,
1st Lieut., Air Corps,   Operations Officer.
Communications Officer.

Appendix E

Langley Field Today

Certainly the fact that so many of the 1930s Army Air Corps buildings not only exixt today, but are continuing to serve the Air Force is a testimony to the architectual design and the skilled craftsmen who built them. But one can't forget the legions of maintenance, service and janitorial personnel, military and civilian, who have been the glue that have held the infrastructure together down through the years.

Air Corps GHQ Today
Now Housing Air Combat Command HQ

GHQ Enlisted Barracks Today

The Officers' Club

Typical Langley Field Officers' Family Housing